Exploring American History

A well regulated Militia, being necessary to the security of a free State, the right of the people to keep and bear Arms, shall not be infringed.

— Second Amendment to the United States Constitution

By
Michael J. McHugh
D. H. Montgomery

A PUBLICATION OF
Christian Liberty Press

© Copyright 1992
Printing 2003

Christian Liberty Press
502 W. Euclid Avenue
Arlington Heights, Illinois 60004
USA

ISBN 1-930092-96-2

Table of Contents

"The great comprehensive truths written in letters of living light on every page of our history are these: Human happiness has no perfect security but freedom, freedom none but virtue, virtue none but knowledge; and neither freedom nor virtue has any vigor or immortal hope except in the principles of the Christian faith."

President John Quincy Adams

Photo Credits

Library of Congress: 311, 314, 315 (left), 325, 330, 334, 334, 338

"GIVE THEM WATTS, BOYS!"

A scene previous to battle in the Revolutionary War,
when gun wadding ran short, the chaplain tore to
pieces his Watt's hymn book and distributed it.

Introduction

The object of this book is to present accurately those facts and principles in the lives of some of the chief founders and builders of America that would be of interest and value to pupils pursuing the study of our nation's history. Throughout the book, great care has been taken to tell only such incidents as are believed to rest on reliable authority.

Young people delight in stories. The dramatic, the picturesque, the personal, appeal powerfully to the young mind, leading it to see the past as a living present, and to think the thoughts and experience the feelings of people who now live only in their words and deeds. Accordingly, the events of American history described in this text are made to center around some hero, and will hopefully inspire each student to search further into the details of the various personalities of our nation's history.

The authors have endeavored to bring out the influence of the Christian faith as it relates to the events and people of America's past. Young people in America today must not be sheltered from the knowledge that our nation has a rich Christian heritage.

The words quoted literally in this book are enclosed in double quotation marks; those quoted in substance only are enclosed in single marks; while those attributed by the writer to different speakers have no marks.

In the hope that this text will be a blessing to each student who studies its pages, it is respectfully presented to the public.

Michael J. McHugh

THE NORTHMEN ON THE COAST OF GREENLAND

Chapter One
Leif Ericsson and the Vikings

"Captains of the waves we are --
Kings of the seething foam --
Warriors bold from the Norseland cold --
Far o'er the sea we roam."

Some voyages of the Vikings to North America. Far away in the cold northern countries that we know as Norway and Sweden and Denmark, lived a race of men who called themselves Vikings. They are often called Northmen or Norsemen, but I like best their own name for themselves. Viking means "son of the bay," or "raiding sailor" and the name helps us to know what kind of people they were -- bold and hardy, fond of adventure, and full of love for the great blue ocean that surged into the thousands of bays along their shores. They built many ships, and often made daring voyages to almost every part of Europe, where they often brutalized people who opposed their raids.

If we could have followed these Viking sailors, we would have found some of them going to England and to France, some to Ireland and the smaller islands nearby; but perhaps more than to any other place, they went to build up a Viking colony in Iceland. Their settlements there grew rapidly, and we may read about their farms and hay crops, their sheep and cattle, and as we should expect, about their ships and trade with all the countries nearby.

Would you like to see a Viking ship? It would not look much like one of our ships today, nor would it travel as fast as ships do now. The bow and the stern rose high out of the water, but the middle was lower and had no deck. Each vessel carried from thirty to sixty oarsmen who used oars twenty feet long. A single mast and only one sail, both of which could be taken down when not in use, completed what would seem to us a strange ship. But they were well-built, and in them the Vikings traveled many weeks at a time upon the sea.

Only two years after Iceland was settled, one of these ships was driven westward by a storm, until it reached the land we now call Greenland, and many years later a Viking colony was made there. A few years later, a Viking ship sailed even farther into the unknown west than this. The vessel had started on a voyage from Iceland to Greenland, and the captain had set out, steering by the sun and stars, Viking fashion. But a thick fog came, and neither sun nor stars could be seen. Still, on and on sailed the Viking ship, and after a time welcome land was seen. It was not snow-bound Greenland the ship had reached, however, but a low woody shore that looked very strange to the captain. So he turned back, and it was left for another man to land on the new-found shore.

This man was Leif, son of Eric, or Leif Ericsson, as he is often called. In about the year 1000, Leif set out to search for the new land. After a short voyage Leif and his thirty-five followers saw the shore, and sailed along beside it for some distance. They called one place they saw Slateland, because of its large flat rocks. Another they called Woodland, and another Vinland, because of the wild grapes they found there. In Vinland they spent the winter, and after going home in the spring, told fine stories of the pleasant land they had found.

Where was Vinland? It was in America somewhere, probably in Newfoundland, but just where we cannot tell. That no lasting settlements were made in Vinland by the Vikings we are sure. Some voyages were made to its shores to get wood, but battles with the Indian natives kept the Vikings from making homes in the land they had found. In time they stopped sailing to Vinland, and deserted even the Greenland colonies and the New World was left once more to the Indians. The New World that the Vikings called Vinland was forgotten for over four hundred years. Finally, in the year 1492, a brave explorer named Christopher Columbus rediscovered the land we call America.

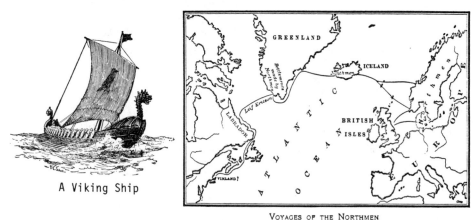

A Viking Ship

Voyages of the Northmen

Comprehension Questions

1. Where did the Viking people live in Europe?
2. Did the Vikings make colonies in Iceland and Greenland?
3. In the year 1000, Leif Ericsson, a Norseman, landed and stayed at a place he called _____, which was probably in Newfoundland.
4. Did the Vikings establish any lasting settlements in America?
5. Who was Leif Ericsson?

Chapter Two
Christopher Columbus

(Born 1451 - Died 1506)

Birth and boyhood of Columbus. Christopher Columbus, the discoverer of America, was born in Genoa, a seaport of Italy, more than five hundred and fifty years ago. His father was a wool-comber. Christopher did not want to learn that trade, but wanted to become a sailor. Seeing the boy's strong liking for the sea, his father sent him to a school where he could learn geography, map-drawing, and whatever else might help him to become, someday, commander of a ship.

When he was fourteen Columbus went to sea. In those days, the Mediterranean Sea swarmed with warships and pirates. Every sailor, no matter if he was but a boy, had to stand ready to fight his way from port to port.

In this exciting life, full of adventure and of danger, Columbus grew to manhood. The rough experiences he then had did much to make him the brave, determined captain and explorer that he afterwards became.

Columbus has a sea-fight; he goes to Lisbon. According to some accounts, Columbus once had a desperate battle with a ship off the coast of Portugal. The fight lasted all day. At length, both vessels caught fire. Columbus jumped from his blazing ship into the sea, and catching hold of a floating oar, managed to swim to the shore about six miles away.

He then went to the port of Lisbon. There he married the daughter of a famous sea captain. For a long time after his marriage Columbus earned his living partly by drawing maps, which he sold to commanders of vessels visiting Lisbon, and partly by making voyages to Africa, Iceland, and other lands.

What men then knew about the world. The maps that Columbus made and sold were very different from those we now have. At that time, only half of the world had been discovered. Europe, Asia, and a small part of Africa were the primary places known. The maps that Columbus had might have shown the earth shaped like a ball, but he supposed it to be much smaller than it really is. No one at this time had sailed around the globe. Therefore, no one knew what lands lay west of the broad Atlantic. For this reason we should look in vain on one of the maps drawn by Columbus for the great continents of North and South America or for Australia or the Pacific Ocean.

"BY SAILING WEST, I SHALL BE ABLE TO REACH THE INDIES."

The plan of Columbus for reaching the Indies by sailing west. While living in Lisbon, Columbus made up his mind to try to do what no other man at that time dared try -- that was to cross the Atlantic Ocean. He thought that by doing so, he could get directly to Asia and the Indies, which, he believed, were opposite Portugal and Spain. If successful, he could open a very profitable trade with the rich countries of the East, where spices, drugs, and silk were brought to Europe. The people of Europe could not reach those countries directly by ships, because they had not yet found their way around the southern point of Africa.

Columbus tries to get help in carrying out his plans. Columbus was too poor to buy even a single ship to undertake such a voyage as he had planned. He asked the king of Portugal to provide some money or vessels, but the king did not want to help. At length, he determined to go to Spain and see if he could get help there.

On the southern coast of Spain, there is a small port named Palos. Within sight of the village of Palos, and within plain sight of the ocean, there was a convent, which is still standing, called the Convent of St. Mary.

One morning a tall, fine-looking man, leading a little boy by the hand, knocked at the door of this convent and begged for a piece of bread and a cup of water for the child. The man was Columbus, whose wife was now dead, and the boy was his son.

The guardian of the convent noticed Columbus standing at the door. He liked his appearance, and coming up, began to talk with him. Columbus frankly told him what he was trying to do. The guardian of the convent listened with great interest; then he gave him a letter to a friend who, he thought, would help him to lay his plans before Ferdinand and Isabella, the king and queen of Spain.

COLUMBUS EXPLAINING HIS PLAN BEFORE FERDINAND AND ISABELLA.

Columbus gets help for his great voyage. Columbus left his son at the convent and set out on his journey, full of bright hopes. But Ferdinand and Isabella could not then see him. After waiting a long time, the traveller was told that he might go before several learned men and tell them about his proposed voyage across the Atlantic.

People who heard what this captain from Lisbon wanted to do thought he had lost his mind. Boys in the streets laughed at him and called him crazy. Columbus waited for help seven years; he then made up his mind that he would wait no longer. Just as he was about to leave Spain, Queen Isabella, who had always felt interested in the brave sailor, resolved to aid him. Two rich sea captains who lived in Palos also decided to take part in the voyage. With the help that Columbus now received, he could get three small vessels. He went in the largest of the vessels--the only one that had an entire deck--as admiral, or commander of the fleet.

Columbus sails. Early on Friday morning, August 3, 1492, Columbus started from Palos to try to cross that ocean which men then called the "Sea of Darkness" -- a name that showed how little they knew of it, and how much they feared it.

We may be pretty sure that the guardian of the convent was one of those who watched the sailing of the little fleet. From the upper windows of the convent he could plainly see the vessels as they left the harbor of Palos.

What happened on the first part of the voyage. Columbus sailed first for the Canary Islands, because from there, he thought it would be a straight line across to Japan and Asia. He was forced to stop at the Canaries from August 12 to September 6, or more than three weeks, to make a new rudder for one of his ships and to change the sails of another.

Finally, all was ready, and he again set out on his voyage toward the west. When the ships sailed so far out on the ocean that the sailors could no longer see any of the islands, they became very frightened. They feared they would never be able to get back to Palos again. They were rough men, used to the sea, but now they bowed their heads and cried like children. Columbus had to work hard to quiet their fears and to encourage them to go forward with the voyage that they already wanted to give up.

What happened after many days at sea. For more than thirty days, the three ships continued on their way toward the west. To the crew every day seemed like a year. From sunrise to sunset nothing was to be seen but water and sky. Eventually, the men began to think that they were sailing on an ocean that had no end. They whispered among themselves that Columbus had gone mad, and that if they continued with him in command they should all be lost.

Santa Maria   Pinta   Nina
The Fleet of Christopher Columbus.

Twice, there was a joyful cry of land! land! But, when they got nearer they saw that what they had thought was land was nothing but banks of clouds. Then some sailors said, let us go to the admiral and tell him that we must turn back. What if he will not listen to us? asked others. Then we will throw him overboard and say, when we reach Palos, that he fell into the sea and was drowned.

But, when the crew went to Columbus and told him that they would go no further, he sternly ordered them to their work, declaring that, whatever might happen, he would not now give up the voyage. Columbus had more courage than his crew because he sincerely believed that his voyage had an important God-ordained purpose, and that God would protect him as he sought to bring the Christian faith to new and strange lands.

Signs of land. The very next day such certain signs of land were seen that even the most faint-hearted took courage. The men had already noticed great flocks of land birds flying westward, as if to guide them. Now some men on one vessel saw a branch of a thorn-bush float by. It was plain that it had not long been broken off the bush, and it was full of red berries.

But a sailor on one of the other vessels found something even better than the thorn-branch. He drew out of the water a carved walking-stick! Everyone saw that such a stick must have been cut and carved by human hands. These two signs could not be doubted. The men now felt sure that they were approaching the shore, and what was more, there were people living in that strange country.

Discovery of land. That evening Columbus begged his crew to keep a sharp lookout, and he promised a velvet coat to the one who would first see land. All of the men were excited, and no man closed his eyes in sleep that night.

Columbus himself stood on a high part of his ship, looking steadily toward the west. About ten o'clock he saw a moving light; it seemed like a torch carried in a man's hand. He called to a companion and asked him if he could see anything of the kind. Yes, he, too, plainly saw the moving light, but soon it disappeared.

Two hours after midnight a cannon was fired from the leading vessel. It was the glad signal that the long-looked-for land was in sight. There it lay directly ahead, about six miles away.

Then Columbus gave the order to furl sails, and the three vessels came to a stop and waited for the dawn. When the sun rose on Friday, October 12, 1492, Columbus saw a beautiful island with many trees growing on it. That was his first sight of the New World.

Columbus lands on the island and names it; people who lived on the island. Attended by the captains of the other two vessels, and by a part of their crews, Columbus set out in a boat for the island. When they landed, all fell on their knees, kissed the ground for joy, and gave thanks to God. Columbus named the island San Salvador (Holy Savior) and took possession of it, by right of discovery, for the king and queen of Spain.

He found that it was inhabited by a copper-colored people who spoke a language he could not understand. These people had never seen a ship or a white man before. They wore no clothing, but painted their bodies with bright colors. The Spaniards made them presents of strings of glass beads and red caps. In return they gave the Spaniards rolls of cotton yarn, tame parrots, and small ornaments of gold.

After staying here a short time Columbus set sail southward, in search of more land and in the hope of finding out where these people got their gold. Columbus also wanted the opportunity to spread the Christian religion to as many foreign lands as possible.

Columbus names the group of islands and their people. As Columbus sailed on, he saw many islands in every direction. He thought that they must be part of the Indies he was seeking. Since he had reached them by travelling west from Spain, he called them the West Indies, and to the red men who lived on them, he gave the name of Indians.

Columbus discovers two very large islands; his vessel is wrecked, and he returns to Spain in another. During the next six weeks, Columbus discovered the island of Cuba. At first, he thought it must be Japan, but afterward he came to the wrong conclusion that it was not an island at all, but part of the mainland of Asia.

THE KING AND QUEEN RECEIVE HIM IN GREAT STATE.

Next he came to the island of Haiti, or San Domingo. Here his ship was wrecked. He took the timber from the wreck and built a fort on the shore. Leaving about forty of his crew in this fort, Columbus set sail for Palos in one of the two remaining vessels.

Columbus arrives at Palos; joy of the people; how Ferdinand and Isabella received him. When the ship of Columbus was seen entering the harbor of Palos, the whole village was wild with excitement. More that seven months had passed since he sailed away from that port, and as nothing had been heard from him, many thought that the vessels and all on board had been lost. They were happy to see their friends and neighbors coming back home. The bells of the churches rang a merry song of welcome; the people crowded the streets, shouting to each other that Columbus, the great navigator, had crossed the "Sea of Darkness" and had returned in safety.

The king and queen were then in Barcelona, a long distance from Palos. To that city Columbus now went. He entered it on horseback, attended by the proudest and richest noblemen of Spain. He brought with him six Indians from the West Indies. They were gaily painted and wore bright feathers in their hair. Then many men followed, carrying rare birds, plants, and gold and silver ornaments, all found in the New World. These were presents for the king and queen. Ferdinand and Isabella received Columbus with great honor. When he had told them the story of his wonderful voyage, they sank on their knees and gave praise to God; all who were present followed their example.

The last voyages of Columbus. Columbus made three more voyages across the Atlantic. He discovered more islands near the coast of America, and he touched the coast of Central America and of South America. He never set foot on any part of what is now the mainland of the United States, and he always thought that the land he had reached was part of Asia. He had rediscovered a new world, but he did not know it. All that he knew was how to get to it and how to show others the way.

Columbus in his old age. The last days of this great man were very sad. The king was disappointed because he brought back no gold to amount to anything. The Spanish governor of San Domingo hated Columbus, and when he landed at that island on one of his voyages, he arrested him and sent him back to Spain in chains. He was immediately set at liberty, but he could not forget the insult. He kept the chains hanging on the wall of his room, and asked to have them buried with him.

IN CHAINS.

Columbus was now an old man; his health was broken, he was poor, in debt, and without a home. Once he wrote to the king and queen saying, "I have not a hair upon me that is not gray, my body is weak, and all that was left to me...has been taken away and sold, even the coat which I wore."

Not long after he came back to Spain to stay, the queen died. Then Columbus felt that he had lost his best friend. He gave up hope and said, "I have done all that I could do; I leave the rest to God."

His death and burial. Columbus died full of sadness-- maybe it would not be too much to say that he died of a broken heart.

He was first buried in Spain; then his body was taken up and carried to San Domingo, where he had wished to be buried. It is hard to say where the body of Columbus found its final resting place. But wherever the grave of the great sailor may be, his memory will live in every heart capable of respecting a brave man; for he first dared to cross the " Sea of Darkness," and he rediscovered the forgotten land of America.

Summary. In 1492 Christopher Columbus set sail from Spain to find a direct way across the Atlantic to Asia and the Indies. He did not get to Asia, but he did better: he discovered America. He died thinking that the new lands he had found were part of Asia; but by his daring voyage he first showed the people of Europe how to get to the New World.

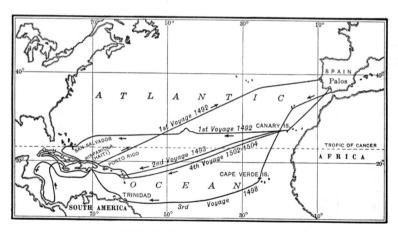

THE FOUR VOYAGES OF COLUMBUS.

Comprehension Questions

1. When and where was Columbus born?
2. What did he do in Lisbon?
3. How much of the world was then known?
4. Why did he go to Spain?
5. How did Columbus finally get help?
6. When did he sail?
7. What happened on the first part of the voyage?
8. Did Columbus think he landed on the Indies?
9. What did Columbus name the island he first landed upon?
10. Did Columbus ever land on any part of what is now the United States?
11. What happened to Columbus in his old age?

Coat of arms of Columbus

Columbus watching for Land.

Chapter Three
John Cabot

(Lived in England from 1472-1498)

John Cabot discovers the continent of North America. When Columbus set out on his first voyage across the Atlantic in 1492, John Cabot, an Italian merchant, was living in Bristol, England. When the news reached that city that Columbus had discovered the West Indies, Cabot begged Henry VII, king of England, to let him see if he could find a shorter way to the Indies than that of Columbus. The king gave his consent; and in the spring of 1497 John Cabot, with his son Sebastian, sailed from Bristol. They headed their vessels toward the northwest; by going in that direction they hoped to get to those parts of Asia and the Spice Islands that were known to Europe, which Columbus had failed to reach.

Early one bright morning near the end of June 1497, they saw land in the west. It was probably Cape Breton Island, a part of Nova Scotia. John Cabot named it "The Land First Seen." Up to this time Columbus had discovered only the West Indies, but John Cabot now saw the continent of North America. No English explorer had ever seen it before. There it lay, a great, lonely land, shaggy with forests, with not a house or a human being in sight.

John Cabot takes possession of the country for the king of England. Cabot went ashore with his son and some of his crew. In the vast, silent wilderness they set up a large cross. Near to it they planted two flagpoles, and hoisted the English flag on one, and the flag of Venice, the city where John Cabot had lived in Italy, on the other. Then they took possession of the land for Henry VII. It was in this way that the English came to consider that the eastern coast of North America was their property, although they did not begin to make settlements there until nearly a hundred years later.

John Cabot and his son return to Bristol. After sailing through the Gulf of St. Lawrence without finding the passage to Asia for which they were looking, the sailors returned to England.

HENRY VII

The king was so pleased with what John Cabot had discovered that he made him a handsome present; and when the captain, richly dressed in silk, appeared in the street, the people of Bristol would run after him and cheer for the "Great Admiral," as they called him.

What the Cabots carried back to England from America. The Cabots took back to England some Indian traps for catching game and some wild turkeys, an American bird the English had never seen, but whose acquaintance they were not sorry to make. They also brought the rib of a whale, which they had found on the beach in Nova Scotia.

Near to where the Cabots probably lived in Bristol, there is a famous old church. It was built long before the discovery of America, and Queen Elizabeth I said that it was the most beautiful building of its kind in all England. In that church hangs the rib of a whale. It is believed to be the one the Cabots brought home with them. It reminds all who see it of that voyage in 1497 by which England claimed possession of a very large part of the continent of North America.

The second voyage of the Cabots; how they sailed along the eastern shores of North America. About a year later, the Cabots set out on a second voyage to the west. They reached the gloomy cliffs of Labrador on the northeastern coast of North America, and they passed many large icebergs. They saw numbers of Indians dressed in the skins of wild beasts, and polar bears as white as snow. These bears were great swimmers, and would dive into the sea and come up with a large fish in their claws. As it did not look to the Cabots as if the polar bears and the icebergs would guide them to the warm countries of Asia and the Spice Islands, they turned around and went south. They sailed along what is now the eastern coast of the United States for a very long distance. However, since they did not find any passage through to the countries they were seeking, they returned to England.

The English now began to see what a large piece of land they had found beyond the Atlantic. They could not tell, however, whether it was a separate continent or a part of Asia. Like everybody in Europe, they called it the New World; but all that name really meant then was simply the new lands across the sea.

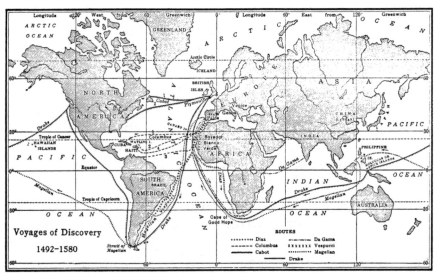

Voyages of Discovery
1492–1580

How the New World came to be called America. Not many years after this the New World received the name by which we now call it. An Italian navigator whose name was Amerigo Vespucci made a voyage to it after it had been discovered by Columbus and the Cabots. He wrote an account of what he saw, and as this was the first printed description of the continent, it was given the name of AMERICA.

Summary. In 1497 John Cabot and his son, Sebastian, from Bristol, England, discovered the mainland or continent of North America, and took possession of it for England. The next year they came over and sailed along the eastern coast of what is now the United States.

An Italian whose name was Amerigo Vespucci visited the New World and afterward wrote the first published account of the mainland. For this reason, the new land was named after him, AMERICA.

Comprehension Questions

1. Who was John Cabot?
2. Who sailed with him?
3. What town in England did the Cabots sail from?
4. What did the chapter say about the second voyage of the Cabots?
5. How did the New World come to be called America?

John Cabot

Map showing how much of the continent of North America was discovered by John Cabot and his son

Chapter Four
Ponce de Leon, Balboa, and De Soto

(Period of Discovery, 1513-1542)

The magic fountain; Ponce de Leon discovers Florida; Balboa discovers the Pacific Ocean. The Indians on the West Indies Islands believed there was a wonderful fountain in a land to the west of them. They said that if an old man should bathe in its waters, he would become a boy again. Ponce de Leon, a Spanish soldier who was getting gray and wrinkled, set out to find this magic fountain, for he thought there was more fun in being a boy than in growing old.

He did not find the fountain, and so his hair grew grayer than ever and his wrinkles grew deeper. But in 1513 he discovered a land bright with flowers, which he named Florida. He took possession of it for Spain.

The same year another Spaniard, named Vasco de Balboa, set out to explore the Isthmus of Panama. One day he climbed to the top of a very high hill, and discovered that vast ocean -- the greatest of all the oceans of the globe -- which we call the Pacific.

Hernando de Soto discovers the Mississippi. Long after Balboa and Ponce de Leon were dead, a Spaniard named Hernando de Soto landed in Florida and marched through the country in search of gold mines.

During his long and weary wanderings, he came to a river more than a mile across. The Indians told him it was the

Mississippi, or the Great River. In discovering it, De Soto had found the largest river in North America. He had also found his own grave, for he died shortly afterward, and was secretly buried at midnight in its muddy waters.

Hernando De Soto.

PONCE DE LEON.

Balboa.

The Spaniards build St. Augustine; we buy Florida in 1819. More than twenty years after the burial of De Soto, a Spanish soldier named Melendez went to Florida and built a fort on the eastern coast. This was in 1565. The fort became the center of a settlement named St. Augustine. It is the oldest city built by European settlers, not only in what is now the United States, but in all of North America.

In 1819, or more than two hundred and fifty years after St. Augustine was begun, Spain sold Florida to the United States.

Summary. Ponce de Leon discovered Florida; another Spaniard, named Balboa, discovered the Pacific; and still another, named De Soto, discovered the Mississippi. In 1565, the Spaniards began to build St. Augustine in Florida. It is the oldest city built by European men in the United States or in all of North America.

Comprehension Questions

1. What did Ponce de Leon think the "magic" fountain could do?
2. What did Ponce de Leon do?
3. What body of water did Balboa discover?
4 What great river did Hernando de Soto discover?
5. What is the name of the oldest city built by Europeans in North America?

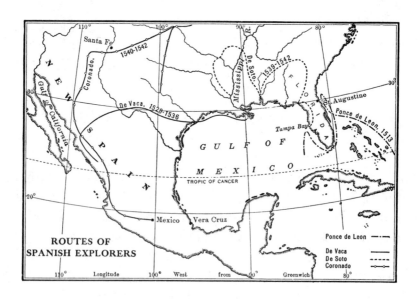

Chapter Five
Sir Walter Raleigh

(Born 1552 - Died 1618)

Walter Raleigh sends two ships to America; how the Indians received the Englishmen. Although John Cabot discovered the continent of North America in 1497 and took possession of the land for England, the English themselves did not try to settle here until nearly a hundred years later. In 1584, a young man named Walter Raleigh, who was a

great favorite of Queen Elizabeth I, sent out two ships to America. The captains of these vessels landed on Roanoke Island, off the coast of what is now the state of North Carolina. They found the island covered with tall red cedars and with vines thick with clusters of wild grapes. The Indians called this place the "Good Land." They were pleased to see the Englishmen, and they invited them to a great feast of roast turkey, venison, melons, and nuts.

Queen Elizabeth names the country Virginia; first settlers; what they sent Walter Raleigh. When the two captains returned to England, Queen Elizabeth I (the "Virgin Queen," as she was called) was delighted with what she heard of the "Good Land." She named it Virginia in honor of herself. She also gave Raleigh a title of honor. From that time he was no longer simply called Mr. Raleigh, but Sir Walter Raleigh.

Sir Walter shipped over English people as emigrants to settle in Virginia during 1585. They sent back to him, as a present, two famous American plants: one called tobacco, the other the potato. The queen had given Sir Walter a fine estate in Ireland, and he set out both plants in his garden. The tobacco plant did not grow very well there, but the potato did; and after a short time thousands of farmers began to raise that vegetable throughout Ireland and England. As far back as that time -- or more than four hundred years ago -- America was beginning to feed the people of the Old World.

The Virginia settlement destroyed. Sir Walter spent immense sums of money on his settlement in Virginia, but it did not succeed. One of the settlers, named Dare, had a daughter born there. He named her Virginia Dare. She was the first English child born in America. But the little girl, with her father and mother and all the rest of the settlers, disappeared. It is supposed that they were killed by the Indians or that they wandered away and starved to death; but all that we really know is that not one of them was ever seen again.

Last days of Sir Walter Raleigh. After Queen Elizabeth died, King James became ruler of England. He accused Sir Walter of trying to take away his crown in order to make someone else ruler over the country. Sir Walter was sent to prison and kept there for many years. Eventually, King James released him in order to send him to South America to get gold. When Sir Walter returned to London without any gold, the greedy king accused him of having disobeyed him because he had fought with some Spaniards. Raleigh was condemned to death and was beheaded.

JAMESTOWN IN 1622.
From an old print.

But Sir Walter's attempt to settle Virginia led other Englishmen to try. Before he died they built a town, called Jamestown, on the coast. We shall soon read about the history of that town. The English held Virginia from that time until it became part of the United States.

Summary. Sir Walter Raleigh sent over men from England to explore the coast of America. Queen Elizabeth named the country they visited Virginia. Raleigh then shipped emigrants over to make a settlement. These emigrants sent him two American plants, tobacco and the potato; the people of Great Britain and Ireland came to like them both. Sir Walter's settlement failed, but his example led other Englishmen to try to make one. Before he was beheaded, they had succeeded in developing a prosperous settlement in the colony of Virginia.

Comprehension Questions

1. Who was Sir Walter Raleigh?
2. What name did Queen Elizabeth give to the country?
3. What American plants did the emigrants send him?
4. What did he do with those plants?
5. What happened to the Virginia settlement?
6. How did Sir Walter Raleigh die?

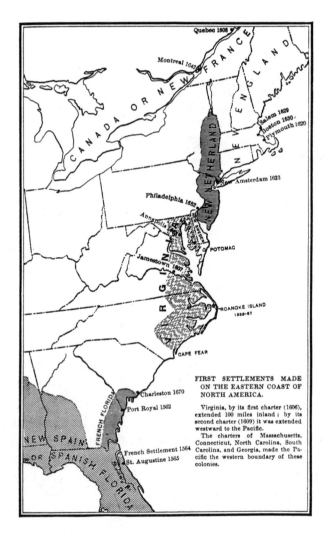

FIRST SETTLEMENTS MADE ON THE EASTERN COAST OF NORTH AMERICA.

Virginia, by its first charter (1606), extended 100 miles inland ; by its second charter (1609) it was extended westward to the Pacific.

The charters of Massachusetts, Connecticut, North Carolina, South Carolina, and Georgia, made the Pacific the western boundary of these colonies.

Chapter Six
Captain John Smith

(Born 1579 - Died 1631)

New and successful attempt to make a settlement in Virginia; Captain John Smith. One of the leaders in the new expedition who set out to make a settlement in Virginia while Raleigh was in prison, was Captain John Smith. He began life as a clerk in England. Not liking his work, he ran away and turned soldier. After many strange adventures, he was captured by the Turks and sold as a slave. His master, who was a Turk, placed a heavy iron collar around his neck and forced him to thresh grain with a big wooden club. One day the Turk rode up and struck his slave with his riding-whip. This was more than Smith could bear; he rushed at his master, and with one blow of his club he killed the foolish Turk. He then mounted the dead man's horse and escaped. After a time he returned to England, but as England seemed a little dull to Captain Smith, he decided to join some emigrants who were going to Virginia.

CAPTAIN JOHN SMITH.

Captain John Smith

What happened to Captain Smith on the voyage; the landing at Jamestown; what the settlers wanted to do; Smith's plan. On the way to America, Smith was accused of plotting to murder the chief men among the emigrants so that he might make himself "King of Virginia." The accusation was false, but he was put in irons and kept a prisoner for the rest of the voyage.

In the spring of 1607 the emigrants reached Chesapeake Bay and sailed up a river, which they named the James River in honor of King James I of England. When they landed they named the settlement Jamestown for the same reason. Here they built a log fort, and placed three or four small cannon on its walls. Most of the men who settled Jamestown came hoping to find mines of gold in Virginia, or else a way through to the Pacific Ocean and the Indies, which they thought could not be very far away. But Captain Smith wanted to help his countrymen to make homes here for themselves and their children.

Smith's trial; how the settlers lived; the first English church; sickness; attempted desertion. As soon as Captain Smith landed, he demanded to be tried by a jury of twelve men. The trial took place. It was the first English court and the first English jury that ever sat in America. The captain proved his innocence and was set free. His chief accuser was required to pay him a large sum of money for damages. Smith kindly gave this money to help the settlement.

As the weather was warm, the emigrants did not begin building log cabins immediately, but slept on the ground, sheltered by boughs of trees. For a church they had an old tent, in which they met on Sunday. They were all members of the Church of England (the Anglican Church).

When the cold weather came, many people became sick. Soon the whole settlement was like a hospital. Sometimes three or four would die in one night. Captain Smith, though not well himself, did everything he could for those who needed his help.

When the sickness was over, some of the settlers were so unhappy that they determined to seize the only vessel there was at Jamestown and go back to England. Captain Smith turned the cannon of the fort against them. The deserters saw that if they tried to leave the harbor he would knock their vessel to pieces, so they came back. One of the leaders of these men was tried and shot; the other was sent to England in disgrace.

The Indians of Virginia. When the Indians of America first met the white men, they were usually friendly to them. This did not last long, because often the whites treated the Indians very badly. In fact, the Spaniards made slaves of the Indians and whipped many of them to death. But these were generally the Indians of the West Indies and South America. Some of the Indian tribes of North America, especially those in what is now New York State, were terribly fierce and a match for the Spaniards in cruelty.

The Indians in the east did not build cities, but lived in small villages. These villages were made up of huts, covered with the bark of trees. Such huts were called wigwams. The women did nearly all the work, such as building the wigwams and hoeing corn and tobacco. The men hunted and made war. Instead of guns, the Indians had bows and arrows. With these, they could bring down a deer or a squirrel quite as well as a white man could with a rifle. They had no iron, but made hatchets and knives out of sharp, flat stones. They never built roads, for they had no wagons, and in the eastern part of America they did not use horses; but they could find their way with ease through the thickest forest. When they came to a river they swam across it, so they had no need of bridges. For boats, they made canoes of birch bark. These canoes were almost as light as paper, yet they were very strong and handsome, and they "floated on the river like a yellow leaf in autumn." In them, they could go hundreds of miles quickly and silently. So every river and stream throughout North America became a roadway to the Indian.

Captain Smith goes in search of the Pacific; he is captured by Indians. After that first long, hot summer was over, some of the settlers wished to explore the country and see if they could find a short way through to the Pacific Ocean.

Captain Smith led the expedition. The Indians attacked them, killed three of the men, and took the captain prisoner. To amuse the Indians, Smith showed them his pocket compass. When the warriors saw that the needle always pointed toward the north, they were greatly astonished; and instead of killing their prisoner, they decided to take him to their chief. This chief was named Powhatan. He was a tall, grim-looking old man who hated the settlers at Jamestown, because he believed that they had come to steal the land from the Indians.

Smith's life is saved by Pocahontas; her marriage to John Rolfe. Smith was dragged into the chief's wigwam; his head was laid on a large, flat stone, and a tall warrior with a big club stood ready to smash his head. Just as Powhatan was about to cry "Strike!" his daughter Pocahontas, a girl of twelve or thirteen, ran up, and putting her arms around the prisoner's head, laid her own head on his. Now let the Indian with his uplifted club strike, if he dare.

Instead of being angry with his daughter, Powhatan promised her that he would spare Smith's life. When an Indian made such a promise, he kept it, so the captain knew that his head was safe. Powhatan released his prisoner and soon sent him back to Jamestown, and Pocahontas, followed by many Indians, carried to the settlers presents of corn and venison.

Some years after this the Indian maiden married John Rolfe, an Englishman who had come to Virginia. They went to London, and Pocahontas died not far from that city. She left a son, and from that son came some noted Virginians. One of them was John Randolph. He was a famous man in his day, and he always spoke with pride of the Indian princess, as he called her.

Captain Smith is made governor of Jamestown; the gold-diggers; "Corn, or your life!" More emigrants came over from England, and Captain Smith was now made governor of Jamestown. Some of the emigrants found some glittering earth which they thought was gold. Soon nearly everyone was hard at work digging it. Smith laughed at them, but they insisted on loading a ship with the worthless stuff and sending it to London. That was the last that was heard of it.

A light bark canoe, easily carried

The people had wasted their time digging this shining dirt when they should have been hoeing their gardens. Soon they began to run out of food. The captain started off with a party of men to buy corn from the Indians. The Indians made up an evil plot to kill the whole party. Fortunately, Smith discovered the plan. Seizing the chief by the hair, he pressed the muzzle of a pistol against his heart and gave him his choice: "Corn, or your life!" He received the corn, and plenty of it.

"He who will not work shall not eat." Captain Smith then ordered part of the men to plant corn, so that they might raise what they needed. The rest of the settlers he took with him into the woods to chop down trees and saw them into boards to send to England. Many tried to escape from this labor, but Smith said, "Men who are able to dig for gold can chop." Then he made this rule: "He who will not work shall not eat." Rather than lose his dinner, the laziest man now took his axe and ran off for the woods.

Captain Smith's cold-water cure. Although the choppers worked, they grumbled. They liked to see the chips fly and to hear the great trees "thunder as they fell," but the axe-handles raised blisters on their fingers. These blisters made the men swear, so that commonly one would hear "a loud oath" at every third stroke of the axe. Smith said the swearing must be stopped. He had each man's oaths numbered. When the day's work was done, every offender was called up. His oaths were counted; then he was told to hold up his right hand, and a can of cold water was poured down his sleeve for each oath. This new style of water-cure did wonders. In a short time hardly a single grumble would be heard in a whole week; it was just chop, chop, chop; and the madder the men became, the more the chips would fly.

Captain Smith meets with an accident and goes back to England; his return to America; his death. Captain Smith had not been governor very long when he met with a terrible accident. He was out in a boat, and a bag of gunpowder he had with him exploded. He was so badly hurt that he had to go back to England to get proper treatment for his wounds.

He returned to America several years later, explored the coast north of Virginia, and gave it the name of New

England, but he never went back to Jamestown again. He died in London, and was buried in a famous old church in that city.

What Captain Smith did for Virginia. Captain John Smith was in Virginia less than three years; yet in that short time he did a great deal. First, he saved the settlers from starving, by making the Indians sell them corn. Next, by his courage, he saved them from the attacks of the Indians. Lastly, he taught them how to work. Had it not been for him, the people of Jamestown would probably have lost all heart and gone back to England. He insisted on staying; and so, through him, the English held their first real foothold in America. But this was not all; he wrote two books on Virginia, describing the soil, the trees, the animals, and the Indians. He also made some excellent maps of Virginia and of New England. These books and maps taught the English people many things about this country, and were a great help to those who wished to travel to America. For these reasons, Captain Smith has rightfully been called the "Father of Virginia."

Black slaves sent to Virginia; tobacco. About ten years after Captain Smith left Jamestown, the commander of a Dutch ship brought many black slaves to Virginia (1619) and sold them to the settlers. That was the beginning of slavery in this country. Later, when other English settlements had been made, they also bought slaves; and so, after a time, every settlement both north and south owned slaves. The people of Virginia used most of their slaves in raising tobacco. They sold this in England; and as it generally brought a good price, many of the planters became quite rich. Sadly, the moral evil of slavery by race would take many years to die away from American society.

Bacon's war against Governor Berkeley; Jamestown burned. Long after Captain Smith was in his grave, Sir William Berkeley was made governor of Virginia by the king of England. Governor Berkeley treated the people very badly. Finally, a young planter named Nathaniel Bacon raised a small army and marched against the governor, who was in Jamestown. The governor, finding that he had few friends to fight for him, moved quickly to get out of the place. Bacon then entered it with his men; but he knew that, if necessary, the king would send soldiers from England to aid the governor in getting it back. So he set fire to the place and burned it. It was never built up again, and only a crumbling church tower and a few gravestones can now be seen where Jamestown once stood. Those ruins mark the first English town settled in America.

What happened later in Virginia; the Revolution; Washington; four presidents. Although Jamestown was destroyed, Virginia kept growing in strength and wealth. What was better still, the country grew in the number of its great men. The king of England continued to rule America until 1776, when many of the people of Virginia demanded that independence should be declared. The great war of independence overthrew the king's power and made us free. The military leader of that war was a Virginia planter named George Washington.

POCAHONTAS.

After we had gained the victory and peace was made, we chose presidents to govern the country. Four out of five of our first presidents, beginning with Washington, came from Virginia. For this reason that state has sometimes been called the "Mother of Presidents." One of the most famous men during the War of Independence, Patrick Henry, was a Virginian and ruled faithfully as governor of Virginia for several years.

Summary. In 1607 Captain John Smith, with several other emigrants, made the first lasting settlement built by Englishmen in America. Through Captain Smith's energy and courage, Jamestown, Virginia, took firm root. Virginia was the first state to demand the independence of America, and Washington, who was a Virginian, led the War for American Independence and helped to free the colonies from English rule.

Comprehension Questions

1. Where did the church in Jamestown originally meet?
2. Did the Indians in the East build cities?
3. What type of houses did the Indians live in?
4. Did they have guns?
5. Did they have horses and wagons?
6. What happened to Captain Smith when he went in search of the Pacific?
7. What happened to Jamestown?
8. What did the War for American Independence do?
9. Who was the great military leader of the American army?
10. Why is Virginia sometimes called the "Mother of Presidents"?
11. Who was Patrick Henry?

The old church tower at Jamestown

Chapter Seven
Captain Henry Hudson

(Voyages from 1607 to 1611)

Captain Hudson tries to find a northwest passage to China and the Indies. When Captain John Smith sailed for Virginia, he left in London a friend, named Henry Hudson, who was considered to be one of the best sea-captains in England.

While Smith was in Jamestown, a company of London merchants sent out Captain Hudson to try to find a passage to China and the Indies. When he left England, he sailed to the northwest, hoping that he could find a way open to the Pacific across the North Pole or not far below it.

He knew that if he found such a passage, it would be much shorter than a voyage round the globe farther south; because, as anyone can see, it is not so far around the top of an apple, near the stem, as it is around the middle. Hudson could not find the passage he was looking for; but he saw mountains of ice, and he went nearer to the North Pole than anyone had ever gone before.

The Dutch hire Captain Hudson; he sails for America. The Dutch people in Holland had heard of Hudson's voyage, and a company of merchants in that country hired the brave sailor to see if he could find a passage to Asia by sailing to the northeast.

He set out from the port of Amsterdam, in 1609, in a vessel named the *Half Moon*. After he had gone quite a long distance, the sailors got so tired of seeing nothing but fog and ice that they refused to go any further.

THE "HALF-MOON" IN THE HUDSON RIVER.

Then Captain Hudson turned his ship around and sailed for the coast of North America. He did that because his friend, Captain Smith of Virginia, had sent him a letter, with a map, which made him think that he could find such a passage as he wanted north of Chesapeake Bay.

Captain Hudson reaches America and finds the "Great River." Hudson sailed to Chesapeake Bay; but the weather was so stormy that he thought it would not be safe to enter it. Therefore, he sailed northward along the coast. In September 1609, he entered a beautiful bay, formed by the spreading out of a large river. At that point the stream is more than a mile wide, and he called it the "Great River." On the eastern side of it, not far from its mouth, there is a long, narrow island: the Indians of that day called it Manhattan Island.

The tides in the "Great River"— Captain Hudson begins to sail up the stream. One of the remarkable things about the river that Hudson had discovered was that it had hardly any current, and the tide from the ocean moved upstream for more than a hundred and fifty miles. If no fresh water ran in from the hills, the sea would fill the channel for a long distance, and so make a kind of salt-water river of it. Hudson noticed how salty it was, and that made him think he had finally found a passage that would lead him through from the Atlantic to the Pacific. He was

delighted with all he saw, and said, "This is as beautiful a land as one can tread upon." Soon he began to sail up the stream, wondering what he would see and whether he would come out on an ocean that would take him to Asia.

Hudson's voyage on the "Great River"— his feast with the Indians. At first he drifted along, carried by the tide, under the shadow of a great natural wall of rock. That wall, which we now call the Palisades, is from four hundred to six hundred feet high; it extends for nearly twenty miles along the western shore of the river.

Then some distance farther up, Captain Hudson came to a place where the river winds its way through great forest-covered hills, called the Highlands. At the end of the fifth day he came to a point on the eastern bank above the Highlands, where the city of Hudson now stands. Here an old Indian chief invited him to go ashore. Hudson had found the Indians, as he said "very loving"; so he accepted the invitation. The Indians made a great feast for the captain. They gave him not only roast pigeons, but also a roast dog, which they cooked in his honor.

These Indians had never seen a white man before. They thought that the English captain, in his bright scarlet coat trimmed with gold lace, had come down from the sky to visit them. What puzzled them the most, however, was that he had such a pale face.

At the end of the feast Hudson rose to go, but the Indians begged him to stay all night. Then one of them stood up, gathered all the arrows, broke them to pieces, and threw them into the fire, in order to show the captain that he need not be afraid to stay with them.

Captain Hudson reaches the end of his voyage and turns back; trouble with the Indians. Captain Hudson went back to his ship and continued up the river until he had reached a point about a hundred and fifty miles from its mouth. Here the city of Albany now stands. He found that the water was growing shallow, and he feared that if the *Half Moon* went farther she would run aground. It was clear to him, too, that wherever the river might lead, he was unlikely to find it a short way through to China.

On the way down stream a dishonest Indian, who had come out in a canoe, managed to steal something from the ship. One of the crew happened to see the Indian as he was slyly slipping off the ship; picking up a gun he fired and killed him. After that, Hudson's men had several fights with the Indians.

Hudson returns to Europe; the "Great River" is called by his name; his death. Early in October the captain set sail for Europe. Ever since that time the beautiful river that he explored has been called the Hudson, in his honor.

The next year Captain Hudson made another voyage, and entered that immense bay in the northern part of America which we now know as Hudson Bay. There he got into trouble with his men. Some of them grabbed him and set him adrift in a small boat with a few others. Nothing more was ever heard of the brave English sailor. The bay that bears his name is probably his grave.

The Dutch take possession of the land on the Hudson and call it New Netherland; how New Netherland became New York. When the Dutch in Holland heard that Captain Hudson had found a country where the Indians had plenty of rich furs to sell, they sent out people to trade with them. Holland is also called the Netherlands, which means, the Low Lands. When the Dutch took possession of the country on the Hudson (1614), they gave it the name of New Netherland, for the same reason that the English called one part of their possessions in America New England. In the course of a few years, the Dutch built (1615) a fort and some log cabins on the lower end of Manhattan island. After a time they named this little settlement New Amsterdam, in remembrance of the port of Amsterdam in Holland from which Hudson sailed.

After the Dutch had held the country of New Netherland for about fifty years, the English (1664) took it. They changed its name to New York, in honor of the Duke of York, who was brother to the king. The English also changed the name of New Amsterdam to New York City.

View of New Amsterdam in 1656

The New York "Sons of Liberty" in the Revolution; what Henry Hudson would say of the city now. More than a hundred years after this the young men of New York, the "Sons of Liberty," as they called themselves, made ready with the "Sons of Liberty" in other states to do their full part, under the lead of General Washington, in the great War for American Independence--that war by which we gained our freedom from the rule of the king of England, and became the United States of America.

THE HALF-MOON ON THE HUDSON.

The silent harbor where Henry Hudson saw a few Indian canoes is now one of the busiest seaports in the world. The great Statue of Liberty stands at its entrance. To it fleets of ships are constantly coming from all parts of the globe; from it other fleets of vessels are constantly going. If Captain Hudson could see the river which bears his name, and Manhattan Island now covered with miles of buildings which make the largest and wealthiest city in America, he might say: There is no need of my looking any further for the riches of China and the Indies, for I have found them here.

Summary. In 1609 Henry Hudson, an English sea-captain, then working under the Dutch, discovered the river now called by his name. The Dutch took possession of the country on the river, named it New Netherland, and built a small settlement on Manhattan Island. Many years later the English seized the country and named it New York. The settlement on Manhattan Island then became New York City. It is now one of the largest and wealthiest cities in the United States and one of the greatest seaports for shipping and trade in the world.

Comprehension Questions

1. Who was Henry Hudson?
2. What did he try to find?
3. What is the river he discovered called now?
4. What country seized New Netherland?
5. What name did they give it?
6. What would Hudson say if he could see New York City today?

Chapter Eight
Captain Miles Standish

(Born 1584 - Died 1656)

The English Pilgrims in Holland; why they left England. When the news of Henry Hudson's discovery of the Hudson River reached Holland, many Englishmen were living in the Dutch city of Leyden. These people were mostly farmers who had fled from Scrooby and neighboring villages in the northeast of England. They called themselves Pilgrims, because they were wanderers who were in search of freedom to worship God as the Bible commands.

THE PILGRIMS IN
ENGLAND AND HOLLAND
SCALE OF MILES

Miles Standish in Armor.

The Pilgrims left England because King James I would not let them hold their church meetings in peace. He thought, as most kings then did, that everybody in England should belong to the same church and worship God in the same way that he did. He was afraid that if people were allowed to go to whatever church they thought best, it would lead to disputes and quarrels, which would end by breaking his kingdom to pieces. Quite a number of Englishmen, seeing that they could not have religious liberty at home, escaped with their wives and children to Holland, for there the Dutch were willing to let them worship God in the way that the Bible commanded.

Why the Pilgrims wished to leave Holland and go to America. The Pilgrims were not happy in Holland. They saw that, if they stayed in that country, their children would grow up to be more Dutch than English. They saw too that they could not hope to get land in Holland. They resolved, therefore, to go to America, where they could get farms for nothing, and where their children would never forget the English language or the good old English customs and laws. In the wilderness they could not only enjoy entire religious freedom, but they could build up a settlement that would surely be their own.

The Pilgrims, with Captain Miles Standish, sail for England and then for America; they reach Cape Cod and choose a governor there. In 1620 a company of Pilgrims sailed for England on their way to America. Captain Miles Standish, an English soldier who had fought in Holland, joined them. He did not belong to the Pilgrim church, but he had become a great friend to those who did.

About a hundred of these people sailed from Plymouth, England, for the New World in the ship *Mayflower*. Many of those who went were children and young people. The Pilgrims had a long, rough passage across the Atlantic Ocean. Toward the last of November (1620), they saw land.

It was Cape Cod, that narrow strip of sand more than sixty miles long, which looks on a map like an arm bent at the elbow.

THE "MAYFLOWER."

Finding that it would be difficult to go further, the Pilgrims decided to land and explore the cape; so the *Mayflower* entered Cape Cod Harbor, inside the half-shut fist, and then came to anchor.

Before they landed, the Pilgrims held a meeting in the cabin, and prepared a written agreement to establish a government for the settlement. They signed the agreement, called the Mayflower Compact, and then chose John Carver as their first governor. This Compact set forth the main purpose for the new colony, to establish a society that would "glorify God and advance the Christian faith...."

Wash-day; what Standish and his men found on the cape. On the first Monday after they had reached the cape, all the women went on shore to wash, and so Monday has been kept as wash-day in New England ever since. Shortly after that, Captain Miles Standish, with several men, started off to see the country. They found some Indian corn buried in the sand; and a little farther on a young man named William Bradford, who afterward became governor, stepped into an Indian deer-trap. It jerked him up by the leg in a way that must have made even the soberest Pilgrim smile.

Captain Standish and his men set sail in a boat for a blue hill in the west, and find Plymouth Rock; Plymouth Harbor; landing from the Mayflower. On clear days the people on board the *Mayflower*, anchored in Cape Cod Harbor, could see a blue hill on the mainland, in the west, about forty miles away. To that blue hill, Standish and some others determined to go. Taking a sailboat they started off. A few days later they passed the hill, which the Indians called Manomet, and entered a fine harbor. There, on December 21, 1620, the shortest day in the year, they landed on that famous stone which is now known throughout the world as Plymouth Rock.

PLYMOUTH ROCK.

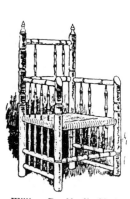

William Bradford's Chair.

Standish, with the others, went back to the *Mayflower* with a good report. They had found just what they wanted: an excellent harbor where ships from England could come in; a brook with good drinking water; and last of all, a piece of land that was nearly free from trees, so that nothing would hinder their planting corn early in the spring. Captain John Smith of Virginia had been there before them, and had named the place Plymouth on his map of New England. The Pilgrims liked the name, and so made up their minds to keep it. The *Mayflower* soon sailed for Plymouth, and the Pilgrims began to build the log cabins of their little settlement.

Sickness and Death. During that first winter nearly half the Pilgrims died. Captain Standish showed himself to be as good a nurse as he was a soldier. He, with Governor Carver and their minister, Elder Brewster, cooked, washed, waited on the sick, and did everything that kind hearts and willing hands could do to help their suffering friends. But the men who had begun to build houses had to stop that work to dig graves. When these graves were filled, they were smoothed down flat, so that no prowling Indian should count them and see how few Pilgrims there were left.

Samoset, Squanto, and Massasoit visit the Pilgrims. One day in the spring the Pilgrims were startled at seeing an Indian walk boldly into their little settlement. He cried out in good English, "Welcome! welcome!" This visitor was named Samoset; he had met some sailors years before, and had learned several English words from them.

The next time Samoset came he brought with him another Indian, whose name was Squanto. Squanto was the only one left of the tribe that had once lived at Plymouth. All the rest had died of a dreadful sickness, or plague. He had been stolen by some sailors and carried to England; there he had learned the English language. After his return, he had joined an Indian tribe that lived about thirty miles farther west. The chief of that tribe was named Massasoit, and Squanto said that he was coming soon to visit the Pilgrims. In about an hour Massasoit, with some sixty warriors, appeared on a hill just outside the settlement. The Indians had painted their faces in their very gayest style -- black, red, and yellow. If paint could make them handsome, they were determined to look their best.

Plymouth in the Early Days.

Massasoit and Governor Carver make a treaty of friendship; how Thanksgiving was kept; what Squanto did for the Pilgrims. Captain Standish, attended by a guard of honor, went out and brought the chief to Governor Carver. Then Massasoit and the governor made a solemn promise or treaty, in which they agreed that the Indians of his tribe and the Pilgrims should live like friends and brothers, doing all they could to help each other. That promise was kept for more than fifty years; it was never broken until long after the two men who made it were in their graves.

When the Pilgrims had their first Thanksgiving feast to thank God for His blessings, they invited Massasoit and his men to come and share it. The Indians brought venison and other good things; there were plenty of wild turkeys roasted; and so they all sat down together to a great dinner, and had a merry time in the wilderness.

Squanto was of great help to the Pilgrims. He showed them how to catch eels, where to go fishing, when to plant their corn, and how to put a fish in every hill to make the corn grow faster. After a while, he came to live with the Pilgrims. Squanto liked them so much that, just before he died, he begged Governor Bradford to pray that he might go to the Pilgrim's heaven.

Canonicus dares Governor Bradford to fight; the palisade; the fort and meeting-house. West of where Massasoit lived, there were some Indians on the shore of Narragansett Bay, in what is now Rhode Island. Their chief was named Canonicus, and he was no friend to Massasoit or to the Pilgrims. Canonicus thought he could frighten the Pilgrim settlers away; so he sent a bundle of sharp, new arrows, tied round with a rattlesnake skin, to Governor Bradford. That meant that he dared the governor and his men to come out and fight. Governor Bradford threw away the arrows, and then filled the snake-skin to the mouth with powder and ball. This was sent back to Canonicus. When he saw it, he was afraid to touch it, for he knew that Miles Standish's bullets could whistle louder and cut deeper than his Indian arrows.

Although the Pilgrims did not believe that Canonicus would attack them, they thought it best to build a very high, strong fence, called a palisade, around the town. They also built a log fort on one of the hills, and used the lower part of the fort for a church. Every Sunday all the people, with Captain Standish at the head, marched to their meeting-house, where a man stood on guard outside. Each Pilgrim carried his gun, and set it down near him. With one ear he listened sharply to the preacher; with the other he listened just as sharply for the cry, Indians! Indians! But the Indians never came.

The new settlers; trouble with the Indians in their neighborhood; Captain Standish's fight with the Indian warriors. By and by more emigrants came from England and settled about twenty-five miles north of Plymouth, at a place that is now called Weymouth. The Indians in that neighborhood did not like these new settlers, and they made up their minds to come upon them suddenly and murder them.

CAPTAIN MILES STANDISH THE CHOSEN MILITARY LEADER.

Governor Bradford sent Captain Standish, with a few men, to see how great the danger was. He found the Indians very bold. One of them came up to him carrying a long knife. He held it up, to show how sharp it was, and then patting it, he said, "By and by, it shall eat, but not speak." Presently another Indian came up. He was a big fellow, much larger and stronger than Standish. He, too, had a long knife, as keen as a razor. "Ah," said he to Standish, "so this is the mighty captain the white men have sent to destroy us! He is a little man; let him go and work with the women."

The captain's blood was on fire with rage, but he said not a word. His time had not yet come. The next day the Pilgrims and the Indians met in a log cabin. Standish made a sign to one of his men, and he shut the door fast. Then the captain sprang like a tiger at the big warrior who had laughed at him, and snatching his long knife from him, he plunged it into his heart. A hand-to-hand fight followed between the Pilgrims and the Indians. The Pilgrims gained the victory, and carried back the head of the Indian chief in triumph to Plymouth. Captain Standish's bold action saved both of the English settlements from destruction.

The remainder of Miles Standish's life. Standish did more things for the Pilgrims than fight for them; for he went to England, bought goods for them, and borrowed money to help them.

He lived to be an old man. At his death he left, among other things, three well-worn Bibles and three good guns. In those days, the men who read the Bible most were those who fought the hardest.

Near Plymouth, there is a high hill called Captain's Hill. That was where Standish made his home during the last part of his life. A granite monument, over a hundred feet high, stands on top of the hill. On it is a statue of the brave captain looking toward the sea. He was one of the makers of America.

GOV. JOHN WINTHROP.

Governor John Winthrop founds Boston. Ten years after the Pilgrims landed at Plymouth, a large company of English people under the leadership of Governor John Winthrop came to New England. They were called Puritans; they, too, were seeking that religious freedom which was denied them in the old country. One of the vessels that brought over these new settlers was named the *Mayflower*. She might have been the very ship that in 1620 brought the Pilgrims to these shores.

Governor Winthrop's company named the place where they settled Boston, in grateful remembrance of the beautiful old city of Boston, England, from which some of the chief emigrants came. The new settlement was called the Massachusetts Bay Colony. Massachusetts was the Indian name for the Blue Hills, near Boston. The Plymouth Colony was now often called the Old Colony, because it had been settled first. After many years, these two colonies were united, and still later they became the state of Massachusetts.

How other New England colonies grew up; the Revolution. By the time Governor Winthrop arrived, English settlements had been made in Maine, New Hampshire, and later (1724) in the country which afterward became the state of Vermont. Connecticut and Rhode Island were first settled by emigrants who came from Massachusetts.

Early New England

When the Revolution broke out, the people throughout New England took up arms in defense of their God-given rights. The first bloody battle of the war was shed on the soil of Massachusetts, near Boston.

Summary. The Pilgrims landed at Plymouth, New England, in 1620. One of the chief men who came with them was Captain Miles Standish. Had it not been for his help, the Indians might have destroyed the settlement. In 1630 Governor John Winthrop, with a large company of Puritan emigrants from England, settled Boston. The first battle of the War for American Independence was fought near Boston.

Comprehension Questions

1. Why did some Englishmen in Holland call themselves Pilgrims?
2. Why had they left England?
3. Why did they now wish to go to America?
4. Who was Miles Standish?
5. From what place in England, and in what ship, did the Pilgrims sail?
6. Why did the Pilgrims hold the first Thanksgiving?
7. What did the Pilgrims build to protect them from the Indians?
8. What else did Miles Standish do besides fight?
9. Who was the first Governor of the Boston settlement?

Puritans on Horseback.

Chapter Nine
Lord Baltimore

(Born 1580 - Died 1632)

Lord Baltimore's settlement in Newfoundland; how Catholics were then treated in England. While Captain Miles Standish was helping build up Plymouth, Lord Baltimore, an English nobleman, was trying to make a settlement on the cold, foggy island of Newfoundland.

Lord Baltimore had been brought up a Protestant, but had become a Catholic. At that time, Catholics were treated very cruelly in England. They were ordered by law to attend the Church of England. They did not like that church any better than the Pilgrims did; but if they failed to attend it, they had to take their choice between paying a large sum of money or going to prison.

Lord Baltimore hoped to make a home for himself and for other English Catholics in the wilderness of Newfoundland, where there would be no one to trouble them. But, the unfortunate settlers were unable to live in Newfoundland because of the cold weather. They had winter a good part of the year, and fog during all of it. They could grow nothing, because, as one man said, the soil was either rock or swamp: the rock was as hard as iron; the swamp was so deep that you could not touch bottom with a ten-foot pole.

The king of England gives Lord Baltimore part of Virginia, and names it Maryland; what Lord Baltimore paid for it. King Charles I of England was a good friend to Lord Baltimore; and when the settlement in Newfoundland was given up, he made him a present of an large three-cornered piece of land in America. This piece was cut out of Virginia, north of the Potomac River.

GEORGE CALVERT (LORD BALTIMORE).

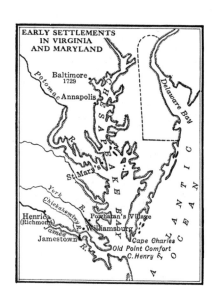

The king's wife, who was called Queen Mary, was a French Catholic. In her honor, Charles named the country he had given Lord Baltimore, Mary Land, or Maryland. He could not have chosen a better name, because Maryland was to be a shelter for many English people who believed in the same religion that the queen did.

All that Lord Baltimore was to pay for Maryland, with its twelve thousand square miles of land and water, was two Indian arrows. These he agreed to send every spring to the royal palace of Windsor Castle, near London. The arrows would be worth nothing whatever to the king, but they were sent as a kind of yearly rent. They showed that, though Lord Baltimore had the use of Maryland, and could do pretty much as he pleased with it, still the king did not surrender all control of it. In Virginia and in New England the king had granted all land to groups of persons, and he had been particular to tell them just what they must or must not do; but he gave Maryland to one man only. More than this, he promised to let Lord Baltimore have his own way in everything, so long as he made no laws in Maryland that were contrary to the laws of England. So, Lord Baltimore had greater privileges than any other holder of land in America at that time.

Lord Baltimore dies; his son sends emigrants to Maryland; the landing; the Indians; St. Mary's. Lord Baltimore died before he could get ready to come to America. His eldest son then became the next Lord Baltimore. He sent over many emigrants; part of them were Catholics, and part were Protestants, but all were to have equal rights in Maryland. In the spring of 1634, these people landed on a little island near the mouth of the Potomac River. There they cut down a tree and made a large cross; then, kneeling around that cross, they all joined in prayer to God for their safe journey.

A little later they landed on the shore of the river. There they met some Indians. Under a huge mulberry tree they bargained with the Indians for a place to build a town, and paid for the land in hatchets, knives, and beads.

The Indians were greatly amazed at the size of the ship in which the white men came. They thought that it was made like their canoes, and that it was simply the trunk of a tree hollowed out. They wondered where the English could have found a tree big enough to make it.

The emigrants named their settlement St. Mary's. The Indians and the settlers lived and worked together, side by side. The Indians showed the emigrants how to hunt in the forest, and the Indian women taught the white women how to make corn meal, and to bake Johnny-cake before the open fire.

Maryland, the home of religious liberty. Maryland was different from the other English colonies in America, because everyone there, whether Catholic or Protestant, had the right to worship God in his own way. In that humble little village of St. Mary's, made up of thirty or forty log huts and wigwams in the woods, "religious liberty had its only home in the wide world."

But more than this, Lord Baltimore, who was a Protestant, kindly invited people who had been driven out of the other settlements on account of their religion to come and live in Maryland. He gave a hearty welcome to all, whether they thought as he did or not. How sad it is that so many people in America today have forgotten the importance of religious liberty.

Maryland falls into trouble; the city of Baltimore is built. This happy time of peace did not last long. Some of the Virginians were very angry because the king had given Lord Baltimore part of what they thought was their land. They fought with the new settlers and gave them much trouble.

Things continued to get worse. Men went to Maryland and undertook to drive out the Catholics. Sometimes they acted in a very shameful manner toward Lord Baltimore and his friends; among other things, they put Father White in irons and sent him back to England as a prisoner. Lord Baltimore had spent a great deal of money in building up the settlement, but his right to the land was taken away from him for a time, and all who dared to defend him were badly treated.

St. Mary's never grew to be much of a place, but not quite a hundred years after the English landed there, a new and beautiful city was begun (1729) in Maryland. It was named Baltimore, in honor of that Lord Baltimore who sent out the first emigrants.

Summary. King Charles I of England gave Lord Baltimore a part of Virginia and named it Maryland, in honor of his wife, Queen Mary. A company of emigrants came out to Maryland in 1634. It was the first settlement in America in which all Christian people had entire liberty to worship God in whatever way they thought right. That liberty they owed to Lord Baltimore's son who was a Bible-believing Christian.

Comprehension Questions

1. Who was Lord Baltimore, and what did he try to do in Newfoundland?
2. How were Catholics then treated in England?
3. What was Lord Baltimore to pay for Maryland?
4. What wonderful freedom found its home in Maryland?
5. Did a city called Baltimore develop and prosper over time?

Chapter Ten
Roger Williams

(Born 1600 - Died 1684)

Roger Williams comes to Boston; he preaches in Salem and in Plymouth; his friendship for the Indians. Shortly after Governor John Winthrop and his company settled Boston, a young minister named Roger Williams came over from England to join them.

Mr. Williams soon became a great friend to the Indians, and while he preached at Salem, near Boston, and at Plymouth, he came to know many of them. He made great effort to learn their language, and he spent much time talking with the chief Massasoit and his men in their dirty, smoky wigwams. He made the Indians feel that, as he said, his whole heart's desire was to do them good. For this reason, they were always glad to see him and ready to help him. A time came, as we shall soon see, when they were able to do as much for him as he could do for them.

Who owned the greater part of America? what the king of England thought; what Roger Williams thought and said. The company that had settled Boston held the land by permission of the king of England. The king considered that most of the land in America belonged to him, because John Cabot had discovered it. But Roger Williams said that the English king had no right to the land unless he bought it from the Indians, who were living here when the English came.

Now the people of Massachusetts were always quite willing to pay the Indians a fair price for whatever land they wanted, but many of them were afraid to have Mr. Williams preach and write as he did. They believed that if they allowed him to continue speaking out so boldly against the king, the English monarch would get so angry that he would take Massachusetts away from them and give it to a new group. In that case, those who had settled there would lose everything. For this reason, the people of Boston tried to make the young minister agree to keep silent on this subject.

Rogers Williams Fleeing Through the Woods.

A policeman is sent to arrest Roger Williams; he escapes to the woods, and goes to Mount Hope. Mr. Williams was not the kind to keep silent. So the chief men of Boston sent a policeman down to Salem, with orders to grab him and send him back to England. When he heard that the police were after him, Mr. Williams slipped quietly out of his house and escaped to the woods.

There was a heavy depth of snow on the ground, but the young man made up his mind that he would go to his old friend Massasoit, and ask him to help him in his trouble.

Massasoit lived near Mount Hope, in what is now Rhode Island, about eighty miles southwest from Salem. There were no roads through the woods, and it was a long, dreary journey to make on foot but Mr. Williams did not hesitate. He took a hatchet to chop firewood, a flint and steel to strike fire with -- for in those days people had no matches -- and last of all, a pocket compass to aid him in finding his way through the thick forest.

All day he waded wearily on through the deep snow, only stopping now and then to rest or to look at his compass and make sure that he was going in the right direction. At night, he would gather wood enough to make a little fire to warm himself or to melt some snow to drink. Then he would cut down a few branches for a bed, or if he was blest enough to find a large, hollow tree, he would creep into that. There he would fall asleep while listening to the howling of the wind or to the fiercer howling of the hungry wolves prowling around the woods.

At length, after much suffering from cold and lack of food, he managed to reach Massasoit's wigwam. There the big-hearted Indian chief gave him a warm welcome. He took him into his poor cabin and kept him until spring -- there was no rent bill to pay. All the Indians liked the young minister, and even Canonicus, that savage chief of a neighboring tribe, who had dared Governor Bradford to fight, said that he "loved him as his own son."

Roger Williams at Seekonk; "What cheer, friend?"
When the warm days came, in the spring of 1636, Mr.
Williams began building a log hut for himself at Seekonk, on
the east bank of the Seekonk River. But he was told that his
cabin stood on ground owned by the people of Massachusetts;
so he, with a few friends who had joined him, took a canoe
and paddled down stream to find a new place to build.

BUILDING A LOG CABIN

"What cheer, friend? what cheer?" shouted some Indians who
were standing on a rock on the western bank of the river.
That was the Indian way of saying: How do you do? He
landed on what is now called "What Cheer Rock," and had a
talk with the Indian men. They told him that there was a
fine spring of water round the point of land a little farther
down. He went there, and liked the spot so much that he
decided to stay. His friend Canonicus owned the land, and
he gladly let him have what he needed. Roger Williams
believed that a kind Providence had guided him to this
pleasant place, and so he named it PROVIDENCE.

Providence was the first settlement made in America that set its doors wide open to everyone who wished to come and live there. This great and good work was done by Roger Williams. Providence eventually grew to be the chief city in the state of Rhode Island. When the Revolution began, every man and boy in the state, from sixteen to sixty, stood ready to fight for liberty and against English rule.

Summary. Roger Williams, a young minister from Salem, Massachusetts, declared that the Indians, and not the king of England, owned the land in America. The governor of Massachusetts was afraid that if Mr. Williams continued to say these things, the king would hear of it and would take away the land held by the people of Boston and the other settlements. Therefore, he sent a policeman to arrest the young minister and put him on board a ship going back to England. When Mr. Williams learned of this, he fled to the Indian chief, Massasoit. In 1636, Roger Williams began building Providence the first settlement in what eventually became the state of Rhode Island.

Comprehension Questions

1. Who was Roger Williams?
2. Who did Mr. Williams think first owned the land in America?
3. How did many of the people of Massachusetts feel about Mr. Williams?
4. Why did Mr. Williams name the settlement Providence?
5. What became of the city of Providence?
6. In what year did Roger Williams begin to build the place known as Providence?

Chapter Eleven
King Philip

(Time of the Indian War, 1675-1676)

Death of Massasoit; Wamsutta and Philip; Wamsutta's sudden death. When the Indian chief Massasoit died, the people of Plymouth lost one of their best friends. Massasoit left two sons, one named Wamsutta, who became chief in his father's place, and the other called Philip. They both lived near Mount Hope, in Rhode Island.

The governor of Plymouth heard that Wamsutta was stirring up the Indians to make war on the settlers, and he ordered the Indian chief to come to him and give an account of himself. Wamsutta went, but on his way back he suddenly fell sick, and soon after he reached home he died. His young wife was a woman who was respected by her tribe, and she told them that she felt sure the settlers had poisoned her husband in order to get rid of him. This was not true, but the Indians believed it.

Philip becomes chief; why he hated the settlers; how the settlers had obtained possession of the Indian lands. Philip now became chief. He called himself "King Philip." His palace was a wigwam made of bark. On great occasions, he wore a bright red blanket and a kind of crown made of a broad belt ornamented with shells. King Philip hated the settlers because he believed they had murdered his brother. He also saw the settlers were growing stronger in numbers every year, while the Indians were becoming weaker.

King Philip

When the Pilgrims landed at Plymouth, Massasoit, Philip's father, held all the country from Cape Cod back to the eastern shores of Narragansett Bay, a strip of land about thirty miles wide. The white settlers bought a small piece of this land. After a while they bought more, and so they continued until, in about fifty years, they owned nearly all of what Massasoit's tribe had once owned. The Indians had nothing left but two little pieces of land, which were nearly surrounded by the waters of Narragansett Bay. Here they felt that they were shut up almost like prisoners, and that the settlers watched everything that they did.

How King Philip felt; signs of the coming war; the "Praying Indians"; the murder. King Philip was a very proud man; as proud, in fact, as the king of England. He could not bear to see his people losing power. He thought that if the Indians did not rise and drive out the white men, then the white men would surely drive out the Indians. Most of the Indians now had guns, and could use them almost as well as the settlers could; so Philip thought that it was best to fight.

King Philip.

Although many Indians now hated the white settlers, this was not true of all. A minister, named John Eliot, had persuaded some of the Indians near Boston to give up their pagan religion, and to try to live like peace-loving Christians. These were called "Praying Indians." One of them who knew King Philip well told the settlers that Philip's warriors were grinding their hatchets sharp for war. Soon afterward this "Praying Indian" was found murdered. The settlers accused three of Philip's men of having killed him. They were tried, found guilty, and hanged.

Beginning of the war at Swansea; burning of Brookfield. Then Philip's warriors began the war in the summer of 1675. Some settlers were going home from church in the town of Swansea, Massachusetts; they had gone to pray that there might be no fighting. As they walked along, talking together, two guns were fired out of the bushes. One of the Pilgrim men fell dead in the road, and another was badly hurt.

The shots were fired by Indians. This was the way they always fought when they could. They were not cowards; but they did not come out and fight boldly, but would fire from behind trees and rocks. Frequently a settler would be killed without even seeing who shot him.

At first, the fighting was mainly in those villages near Plymouth Colony that were nearest Narragansett Bay; then it spread to the valley of the Connecticut River. Deerfield, Springfield, Brookfield, Groton, and many other places in Massachusetts were attacked. The Indians would creep up quietly in the night, burn the houses, carry off the women and children as prisoners if they could, kill the men and take their scalps home and hang them in their wigwams.

At Brookfield the settlers left their houses, and gathered in one strong house for defense. The Indians burned all the houses but that one, and did their best to burn it, too. They shot blazing arrows into the shingles of the roof. When the Indians saw that the shingles had caught, and were beginning to flame up, they danced for joy, and roared like wild bulls. But the men in the house managed to put out the fire on the roof. Then the wicked warriors got a cart, filled it with hay, set it on fire, and pushed it up against the house.

This time they thought that they would surely burn the settlers out; but just then a heavy rain shower came up, and extinguished the fire. A little later, some soldiers marched into the village, and saved the people in the house.

"KING PHILIP'S" WAR

The fight at Hadley; what Colonel Goffe did. At Hadley, the people were in the meeting-house when the terrible Indian war-whoop rang through the village. The warriors drove back those who dared to go out against them, and it seemed as though the village would be destroyed.

Suddenly, a white-haired old man, sword in hand, appeared among the settlers. No one knew who he was; but he called to them to follow him, as a captain calls to his men, and they obeyed him. The astonished Indians turned and ran. When all was over, the townspeople looked for their brave leader, but he was gone; they never saw him again. Many thought that he was an angel who had been sent to save them. But the angel was Colonel Goffe, an Englishman, one of the judges who, after the Civil War in England, had sentenced King Charles the First to death. He had escaped to America after the son of King Charles I took the throne; and fortunately for the people of Hadley, he was hiding in the house of a friend in that village when the Indians attacked.

How a woman drove off an Indian. In this dreadful war with the Indians, there were times when even the women had to fight for their lives. In one case, a woman had been left in a house with two young children. She heard a noise at the window, and looking up, saw an Indian trying to raise the curtain. Quickly she put her two little children under two large brass kettles which stood near. Then, grabbing a shovelful of red-hot coals from the open fire, she stood ready, and just as the Indian thrust his head into the room, she dashed the coals right into his face and eyes. With a yell of agony the Indian let go his hold, dropped to the ground as though he had been shot, and ran howling into the woods.

The great swamp fight; burning the Indian wigwams; what the Chief Canonchet said. During the summer and autumn of 1675 the Indians on the west side of Narragansett Bay took no open part in King Philip's War. But the next winter, the settlers found that these Indians were secretly receiving and sheltering the cruel Indians who had been wounded in fighting for their proud chief. For that reason, the settlers determined to raise a large army and attack them. The Indians had gathered in a fort on an island in a swamp. This fort was a very difficult place to reach. It was built from the trunks of trees set upright in the ground. It was so strong that the Indian warriors felt safe.

Starting very early in the morning, the attacking party waded fifteen miles through deep snow. Many of them had their hands and feet badly frozen. One of the chief men in leading the attack was Captain Benjamin Church of Plymouth. He was a very brave soldier and knew all about Indian life and Indian fighting. In the battle, he was struck by two bullets, and so badly wounded that he could not move a step further; but he made one of his men hold him up, and shouted to his soldiers to go ahead. The fight was a very hard one, but finally the fort was taken. More than two hundred and fifty men in the attacking party were killed or wounded; the Indians lost as many as a thousand.

After the battle was over, Captain Church begged the men not to burn the wigwams inside the fort, for there were a great number of old men and women and little Indian children in the wigwams. But the men were very angry with the Indians, and would not listen to him. They set the wigwams on fire, and burned many of these poor people to death.

Canonchet, the chief of the tribe, was taken prisoner. The settlers told him they would spare his life if he would try to make peace. "No," said he, "we will all fight to the last man rather than become slaves." He was then told that he must be shot. "I like it well," said he. "I wish to die before my heart becomes soft, or I say anything unworthy of myself." This proud and fierce warrior was so blinded by hatred that he was willing to die rather than seek to live at peace with his fellow man.

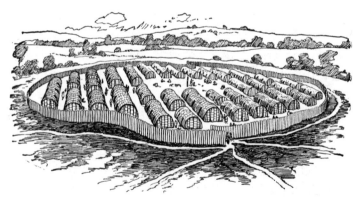

This was a village of wigwams, surrounded by a palisade.

Philip's wife and son are taken prisoner; Philip is shot; end of war. The next summer Captain Church, with many "brisk Bridgewater lads," chased King Philip and his men, and took many Indian prisoners. Among those taken captive were King Philip's wife and his little boy. When Philip heard of it he cried out, "My heart breaks; now I am ready to die." He had good reason for saying so. His stubbornness and pride brought misery and death to his own wife and children. King Philip refused to call an end to a war that never should have started.

Not long after that, King Philip himself was shot. He had been hunted like a wild beast from place to place. At last he had returned to see his old home at Mount Hope once more. Shortly after his return, the Indian warrior was shot to death by Captain Church during a fight.

King Philip's death brought the war to an end. It had lasted a little over a year, from the early summer of 1675 to the latter part of the summer of 1676. In that short time the Indians had killed between five and six hundred New England settlers, and had burned thirteen villages to ashes, besides partly burning a great many more. The war cost so much money that many people were made poor by it. But the strength of the Indians was broken, and they never dared to trouble the people of southern New England again.

Summary. In 1675, King Philip began a great Indian war against the people of southern New England. His object was to kill off the white settlers, and get back the land for the Indians. He did kill a large number, and he destroyed many villages; but in the end the settlers gained the victory. Philip's wife and child were killed and he was shot. The Indians never attempted another war in this part of the country.

Exploring American History

Comprehension Questions

1. Who was Wamsutta?
2. Who was "King Philip"?
3. Who were the "Praying Indians"?
4. Tell how a woman drove off an Indian.
5. What happened to King Philip himself?
6. Who won King Philip's war?

Distribution of
INDIAN TRIBES
SCALE OF MILES
0   100   200   300   400

Chapter Twelve
William Penn

(Born 1644 - Died 1718)

King Charles the Second gives William Penn a great piece of land, and names it Pennsylvania. King Charles II of England owed a large sum of money to a young Englishman named William Penn. The king was fond of pleasure, and he spent so much money on himself and his friends that he had none left to pay his just debts. Penn knew this; so he told His Majesty that if he would give him a piece of wild land in America, he would ask nothing more.

Charles was very glad to settle the account so easily. He therefore, gave Penn a great territory north of Maryland and west of the Delaware River. This territory was nearly as large as England. The king named it Pennsylvania, a word that means Penn's Woods. At that time, the land was not thought to be worth much. No one knew yet that beneath Penn's Woods there were immense mines of coal and iron, which would one day be of greater value that all the riches of the king of England.

William Penn's religion; what he wanted to do with his American land. Penn belonged to a religious society called the Society of Friends; today they are generally spoken of as Quakers. They are a people who try to find out what is right by asking their own hearts and by studying the Bible. They believe that no person should be shown more respect than another; and at that time, they would not take off their hats even to the king himself. The vast majority of settlers viewed the Quakers as rebellious extremists, for they rejected the Bible as the ultimate authority for faith and life while they sought extra-Biblical revelation.

Penn wanted the land that had been given him here as a place where the Friends or Quakers might go and settle. A little later the whole of what is now the state of New Jersey was bought by Penn and other Quakers for the same purpose. We have seen that neither the Pilgrims nor the Catholics had any real peace in England. The Quakers suffered even more; they were often cruelly whipped and thrown into dark and dirty prisons, where many died from the bad treatment they received. William Penn himself had been shut up in jail four times because of his religion. Although he was no longer in such danger, because the king was his friend, he wanted to provide a safe place for others who were not as well off as he.

Penn sends out emigrants to Pennsylvania; he gets ready to go himself; his conversation with the king. Penn soon sent out some people who were anxious to settle in Pennsylvania. The next year, 1682, he made ready to sail himself with a hundred more emigrants. Just before he started, he called on the king in his palace in London. The king liked to joke, and he said to Penn that he should never expect to see him again, for he thought that the Indians would be sure to catch such a good-looking young man as Penn was and eat him. 'But, Friend Charles,' said Penn, 'I mean to buy the land from the Indians, so they will remain on good terms with me and not eat me.' 'Buy their lands!' exclaimed the king. 'Why, is not the whole of America mine?' 'Certainly not,' answered Penn. 'What!' replied the king; 'didn't my people discover it? and so haven't I the right to it?' 'Well, Friend Charles,' said Penn, 'suppose a canoe, full of Indians, should cross the sea and they should discover England, would that make it theirs? Would you surrender the country to them?' The king did not know what to say to this; it was a new way of looking at the matter. He probably said to himself, these Quakers are a strange people; they seem to think that even American savages have rights that should be respected.

Penn starts the city of Philadelphia; his treaty with the Indians; his visit with them; how the Indians and the Quakers worked together. When William Penn reached America in 1682, he sailed up the broad and beautiful Delaware River for nearly a hundred miles. There he stopped, and decided to build a city on its banks. He gave the place the Bible name of Philadelphia, or the City of Brotherly Love, because he hoped that all its citizens would live together like brothers. The streets were named from the trees then growing on the land, and so today many still bear names like Walnut, Pine, Cedar, and Vine.

Penn said, "We intend to sit down lovingly among the Indians." In the beginning, he held a great meeting with them under a wide-spreading elm. The tree stood in what is now a part of Philadelphia. Here Penn and the Indians made a treaty, or agreement, by which they promised each other that they would live together as friends as long as the water should run in the rivers, or the sun shine in the sky.

William Penn's Treaty with the Indians.

Nearly a hundred years later while the Revolutionary War was going on, the British army took possession of the city. It was cold, winter weather, and the men wanted firewood, but the English general thought so much of William Penn that he set a guard of soldiers around that great elm, to prevent anyone from chopping it down.

Not long after the great meeting under the elm, Penn visited some of the Indians in their wigwams. They treated him to a meal of roasted acorns. After their feast, some of the young warriors began to run and leap about, to show the Englishman what they could do. When Penn was in college at Oxford he had liked doing such things himself. The sight of the Indian boys made him feel like a boy again, so he sprang up from the ground and beat them all at hop, skip, and jump. This completely won the hearts of the Indians.

From that time, for sixty years, the Pennsylvania settlers and the Indians were best friends. The Indians said, "The Quakers are honest men; they do no harm; they are welcome to come here." In New England there had been, as we have seen, a terrible war with the Indians, but in Pennsylvania there were no major wars for many years.

How Philadelphia grew; what was done there in the Revolution; William Penn's last years and death. Philadelphia grew very fast. William Penn let the people have land very cheap, and he said to them, "You shall be governed by laws of your own making." Even after Philadelphia became a large town, it had no poorhouse, for none was needed; everybody seemed to be able to take care of himself.

When the Revolution began, the people of Pennsylvania and of the country north and south of it sent men to Philadelphia to decide what should be done. This meeting was called the First Continental Congress. It was held in the old State House, a building that is still standing. There in 1776, Congress declared the United States of America independent of England. In the war, the people of Delaware and New Jersey fought side by side with those of Pennsylvania.

William Penn spent a great deal of money in helping Philadelphia and other settlements. After he returned to England he was put in prison for debt by a wicked fellow he had employed. He did not owe the money, and he proved that the man who said that he did was no better than a thief. Penn was released from prison, but his long confinement in jail had broken his health down. When he died the Indians of Pennsylvania sent his widow some beautiful furs, in remembrance of their "Brother Penn," as they called him. They said that the furs were to make her a cloak, "to protect her while she passed through this thorny wilderness without her guide."

PENN PAYING FOR HIS LAND

About twenty-five miles west of London, on a country road within sight of the towers of Windsor Castle, there stands a Friends' meeting-house, or Quaker church. In the backyard of the meeting-house, William Penn lies buried. For a hundred years or more, there was no mark of any kind to show where he was buried. Now a small stone bearing his name points out the grave of the founder of the great state of Pennsylvania.

Summary. Charles II, king of England, owed William Penn, a young English Quaker, a large sum of money. In order to settle the debt, the king gave him a great piece of land in America, and named it Pennsylvania, or Penn's Woods. Penn wished to make a home for Quakers in America, and in 1682 he came over, and began building the city of Philadelphia. When the Revolution broke out, men were sent from all parts of the country to Philadelphia, to hold a meeting called the Continental Congress. In 1776, Congress declared the United States independent from England.

Comprehension Questions

1. To whom did King Charles II owe a large sum of money?
2. How did he pay his debt?
3. What did the king name the country?
4. What does Philadelphia mean?
5. Did the Indians trouble the Quakers?
6. Where is William Penn buried?

Chapter Thirteen
General James Oglethorpe

(Born 1696 - Died 1785)

The twelve English colonies in America; General Oglethorpe makes a settlement in Georgia. We have seen that the first real colony or settlement made in America by the English was in Virginia in 1607. By the beginning of 1733, or in about a hundred and twenty-five years, eleven more had been made -- twelve in all. They stretched along the seacoast, from the farthest coast of Maine to the northern boundary of Florida, which was then owned by the Spaniards.

The two colonies farthest south were North Carolina and South Carolina. In 1733 James Oglethorpe, a brave English soldier who afterward became General Oglethorpe, came over here to make a new settlement. This new one, which made a total of thirteen colonies, was called Georgia in honor of King George II, who gave a piece of land for it, on the seacoast below South Carolina.

What it was that led General Oglethorpe to make this new settlement. General Oglethorpe had a friend in England who was cast into prison for debt. There the unfortunate man was so cruelly treated that he became sick and died, leaving his family in great trouble.

The General felt the death of his friend so much that he began to investigate how other poor debtors lived in the London prisons. He soon found that great numbers of them suffered terribly. The prisons were crowded and filthy. The men shut up in them were ragged and dirty; some of them were held with heavy chains; a good many actually died of starvation.

General Oglethorpe could not bear to see strong men killed off in this manner. He thought that if the best of them (those who were honest and willing to work) could have the chance to earn their living, they would soon do as well as any men. During his effort to help them, he persuaded the king to give the land of Georgia.

James Oglethorpe.

Early Settlements in Georgia.

Building the city of Savannah; what the people of Charleston, South Carolina did; a busy settlement; the alligators. General Oglethorpe took thirty-five families to America in 1733. They settled on a bank of the Savannah River, about twenty miles from the sea. The General laid out a town with broad, straight, handsome streets, and with many small squares or parks. He called the settlement Savannah, from the Indian name of the river on which it stands.

The people of Charleston, South Carolina, were glad to have some English neighbors south of them to help them fight the Spaniards of Florida, who hated the English and wanted to drive them out. They gave the newcomers a hundred head of cattle, a group of hogs, and twenty barrels of rice.

The emigrants began to work with a will, cutting down the forest trees, building houses, and planting gardens. There were no lazy people to be seen at Savannah. Even the children found something to do that was helpful.

Nothing disturbed the people but the alligators. They climbed up the bank from the river to see what was happening. But the boys soon taught them not to be too curious. When one monster was found impudently prowling around the town, they thumped him with sticks until they almost beat the life out of him. Soon the alligators decided not to pay any more visits to the settlers.

Arrival of some German emigrants; "Ebenezer"; "blazing" trees. After a time some German Protestants, who had been cruelly driven out of their native land on account of their religion, came to Georgia. General Oglethorpe gave them a hearty welcome. He had bought land from the Indians, and so there was plenty of room for all. The Germans went up the river, and then went back several miles into the woods; there they picked out a place for a town. They called their settlement by the Bible name of Ebenezer, which means "The Lord hath helped us."

There were no roads through the forests, so the new settlers "blazed" the trees; that is, they chopped a piece of bark off, so that they could find their way through the thick woods when they wanted to go to Savannah. Every tree so marked stood like a guide-post; it showed the traveller which way to go until he came in sight of the next one.

Trying to make silk; the queen's American dress. The settlers hoped to be able to get large quantities of silk to send to England, because the mulberry tree grows wild in Georgia, and its leaves are the favorite food of the silkworm. At first it seemed as if the plan would be successful, and General Oglethorpe took over some Georgia silk as a present to the queen of England. She had a handsome dress made of it for her birthday; it was the first American silk dress ever worn by an English queen. But, after a while it was found that silk could not be produced in Georgia as well as it could in Italy and France, and so in time cotton became the favorite crop.

Keeping out the Spaniards; Georgia powder at Bunker Hill; General Oglethorpe in his old age. The people of Georgia did a good work in keeping out the Spaniards, who were trying to take over the country located just north of Florida. Later, like the settlers in North Carolina and South Carolina, they did their full share in helping to make America independent from the rule of the king of England. When the War of American Independence began, the king had a lot of powder stored in Savannah. The people broke into the building, rolled out the kegs, and carried them off. Part of the powder they kept for themselves, and part they may have sent to Massachusetts; it is likely that the men who fought at Bunker Hill may have loaded their guns with some of the powder given to them by their friends in Savannah. Therefore, the king got it back, but in a different way than he expected.

OGLETHORPE AND THE CHIEFS.

General Oglethorpe spent the closing years of his life in England. He lived to a very old age. Up to the last, he had eyes as bright and keen as a boy's. After the Revolution was over, the king made a treaty, or agreement, by which he promised to let the United States of America live in peace. General Oglethorpe was able to read that treaty without glasses. He had lived to see the colony of Georgia, which he had settled, become a free and independent state.

Summary. In 1733 General James Oglethorpe brought over some emigrants from England, and settled Savannah, Georgia. Georgia was the thirteenth English colony; it was the last one established in this country. General Oglethorpe lived to see it become one of the United States of America.

Comprehension Questions

1. At the beginning of 1733, how many English colonies were there in America?
2. Who was General Oglethorpe?
3. What did he wish to do for the poor debtors?
4. Did the colony of Georgia raise more cotton or silk?
5. What good work did the people of Georgia do?
6. What event did General Oglethorpe enjoy in his old age?

Chapter Fourteen
Benjamin Franklin

(Born 1706 - Died 1790)

Growth of Philadelphia; what a young printer was doing for it. By the year 1733, when the people of Savannah were building their first log cabins, Philadelphia had grown to be the largest city in this country -- though it would take more than seventy such cities to make one as great as Philadelphia is today.

Next to William Penn, the person who did the most for Philadelphia was a young man who had gone from Boston to make his home among the Quakers. He lived in a small house near the market. On a board over the door he had painted his name and business: Benjamin Franklin, Printer.

Franklin's newspaper and almanac; how he worked, standing before kings. Franklin was then publishing a small newspaper called the *Pennsylvania Gazette*. Today we print newspapers with computer-controlled electric power at the rate of one or two thousand a minute; but Franklin, standing in his shirt sleeves at a little press, printed slowly with his own hands. It was slow, hard work, as you could see by the drops of sweat that stood on his forehead. The young man not only wrote most of what he printed in his paper, but he often made his own ink; sometimes he even made his own type. When he ran out of paper he would take a wheelbarrow, go out and buy a load, and wheel it home. Today there are more than one dozen newspapers printed in Philadelphia; then there were only two, and Franklin's was the better of them.

In addition to this paper he published an almanac, which thousands of people bought. In it he printed such sayings as these: "He who would thrive must rise at five," and "If you want a thing well done, do it yourself." But Franklin was not contented with simply printing these sayings; he practiced them as well.

THE FIRST PRINTING PRESS
BROUGHT TO AMERICA.

Sometimes his friends would ask him why he began work so early in the morning, and kept at it so many hours. He would laugh and tell them that his father used to repeat to him this saying of Solomon's: "Seest thou a man diligent in his business? he shall stand before kings; he shall not stand before mean men."

At that time the young printer never expected to stand in the presence of a king; but years later he met with five. One of them, his friend, the king of France, gave him his picture covered with diamonds.

Franklin's boyhood; making tallow candles; he is apprenticed to his brother; how he managed to save money to buy books. Franklin's father was a poor man with a large family. He lived in Boston, and made soap and candles. Benjamin went to school two years; then, when he was ten years old, his father set him to work in his factory, and he finished the rest of his schooling at home. He was now kept busy filling the candle molds with melted tallow, cutting off the ends of the wicks, and running errands.

The boy did not like this type of work; and as he was very fond of books, his father sent him to work in the printing shop of James Franklin, one of Benjamin's brothers. James Franklin paid a small sum of money each week for Benjamin's housing; but the boy told him that if he would let him have half the money to use as he wished, he would house himself. James was glad to do this. Benjamin then stopped eating meat, and while the others went out to dinner, he would stay in the printing office and eat a boiled potato, or a handful of raisins. In this way he saved up several coins every week; and when he had saved enough money he would buy a book.

James Franklin was not only a selfish man, but also a hot-tempered one. When he became angry with his young apprentice, he would beat and knock him around. At length the lad, who was now seventeen, made up his mind that he would run away, and go to New York.

Young Franklin runs away; he goes to New York, and then to Philadelphia. Young Franklin sold some of his books, and with the money paid his passage to New York on a sailing vessel, for in those days there were no airplanes or railroads in America. He could not find work in New York, however, so he decided to move on to Philadelphia. He started to walk across New Jersey to Burlington on the Delaware River, a distance of about fifty miles; there he hoped to get a sailboat going down the river to Philadelphia. Shortly after he set out, it began to rain hard, and the lad was soon wet to the skin and splashed with red mud; but he continued until noon, then took a rest, and on the third day he reached Burlington and found passage down the river.

Benjamin Franklin.

BIRTHPLACE OF BENJAMIN FRANKLIN, BOSTON, MASS.

Franklin's Sunday walk in Philadelphia; the rolls; Miss Read; the Quaker meeting-house. Franklin landed in Philadelphia on a Sunday morning in 1723. He was tired and hungry; he had but a single dollar in the world. As he walked along, he saw a bakeshop open. He went in and bought three great, puffy rolls for a penny each. Then he started up Market Street, where he was one day to have his newspaper office. He had a roll like a small loaf of bread tucked under each arm, and he was eating the other as though it tasted good to him. As he passed a house, he noticed a nice-looking young woman at the door. She seemed to want to laugh, and well she might, for Franklin appeared like a youthful tramp who had been robbing a baker's shop. The young woman was Miss Deborah Read. Several years later Franklin married her. He always said that he could not have been blest with a better wife.

Franklin continued in his walk until he came to the Delaware River. He took a little drink of river water to settle his breakfast, and then gave away the two rolls he had under his arm to a poor woman with a child. On his way back from the river, he followed some people to a Quaker meeting-house. At the meeting no one spoke. Franklin was tired out, and not having any preacher to keep him awake, he soon fell asleep, and slept until the meeting was over. He says, "This was the first house I was in or slept in, in Philadelphia."

Franklin finds work; he goes back to Boston on a visit; he learns to stoop. The next day the young man found some work in a printing office. Six months afterward he decided to go back to Boston to see his friends. He started on his journey with a good suit of clothes, a silver watch, and a well-filled purse.

While in Boston, Franklin went to call on a minister who had written a little book which he had been very fond of reading. As he was coming away from the minister's house, he had to go through a low passageway under a large beam. "Stoop! stoop!" cried out the gentleman; but Franklin did not understand him, and so hit his head a sharp knock against the beam. "Ah," said his friend, as he saw him rubbing his head, "you are young, and have the world before you; stoop as you go through it, and you will miss many hard thumps." Franklin says that this sensible advice, which was thus beat into his head, was of great use because he learned then how to stoop to conquer. Even the Bible tells us that "...he who humbles himself shall be exalted."

Franklin returns to Philadelphia; he goes to London; water against beer. Franklin soon went back to Philadelphia. The governor of Pennsylvania then persuaded him to go to London, telling him that he would help him to get a printing-press and type to start a newspaper in Philadelphia.

When Franklin reached London, he found that the governor was one of those men who promise great things, but do nothing. Instead of buying a press, Franklin had to go to work in a printing office to earn his bread. He stayed in London more than a year. At the office where he worked, the men were great beer drinkers. One of his companions bought six pints a day. He began with a pint before breakfast. Then he took another pint at breakfast, a pint between breakfast and dinner, a pint at dinner, a pint in the afternoon, and last of all, a pint after he had finished work. Franklin drank nothing but water. The others laughed at him, and nicknamed him the "Water-American"; but after a while, they had to confess that he was stronger than they were who drank so much strong beer.

The fact was that Franklin could beat them, both at work and at play. When they went out for a bath in the Thames River, they found that their "Water-American" could swim like a fish. He so astonished them that a rich Londoner tried to persuade him to start a swimming school to teach his sons; but Franklin had stayed in England long enough, and he now decided to go back to Philadelphia.

**Franklin sets up his newspaper; "sawdust pudding";
George Whitefield.** After his return to America, Franklin
labored so diligently that he was soon able to establish a
newspaper of his own. He tried to make it a good one, but
some people thought that he spoke his mind too freely. They
complained of this to him, and explained that if he did not
make his paper to please them, they would stop taking it or
advertising in it.

Franklin heard what they had to say, and then invited them
all to come and have supper with him. They went expecting
a feast, but they found nothing on the table but two dishes of
corn-meal mush and a big pitcher of cold water. That kind of
mush was then eaten only by very poor people. Because it
was yellow and coarse, it was nicknamed "sawdust pudding."

Franklin gave everybody a heaping plateful; and then, filling
his own, he made a hearty supper of it. The others tried to
eat, but could not. After Franklin had finished his supper,
he looked up and said quietly, "My friends, anyone who can
live on 'sawdust pudding' and cold water, as I can, does not
need much help from others." After that, no one went to the
young printer with complaints about his paper. Franklin, as
we have seen, had learned to stoop; but he certainly did not
wish to go stooping through life.

Benjamin Franklin worked hard to make his newspaper
truly serve the needs of the American people. In an effort to
provide his readers with access to important and uplifting
spiritual information, Franklin reprinted a number of
articles and booklets that were written by influential British
evangelist George Whitefield. These articles helped
Whitefield play a leading role in a wonderful period of
revival in the American colonies known as the First Great
Awakening. Rev. Whitefield visited the colonies several

times from 1739-1770, and many newspaper editors like Franklin helped to spread the important truths that Whitefield was trying to bring to the hearts of the American people.

Franklin's plan of life; what he did for Philadelphia. Not many young men can see their own faults, but Franklin could see his. More than that, he tried hard to get rid of them. He kept a little book in which he wrote down his faults. If he wasted half an hour of time or a shilling of money, or said anything that he should not have said, he wrote it down in his book. He carried that book in his pocket all his life, and he studied it as a boy at school studies a hard lesson. From it, he learned three things: first, to do the right thing; next, to do it at the right time; last of all, to do it in the right way.

As he never tired of helping himself to get upward and onward, so, too, he never tired of helping others. He started the first public library in Philadelphia, which was also the first in America. He began the first fire engine company and the first military company in that city. He led the people to pave the muddy streets with stone. He helped to build the first academy, now called the University of Pennsylvania, and he also helped to build the first hospital.

Franklin's experiments with electricity; the wonderful bottle; the picture of the king of England. While doing these things and publishing his paper besides, Franklin found time to make experiments with electricity. Very little was then known about this wonderful power, but a Dutchman living in Leyden, Holland, had discovered a way of bottling it up in what is called a Leyden Jar. Franklin had one of these jars, and he never tired of seeing what new and strange thing he could do with it.

He made a picture of the king of England with a movable gold crown on his head. Then he connected the crown by a long wire with the Leyden jar. When he wanted some fun, he would dare anyone to go up to the picture and take off the king's crown. Why that's easy enough, a man would say; and would walk up and seize the crown. But as soon he touched it, he would get an electric shock which would make his fingers tingle as they had never tingled before. With a loud Oh! Oh! he would let go of the crown, and stand back in amazement, not knowing what had hurt him.

The electrical kite. But Franklin's greatest experiment was conducted seriously with a kite. He believed that the electricity in the bottle, or Leyden jar, was the same thing as the lightning we see in a thunderstorm. He knew well enough how to get an electric spark from the jar, for with such a spark he had once killed a turkey for dinner. Could he get such a spark from a cloud in the sky?

Franklin and his kite

He thought about it for a long time; then he made a kite out of a silk handkerchief, and fastened a sharp iron point to the upright stick of the kite. One day when a thunderstorm was coming up, Franklin and his son went out to the fields. The kite was raised; then Franklin tied an iron key to the lower end of the string. After waiting some time, he saw the little hair-like threads of the string begin to stand up like the bristles of a brush. He felt certain that the electricity was coming down the string. He put his knuckle close to the key and a spark flew out. Next, he took his Leyden jar and collected the electricity in it. He had made two great discoveries: he had found out that electricity and lightning are the same thing; and he had also found how to fill his bottle directly from the clouds, which no one had ever done before.

Franklin invents the lightning rod; Doctor Franklin.
But Franklin did not stop his work. He reasoned that if he
could draw down electricity from the sky with a kite string,
he could draw it better still with a tall, sharp-pointed iron
rod. He put up such a rod on his house in Philadelphia; it
was the first lightning rod in the world. Soon other people
began to put them up, so this was another gift of his to the
city which he loved. Every good lightning rod that has
since been built to protect buildings has been, in some
degree, a copy of that first one invented by Franklin.

© J. L. G. Ferris

Benjamin Franklin's book shop

People now began to talk, not only in this country but in Europe, about his electrical experiments and discoveries. The oldest college in Scotland gave him a title of honor and called him Doctor -- a word which means a learned man. From this time Franklin the printer was no longer plain Mr. Franklin, but Dr. Franklin.

Dr. Franklin did not think that he had found out all that could be found out about electricity; he believed that he had simply made a beginning, and that other men would discover still greater things that could be done with it. Do you think he was mistaken about that?

Franklin in the Revolutionary War; Franklin and the map of the United States. When the war of the Revolution broke out, Dr. Franklin did a great work for his country. He did not fight battles like Washington, but he did something just as useful. First, he helped write the Declaration of Independence, by which we declared ourselves free from the rule of the king of England; next, he went to France to get aid for us. We were then too poor to pay our soldiers; he convinced the king of France to let us have the money to pay our soldiers.

Franklin lived to see the Revolution ended and America free. When he died, full of years and of honors, he was buried in Philadelphia. Twenty thousand people went to his funeral.

If you wish to see what the country thinks of him, you have only to look at a large map of the United States, and count how many times you find his name on it. You will find that more than two hundred counties and towns are named Franklin.

Summary. Benjamin Franklin was born in Boston over two hundred years ago. He went to Philadelphia when he was seventeen. He started a newspaper there, opened the first public library, and did many other things to help the city. He discovered that lightning and electricity are the same thing, and he invented the lightning rod to protect buildings. In the Revolution, he received large sums of money from the king of France to pay our soldiers and help General Washington fight the battles that won America's freedom.

Comprehension Questions

1. Who did a great deal for Philadelphia?
2. What saying of Solomon's did Franklin's father often repeat to him?
3. What did Franklin do for the city of Philadelphia?
4. What title did a college in Scotland give Franklin?
5. Did Franklin think that anything more would be discovered about electricity?
6. What two things did Franklin do in the Revolution?

READING THE DECLARATION OF INDEPENDENCE TO THE PEOPLE.

Chapter Fifteen
George Washington

(Born 1732 - Died 1799)

A Virginia boy; what he became; what he learned at school; his writing books. In 1732, when Franklin was at work on his newspaper, a boy was born on a plantation in Virginia who was one day to become even greater than the Philadelphia printer.

That boy when he grew up was to be chosen leader of the armies of the Revolution; he was to be elected the first president of the United States; and before he died he was to be known and honored throughout the world. The name of that boy was George Washington.

Washington's father died when George was only eleven years old, leaving him, with his brothers and sisters, to the care of a most excellent and sensible mother. It was that mother's influence, more than anything else, except the influence of the Holy Spirit, which made George the man he became.

George went to a little country school, where he learned to read, write, and work math. By the time he was twelve, he could write a clear, bold letter. In one of his first books, he copied many good rules or sayings. Here is one: Labor to keep alive in your breast that little spark of heavenly fire called conscience.

Washington's sports and games, playing at war; "Captain George." But young Washington was not always copying good sayings, for he was a tall, strong boy, fond of all outdoor sports and games. He was a well meaning boy, but he had a hot temper, and at times his blue eyes flashed fire.

In all trials of strength and all deeds of daring, George took the lead; he could run faster, jump farther, and throw a stone higher than anyone else in the school. When the boys played "soldier," they liked to have "Captain George" as commander. When he drew his wooden sword, and shouted Come on! they would all rush into battle with a wild hurrah. Years afterward, when the real war came, and George Washington drew his sword in real battle, some of his school companions may have fought under their old leader.

The great battle with the colt, and what came of it. Once, however, Washington had a battle of a different kind. It was with a high-spirited young horse which belonged to his mother. Nobody had ever been able to do anything with that colt, and most people were afraid of him. Early one morning, George and some of his brothers were out in the pasture. George looked at the colt prancing about and kicking up his heels. Then he said, "Boys, if you'll help me put a bridle on him, I'll ride him." The boys managed to get the colt into a corner and to slip on the bridle. With a leap, George seated himself firmly on his back. Then the fun began. The colt, wild with rage, ran, jumped, plunged, and reared straight up on his hind legs, hoping to throw his rider off. It was all useless; he might as well have tried to throw off his own skin, for the boy stuck to his back as though he had grown there. Then, making a last desperate bound into the air, the animal burst a blood vessel and fell dead. The battle was over, George was victor, but it had cost the life of Mrs. Washington's favorite colt.

When the boys went in for breakfast, their mother, knowing that they had just come from the pasture, asked how the colt was getting on. "He is dead, madam," said George; "I killed him." "Dead!" exclaimed his mother. "Yes, madam, dead," replied her son. Then he told her just how it happened. When Mrs. Washington heard the story, her face flushed with anger. Then, waiting a moment, she looked steadily at George, and said quietly, "While I regret the loss of my favorite horse, I rejoice in my son, who always speaks the truth."

Washington visits Mount Vernon; he makes the acquaintance of Lord Fairfax. George's eldest brother, Lawrence Washington, had married the daughter of a gentleman named Fairfax, who lived on the banks of the Potomac. Lawrence had a fine home a few miles away on the same river; he called his place Mount Vernon. When he was fourteen, George went to Mount Vernon to stay with his brother, following the death of his father.

Lawrence Washington took George down the river to call on the Fairfaxes. There the lad made the acquaintance of Lord Fairfax, an English nobleman who had come from London. He owned an immense piece of land in Virginia. Lord Fairfax and George soon became great friends. He was a gray-haired man nearly sixty, but he enjoyed having this boy of fourteen as a companion. They spent weeks together on horseback in the fields and woods, hunting deer and foxes.

Lord Fairfax hires Washington to survey his land; how Washington lived in the woods; the Indian war dance. Lord Fairfax's land extended westward more than a hundred miles. It had never been carefully surveyed; and he was told that settlers were moving in beyond the Blue Ridge Mountains, and were building log cabins on his property without asking permission. By the time Washington was sixteen, he had learned surveying; and so Lord Fairfax hired him to measure his land for him. Washington was glad to undertake the work, for he needed the money.

Early in the spring, Washington, in company with another young man, started off, on foot, to do this business. They crossed the Blue Ridge Mountains, and entered the Valley of Virginia, one of the most beautiful valleys in America.

The two young men would work all day in the woods, with a long chain, measuring the land. When evening came, Washington would make a map of what they had measured. Then they would wrap themselves up in their blankets, stretch themselves on the ground at the foot of a tree, and go to sleep under the stars.

Every day they shot some animals: squirrels or wild turkeys, or even a deer. They kindled a fire with flint and steel, and roasted the meat on sticks held over the coals. For plates they had flat pieces of wood; and as wood plates could always be made by a few blows with an axe, they never washed any dishes, but just threw them away, and had a new set for each meal.

While in the valley they met a band of Indians, who stopped and danced a war dance for them. The music was not very good -- for most of it was made by drumming on a deerskin stretched across the top of an old iron pot -- but the dancing could not be beat. The Indians leaped into the air, swung their hatchets, gashed the trees, and yelled until the woods rang.

When Washington returned from his surveying trip, Lord Fairfax was greatly pleased with his work; and the governor of Virginia made him one of the public surveyors. By this new job, he could get work that paid very well.

Washington at the age of twenty-one; the French in the west; the governor of Virginia sends Washington to see the French commander. By the time Washington was twenty-one, he had grown to be over six feet in height. He was as straight as an arrow and as tough as a cannon. He had keen blue eyes that seemed to look into the very heart of things, and his fist was like a blacksmith's sledge hammer. He knew all about the woods, all about Indians, and he could take care of himself anywhere. Best of all, however, he had a humble and caring spirit that helped him avoid the sin of pride.

At this time the English settlers held the country along the seashore as far back as the Allegheny Mountains. West of those mountains the French from Canada were trying to get possession of the land. They had made friends with many

Indians, and with their help, the French hoped to drive out the English and get the whole country for themselves.

The French and Indian War

In order to hold this land in the west, the French had built several forts south of Lake Erie, and they were getting ready to build forts on the Ohio River. The governor of Virginia was determined to put an end to this. He had given young Washington the military title of major; he now sent Major Washington to see the French commander at one of the forts near Lake Erie. Washington was to tell the Frenchman that he had built his forts on land belonging to the English, and that he and his men must either leave or fight.

Major Washington dressed himself like an Indian, and attended by several friendly Indians and by a white man named Gist, who knew the country well, he set out on his journey through what was called the Great Woods.

The entire distance to the farthest fort and back was about a thousand miles. Washington could travel by horseback part of the way, but there were no regular roads, and he had to climb mountains and swim rivers. After several weeks' travel he reached the fort, but the French commander refused to surrender the land. He said that he and his men had come to stay, and that if the English did not like it they must fight.

The journey back; the Indian guide; how Washington found his way through the woods; the adventure with the raft. On the way back, Washington had to leave his horses and come on foot with Gist and an Indian guide sent from the fort. This Indian guide was in the pay of the French, and he intended to murder Washington in the woods. One day he shot at him from behind a tree, but by God's grace, did not hit him. Then Washington and Gist managed to get away from him, and set out to go back to Virginia themselves. There were no paths through the thick forest; but Washington had his compass with him, and with that he could find his way just as the captain of a ship finds his way at sea.

When they reached the Allegheny River, they found it full of floating ice. They worked all day and made a raft of logs. As they were pushing their way across with poles, Washington's pole was struck by a big piece of ice which jerked him out into water ten feet deep. A short time later the two men managed to get to a little island, but as there was no wood on it, they could not make a fire. The weather was bitterly cold, and Washington, who was soaked to the skin, had to take his choice between walking around all night, or trying to sleep on the frozen ground in his wet clothes.

Major Washington becomes Colonel Washington; Fort Necessity; Braddock's defeat. When Major Washington returned to Virginia, the governor made him a colonel. With a hundred and fifty men, Colonel Washington was ordered to set out for the west. He was to "make prisoners, kill or destroy," all Frenchmen who tried to take possession of land on the Ohio River. He built a small log fort, which he named Fort Necessity. Here the French attacked him, with five times as many soldiers as Washington had. Colonel Washington fought like a man who liked to hear the bullets whistle past his ears (as he said he did), but in the end he had to surrender the fort.

Then General Braddock, a noted English soldier, was sent to Virginia by the king to drive the French out of the country. He started with a fine army, and Washington went with him. Washington warned General Braddock that the French and the Indians would hide in the woods and fire at his men from behind trees. But Braddock paid no attention to the warning. On his way through the forest, the brave English general was suddenly struck down by the enemy; half of his soldiers were killed or wounded, and the rest put to flight. Washington had two horses shot from under him, and four bullets went through his coat. It was a narrow escape for the young man. One of those who fought in the battle said, "I expected every moment to see him fall." But God preserved George Washington for greater work.

End of the war with the French; what the king of England wanted to do; how the people here felt toward him. The war with the French lasted several years. It ended with the English gaining possession of the whole of America from the Atlantic Ocean to the Mississippi River. All this part of America was ruled by George III, king of England. The king now determined to send over more soldiers, and to keep them in America to prevent the French in Canada from trying to win back the country they had lost. He wanted the people here in the thirteen colonies to pay the cost of keeping these soldiers. The colonists were not willing to do this because they felt that they could protect themselves without help of any kind. Then the king said, "If the Americans will not give the money, I will take it from them by force, for pay it they must and shall." This was more than the king would have dared say about England; for there, if he wanted money to spend on his army, he had to ask the people for it, and they could give it or not, as they thought best. The Americans said, "We have the same rights as our brothers in England, and the king cannot force us to give a single copper against our will. If he tries to take it from us, we will fight." Some of the greatest men in England agreed with us, and said that they would fight, too, if they were in our place.

The king determines to have the money; the tea-ships, and the "Boston Tea Party." But, George III thought that the Americans did not mean what they said. He tried to make them pay the money through unjust taxes, but they would not. From Maine to Georgia, all the people were of one mind. Then the king tried a different way. Quantities of tea were sent to New York, Boston, Philadelphia, Charleston, and Annapolis. If the tea should be landed and sold, then everyone who bought a pound of it would have to pay six cents more than the regular price. That six cents was a tax, and it went into the king's pocket. The people said, We won't pay that six cents. When the tea reached New York the citizens sent it back to England. They did the same thing at Philadelphia. At Charleston the tea was landed, but it was stored in damp cellars. People would not buy any of it any more than they would buy so much poison, so it all rotted and spoiled. At Annapolis the citizens forced the owner of the tea-ship Peggy Stewart to burn his vessel, tea and all. At Boston, they had a grand "tea party." Several men dressed themselves up like Indians, went on board the tea-ships at night, broke open the chests, and emptied the tea into the harbor.

THE BOSTON "TEA-PARTY"

The king closes the port of Boston; Congress meets at Philadelphia; the names of American and British; what General Gage tried to do. This act of the Bostonians made the king terribly angry, and orders were given to close the port of Boston so that no ships, except the king's warships, could come in or go out. Nearly all trade stopped in the city. Many of the inhabitants began to suffer for lack of food. Throughout the colonies, the people tried their best to help them. The New England towns sent herds of sheep and cattle, New York sent wheat, South Carolina gave two hundred barrels of rice; the other colonies gave liberally in money and provisions. Even in England much sympathy was felt for the distressed people of Boston, and in London a large sum of money was raised to help those whom the king was determined to starve into submission.

The colonies now sent some of their best men to Philadelphia to consider what should be done. As this meeting was made up of those who had come from all parts of the country, it took the name of the General or Continental Congress.

About this time, too, a great change happened. People throughout the country began to call themselves Americans, and to speak of the English troops that the king sent over as British soldiers.

In Boston, General Gage had command of these soldiers. He knew that the Americans were getting ready to fight, and that they had stored up powder and ball at Concord, about twenty miles from Boston. One night he secretly sent out a group of soldiers to march to Concord and destroy what they found there.

Paul Revere; the fight at Lexington and Concord; Bunker Hill. But Paul Revere, a Boston man, was on the watch; and as soon as he found out which way the British were going, he set off at a gallop for Lexington, on the road to Concord. All the way out, he roused people from their sleep, with the cry, "The British are coming!" This daring ride helped to warn the American colonists that British soldiers were coming.

When the king's soldiers reached Lexington, they found the Americans, under Captain Parker, ready for them. Captain Parker said to his men, "Don't fire unless you are fired on; but if they want a war, let it begin here." The fighting did begin there, April 19, 1775; and when the British left the town on their way to Concord, seven Americans lay dead on the grass in front of the village church. At Concord that same day, there was still harder fighting; and on the way back to Boston, many of the British were killed.

Not quite two months later, June 17, 1775, a battle was fought on Bunker Hill in Charlestown, just outside Boston. General Gage thought the Yankees wouldn't fight; but they did fight, in a way that General Gage never forgot. Though the Yankees eventually had to retreat because their powder gave out, the British lost more than a thousand men. The contest at Bunker Hill was the first great battle of the American Revolution, the war that overturned the British power in America, and made us a free people. Many Englishmen thought the king was wrong. They would not fight against us and he was forced to hire many German soldiers and send them to America. These Germans had to fight us, whether they wanted to or not, for their king ordered them to come.

Colonel Washington at Mount Vernon; Congress makes him General Washington, and sends him to take command of the American army. At the time the battle of Bunker Hill was fought, Colonel George Washington was living quietly at Mount Vernon. His brother Lawrence had died, and Mount Vernon was now his home. Washington was very well off; he had a fine estate and plenty of servants to do the work on it; but when he received the call of duty to command the American army, he freely gave up his comforts for the cause of freedom.

MOUNT VERNON.†

Congress now made Colonel Washington general-in-chief of all the forces and sent him to Cambridge, a town just outside Boston, to take command of the American army. It was called the Continental Army because it was raised, not only to fight for the people of Massachusetts, but for all the Americans on the continent, north and south. Washington took command of the army under a great elm on what was then the Commons. Six months later he raised the first American flag over the camp at Cambridge.

American sharpshooters; Washington's need of cannon and powder; the attack on Canada; the British driven out of Boston. Men now came from all parts of the country to join the Continental Army. Many of them were sharpshooters. In one case an officer set up a board with the figure of a man's nose chalked on it, for a mark. A hundred men fired at it at long distance, and sixty hit the nose. The newspapers gave them great praise for their skill and said, "Now, General Gage, look out for your nose."

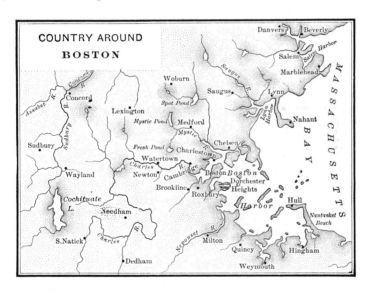

Washington wanted to drive General Gage and the British soldiers out of Boston; but for months he could not get either cannon or powder. Benjamin Franklin said that we would have to fight as the Indians had, with bows and arrows.

While Washington was waiting, a small American force marched against the British in Canada, but when cold weather came on, they nearly starved to death. During this time, our men would sometimes take off their moccasins and gnaw on them while they danced in the snow to keep their bare feet from freezing.

Eventually, Washington received both cannon and powder. He dragged the cannon up to the top of the hills overlooking Boston harbor. He then sent word to General Howe (who had replaced General Gage) that if he did not leave Boston, his ships would be blown to pieces. The British saw that they could not help themselves, so they quickly marched on board their vessels and sailed away. They never came back to Boston again, but went to New York.

THE BRITISH LEAVING BOSTON

The Declaration of Independence; "Down with the king!"; Washington is driven from New York and across the Delaware River. Washington got to New York first. While he was there, Congress, on the 4th of July, 1776, declared the United States independent; that is, entirely free from the rule of the king of England. In New York, there was a gilded lead statue of King George III on horseback. When the news of what Congress had done reached that city, the cry rose: "Down with the king!" That night some of our men pulled down the statue, melted it in a furnace, and cast it into bullets. The next month there was a battle on Long Island, just across from New York City; the British gained the victory. Washington had to leave New York, and Lord Cornwallis, one of the British generals, chased him and his little army clear across the state of New Jersey. It looked at one time as though our men would all be taken prisoners; but Washington managed to seize a number of small boats on the Delaware River and get across into Pennsylvania. As the British had no boats; they could not follow.

Washington's victory at Trenton, New Jersey. Lord Cornwallis left fifteen hundred German soldiers at Trenton on the Delaware. He intended, as soon as the river froze over, to cross on the ice and attack Washington's army. But Washington did not wait for him. On Christmas night (1776) he took many boats, filled them with soldiers, and secretly crossed over to New Jersey. The weather was intensely cold, the river was full of floating ice, and a furious snowstorm set in. Many of our men were ragged and had only old, broken shoes. They suffered terribly, and two of them were frozen to death. However, General Washington never heard one complaint from these brave men.

The Germans at Trenton had been having a jolly Christmas, and had gone to bed, suspecting no danger. Suddenly Washington, with his men, rushed into the little town and captured a thousand German soldiers. It was all done so quickly that the men found themselves prisoners almost before they knew what had happened. The rest of the

Germans escaped to tell Lord Cornwallis how the Americans had beaten them. When Washington had been driven out of New York, many Americans had feared he would be captured. Now they were filled with joy. The battle of Trenton was the first battle won by the Continental Army.

Our victory at Princeton, New Jersey; the British take Philadelphia; winter at Valley Forge; Burgoyne beaten; the king of France agrees to help us. Washington took his thousand prisoners over into Pennsylvania. A few days later he again crossed the Delaware into New Jersey. While Cornwallis was fast asleep in his tent, Washington slipped around him, got to Princeton, and there beat a part of the British army. Cornwallis woke up and heard Washington's cannon. "That's thunder," he said. He was right; it was the thunder of another American victory.

ON GUARD AT VALLEY FORGE

But before the next winter set in, the British had taken Philadelphia, then the capital of the United States. Washington's army was freezing and starving on the hillsides of Valley Forge, about twenty miles northwest of Philadelphia.

Good news was coming, however. The Americans won a great victory at Saratoga, New York, over the British general, Burgoyne. Benjamin Franklin was then in Paris. When he heard that Burgoyne was beaten, he hurried to the palace of the French king to tell him about it. The king of France hated the British, and he agreed to send money, ships, and soldiers to help us. When our men at Valley Forge heard the news, they leaped for joy. Not long after that the British left Philadelphia, and we entered it in triumph.

The war in the south; Jasper; Cowpens; Greene and Cornwallis. While these things were happening in the north, the British sent a fleet of vessels to take Charleston, South Carolina. They hammered away with their big guns at a little log fort under the command of Colonel Moultrie. In the battle, a cannon-ball struck the flagpole on the fort, and cut it in two. The South Carolina flag fell to the ground outside the fort. Sergeant William Jasper leaped down, and while the British shots were striking all around him, seized the flag, climbed back, fastened it to a short staff, and raised it to its place, to show that the Americans would never surrender the fort. The British, after fighting all day, saw that they could do nothing against palmetto logs when defended by such men as Moultrie and Jasper. They sailed away the following day with their ships that had not been destroyed.

Several years later Charleston was taken. Lord Cornwallis then took command of the British army in South Carolina.

General Greene, of Rhode Island, had command of the Americans. He sent Daniel Morgan with his sharpshooters to meet part of the British army at Cowpens; they did meet them, and sent them flying. Then Cornwallis determined to whip General Greene or drive him out of the state. Instead, General Greene forced Cornwallis to retreat into Virginia. He had found North and South Carolina like two hornets' nests, and the farther he ran away from those hornets, the better he was pleased.

Cornwallis and Benedict Arnold; Lafayette; Cornwallis shuts himself up in Yorktown. When Lord Cornwallis came into Virginia, he found Benedict Arnold waiting for him. Arnold had been a general in the American army; Washington gave him the command of the fort at West Point, on the Hudson River, and trusted him as though he were his brother. Arnold deceived him, and secretly offered to surrender the fort to the British. We call a man who is false to his friends and to his country a traitor; it is the most shameful name we can fasten on him. Arnold was a traitor. If we could have caught him, we would have hanged him, but he was clever enough to run away and escape to the British. Now he was burning houses and towns in Virginia, and doing all that he could (as a traitor always will) to destroy those who had once been his best friends. He wanted to stay in Virginia and help Cornwallis, but that general was a brave and honorable man. He despised Arnold, and did not want to have anything to do with him.

A young nobleman named Lafayette had come from France to help us fight against the British. Cornwallis laughed at him and called him a "boy," but he found that General Lafayette was a "boy" who knew how to fight. The British commander moved toward the seacoast; Lafayette followed him; at length Cornwallis shut himself up with his army in Yorktown.

Washington marches against Yorktown, and takes it and the army of Cornwallis. Washington, with his army, was then near New York City, watching the British there. The French king had done as he agreed, and had sent over warships and soldiers to help us; but until this time they had never been able to do much. Now was the chance. Before the British knew what Washington was doing, he had sent the French warships to Yorktown to prevent Cornwallis from getting away by sea. Then, with his own army and a large number of French soldiers, Washington quickly marched south to attack Yorktown by land.

When he arrived there he placed his cannon around the town, and began battering it to pieces. For more than a week he kept firing night and day. One house had over a thousand balls go through it. Eventually, Cornwallis could not hold out any longer, and on October 19, 1781, his army came out and gave themselves up as prisoners.

The Americans formed a line more than a mile long on one side of the road, and the French stood facing them on the other side. The French had on bright clothes, and looked very handsome; the clothes of Washington's men were patched and faded, but their eyes shone with a wonderful light -- the light of victory. The British marched out slowly, between the two lines. Somehow they found it more pleasant to look at the bright uniforms of the French than to look at the eyes of the Americans.

How the news of the taking of Yorktown was carried to Philadelphia; Lord Fairfax. People at a distance noticed that the cannon had suddenly stopped firing. They looked at one another and wondered what it meant. Suddenly a man appeared on horseback riding with all his might toward Philadelphia. As he dashed past, he rose in his stirrups, swung his cap, and shouted with all his might, "Cornwallis is taken! Cornwallis is taken!" Then it was the people's turn to shout, and they made the hills ring with "Hurrah! Hurrah! Hurrah!"

Poor Lord Fairfax, Washington's old friend, had always stood by the king. He was now over ninety. When he heard the cry, "Cornwallis is taken!" it was too much for the old man. He said to his servant, "Come, Joe; carry me to bed, for I'm sure it's high time for me to die."

Tearing down the British flag at New York; Washington goes back to Mount Vernon; he is elected President; his death; Lafayette visits his tomb. The Revolutionary War had lasted seven years: terrible years they were, years of sorrow, suffering, and death. But now the end had come, and America was free. When the British left New York City in December 1783, they nailed the British flag to a high pole on the wharf. A Yankee sailor soon climbed the pole, tore down the flag of England, and hoisted the stars and stripes in its place. That was more than two hundred years ago. Now the English and the Americans have become good friends, and the English people see clearly that the War for Independence ended in the way that was best for both sides.

When it was certain there would be no more fighting, Washington went back to Mount Vernon. He hoped to spend the rest of his life there. But the country needed him, and a few years later it chose him as the first President of the United States.

WASHINGTON TAKES OATH OF OFFICE

Washington assumed the Presidency in New York City, which was then the capital of the United States. A French gentleman, who was there, tells us how Washington, standing in the presence of thousands of people, placed his hand on the Bible, and solemnly swore that with the help of God he would protect and defend the United States of America.

Washington was elected president twice. When he died in 1799, many of the people in England and France joined America in mourning for him, for all men honored his memory.

Lafayette, the brave young Frenchman who fought for us in the Revolution, came to visit us many years afterward. He went to Mount Vernon, where Washington was buried. There he went down into the vault, and kneeling by the side of the coffin, covered his face with his hands, and shed tears of gratitude to think that he had known such a man as Washington, and that Washington had been his friend.

Summary. George Washington, the son of a Virginia planter, became the leader of the armies of the United States in the Revolutionary War. At the close of the war, after he had helped to make America free, he was elected our first President. His name stands today among those of the greatest men in the history of the world. The life of George Washington shows us that God will honor those who honor Him.

Comprehension Questions

1. Where was George Washington born?
2. What job did Lord Fairfax give to Washington when he was only seventeen years old?
3. Describe the event known as the "Boston Tea Party."
4. What was the name of Washington's plantation home?
5. How many years did the Revolutionary War last?
6. Where was the final decisive battle fought?

Chapter Sixteen
John Witherspoon

(Born 1723 - Died 1794)

Christian supporters of the American Revolution; what the Hessian captain said about Presbyterians. Many Christians in America were concerned about the efforts of the British to exert greater control over their American colonies. Eventually, some of them came to believe that independence from Britain was the only way to protect their freedoms.

Christians from many different types of churches supported the War for American Independence. For example, Isaac Backus, a Baptist minister from Massachusetts, said in his sermon the Sunday after the battles of Lexington and Concord that "... it was a foundation point in the constitution of the English government that the people's property shall not be taken from them without their consent..." and therefore, " I declared that I fully believed our cause was just." Congregational pastor Moses Mather from Connecticut wrote a tract in 1775 entitled *America's Appeal*

to the Impartial World, which supported colonial claims against Parliament.

Different church assemblies expressed their support for American independence. The Presbyterian Synod of New York and Philadelphia wrote a letter on May 20, 1775, encouraging its ministers and church members to support the actions of the Continental Congress to oppose British colonial policies. Later, in 1783, the Synod sent a letter to its churches thanking them for their support for the cause of American independence and asking them "...to render thanks to Almighty God, for all of his mercies, spiritual and temporal, and in particular for establishing the Independence of the United States of America." Those attending the meeting of the Philadelphia Baptist Association got up at sunrise on October 23, 1781, after learning about the American victory at Yorktown, Virginia, to thank God for His blessings on this country.

One of the groups most supportive of the patriot cause was the Presbyterians. A Hessian captain, who served with the British army in Pennsylvania, complained that the American Revolution was actually "...an Irish-Scotch Presbyterian Rebellion." An example of Presbyterian support for the war was Rev. James Caldwell, the pastor of a Presbyterian church in New Jersey. During a skirmish near his church, Continental soldiers were running low on paper to use as wadding in their muskets. Caldwell ran into his church and brought out copies of Isaac Watts's hymnals for them to tear apart for wadding. As he did so, he told the soldiers, "Now boys, give 'em Watts!" George Duffield, who was the pastor of a Presbyterian church in Philadelphia and chaplain in the Continental army, chided his congregation for not sending more men into the army.

Christians who were supporters of American independence at times suffered at the hands of the British or the Loyalists. Because of Rev. Mather's fervent support for American independence, he was captured on two different occasions by Loyalists and keep in prison in New York City for several months. The almost unanimous support of Presbyterians for the patriot cause often led the British to vent their anger on Presbyterians and their property. The Synod letter of 1783, which was mentioned earlier, spoke of their "...burnt and wasted churches, and our plundered dwellings, in such places as fell under the power of our adversaries."

John Witherspoon; his theological and political beliefs; his impact on America; the last years of his life. One of the most fervent Presbyterians in his support of American independence was Rev. John Witherspoon, president of the College of New Jersey (now known as Princeton University). At the same time, he was also an unlikely supporter for independence because he was a relatively new resident of America.

Rev. Witherspoon was born in Scotland in 1723 and lived there until 1768, when he moved to the American colonies to become president of the college. He was initially taught at home by his mother, learning to read from the Bible at age four. After the first few years at home, he went to a local grammar school and then went to college at age thirteen. He earned a Master of Arts degree in three years and then studied at a seminary for four more years to prepare for the ministry.

He followed his father into the ministry of the Church of Scotland and pastored two different Presbyterian churches for a total of seventeen years. He married his first wife during his first pastorate. Witherspoon was an faithful pastor who stressed the need for Bible-centered sermons, taught that salvation is by grace alone, spoke of the need for the elect to give an evidence of their faith through good works and morality, and emphasized local control of the church. This combination of evangelical zeal, emphasis on morality and Christian living, and theological orthodoxy

John Witherspoon

made him acceptable to all major factions within the American Presbyterian churches.

Witherspoon had a significant influence on this country through his work at the College of New Jersey. He served as president from 1768 to 1794, teaching several classes and filling the position of professor of divinity at the college. He lived on campus and preached regularly at the Presbyterian church next to his house. Of the 478 men to graduate during his tenure as president of the college, many went on to play an important role in the life of our country. Many became ministers, and several served their states and country in important political and legal positions. His most famous graduate was James Madison, who went on to become Secretary of State and later the fourth President of the United States.

Rev. Witherspoon's impact, however, was not limited to his work at the college. He was an active supporter of American independence. He delivered a sermon on May 17, 1776, entitled *The Dominion of Providence over the Passions of Men*, which was later published for distribution to Scots living in America. In this sermon, he argued that since Britain was requiring total submission by the colonies, the defense of colonial freedoms made necessary the support for colonial independence. Witherspoon was elected as a delegate from New Jersey to the Continental Congress and served from 1776 to 1782. He was the only minister to sign the Declaration of Independence.

After leaving Congress, he spent the next several years at the college but was again elected to public office in 1789, serving in the New Jersey legislature and heading a committee on abolishing the slave trade in New Jersey. His first wife died in October 1789, but he remarried two years later, at the age of 68. He died on November 15, 1794, after being blind for three years.

Other supporters of American independence. Many well-known American Christians played an important role in securing our independence. John Hart, a Baptist deacon from New Jersey, was a signer of the Declaration of Independence. Roger Sherman was a Congregationalist from Connecticut who spent much time and effort supporting America and its independence. He was a faithful church member and deacon who was described by John Adams as "an old Puritan, as honest as an angel and as firm in the cause of American independence as Mount Atlas." He was the only person to sign the Articles of Association (1774), the Declaration of Independence (1776), the Articles of Confederation (1777), and the United States Constitution (1787).

Many Anglicans (also known as Episcopalians) were very important to the success of the Revolutionary War. Two-thirds of the signers of the Declaration of Independence were Episcopalians. George Washington (commander of the American armies during the Revolutionary War and our first President), Alexander Hamilton (army officer in the war, delegate to the Constitutional Convention, and the first Secretary of the Treasury under President Washington), and Patrick Henry (held several elected offices, including being elected governor of the state of Virginia five times, but best known for his stirring call, "Give me liberty or give me death!") are all examples of Anglicans who were active patriots.

Christians who supported Britain; exceptions to the rule. While many Christians supported the patriot cause, not all did. Yet even in those groups which tended to support the British, there were exceptions to the rule.

Supporters of the British cause were most numerous and vigorous in the Church of England (also known as the Anglican or Episcopalian Church), especially in New

England and New York. Many believed that the Word of God required submission to their ruler and to the laws of the land. Therefore, they believed that rebellion against England was wrong. In addition, ministers of the Church of England had to swear that they would not support any effort to harm or depose the English monarch. The services in the Church of England generally included prayers for the king. In spite of the fact that many Anglicans, including many of

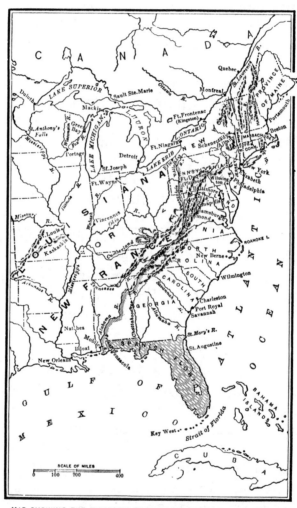

MAP SHOWING THE THIRTEEN ENGLISH COLONIES AND THE FRENCH EXPLORATIONS AND SETTLEMENTS IN THE WEST.

the clergy, were loyal to Britain, it is also clear from what we have already seen that many Anglican church members were active supporters of American independence.

Many in the small Methodist church in America could also be considered Loyalists. The founders of the Methodist movement, Charles and John Wesley, strongly opposed the American revolution. All but one of the Methodist missionaries left America and returned to England. Only Francis Asbury remained in America because he strongly disagreed with the Wesleys' support for the loyalist cause. Another exception to the trend of Methodism toward the loyalist cause was Richard Bassett from Delaware. Mr. Bassett was a devout Methodist and friend of Francis Asbury

Statue of the Minute Man at Concord

who served in the Delaware militia and government during the Revolutionary War. He later was a delegate from Delaware at the Constitutional Convention in 1787 and served in the United States Senate.

Many Roman Catholics also tended toward the loyalist cause, in part because many of the Protestants who had opposed them in the past were now supporting American independence. In spite of this tendency, many individual Catholics were very supportive of the American cause in the Revolutionary War. For example, Daniel Carroll of Maryland and Thomas Fitz Simmons of Pennsylvania were both active in efforts to support the American war effort and later were delegates to the Constitutional Convention.

Many Loyalists left America, either permanently or temporarily. A large portion of the English settlement of Canada resulted from Loyalists who had come from America. Some left because they did not wish to live in a country which they believed had unlawfully revolted against its rightful ruler. Others left because of persecution by supporters of American independence.

Christians who opposed military action. While most Christians in America could be considered either Patriots or Loyalists, some attempted to remain neutral throughout the war because they opposed the use of military force. Such people are generally known as pacifists. Pacifist Christians came from several groups, some of English origin and some from continental Europe.

Most English pacifists were part of the Quaker movement, which was the oldest pacifist group in America. Many had followed William Penn to the colony of Pennsylvania, which was established as a haven for Quakers. All but a few

Quakers opposed all military service or the hiring of substitutes for themselves. They were opposed to paying any war taxes or fines for not having served in the military or provided substitutes. Several hundred individual Quakers were disciplined by their assemblies for paying these war taxes and fines. They also questioned the appropriateness of giving oaths of loyalty to state governments that had come into being through rebellion against their rulers.

Most of the European pacifists had come to America during the 1700s and were Mennonites, Moravians, Dunkers (the name comes from their mode of baptism), or part of the Church of the Brethren. The Mennonites held beliefs that were similar to those of the Quakers, but the others tended to be more flexible. The rest were willing to pay war taxes and fines, hire substitutes, and some even participated in the war in such non-combatant roles as working in hospitals or driving wagons. Some Moravians were even willing to fight in their own self-defense.

Most pacifists eventually supported the patriot position, in spite of their rejection of military service and in spite of the persecution some received from patriots for their positions. The Moravians tended to be more sympathetic to the loyalist cause because they appreciated the greater freedom they had in the colonies in comparison to their earlier lives in Europe and because they had taken oaths of loyalty to Britain when they came to America.

Summary. American Christians were divided in their response to the War for American Independence. Some actively supported the independence of the colonies from England while others remained loyal to Britain. Still others tried to remain neutral because they were opposed to all military action. While there were true men and women of

John Witherspoon

God on all sides, we can be thankful that God blessed the efforts of those who sought to establish the independence of our country. If it had not been for the prayers and work of men like Rev. John Witherspoon, the cause of American independence could have been lost.

Comprehension Questions

1. What did the Loyalists do to Rev. Mather?
2. What church assembly got up at sunrise to thank God for the American victory at Yorktown, Virginia?
3. Why did Rev. Witherspoon come to America?
4. How many ministers signed the Declaration of Independence?
5. Which church brought all but one of its missionaries home to England during the Revolutionary War?
6. Name one of the pacifist groups in America during the time of the Revolutionary War.

THE PRAYER BEFORE THE BATTLE OF BUNKER HILL.

Chapter Seventeen
Daniel Boone

(Born 1734 - Died 1820)

Daniel Boone; what the hunters of the west did; Boone's life in North Carolina. Before Washington began to fight the battles of the Revolution in the east, Daniel Boone and other famous hunters were fighting bears and Indians in what was then called the west. By that war in the woods, these brave and hardy men helped us to settle that part of the country.

Daniel Boone was born in Pennsylvania. His father moved to North Carolina, and Daniel helped cut down the trees around their log cabin in the forest. He ploughed the land, which was thick with stumps, hoed the corn that grew up among those stumps, and then, as there was no mill nearby pounded it into meal for Johnny-cake. He learned how to handle a gun at the same time he did a hoe. The unfortunate deer or racoon that saw young Boone coming toward him, if he had only been bright enough, might have known that he had seen his best days, and that he would soon have the whole Boone family sitting round him at the dinner table.

Boone's wanderings in the western forests; his bear tree. When Daniel had grown to manhood, he wandered off with his gun on his shoulder, and crossing the mountains, entered what is now the state of Tennessee. That whole country was then a wilderness, full of large animals and Indians; and Boone had many a hard fight with each.

More than two hundred and thirty years ago, he cut these words on a beech tree still standing in eastern Tennessee: "D. Boon killed a bar on this tree in the year 1760." You will see if you examine the tree, on which the words can still be read, that Boone could not spell very well; but he could do what the bear cared about a good deal better -- he could shoot straight.

Boone goes hunting in Kentucky; what kind of game he found there; the Indians; the "Dark and Bloody Ground." Nine years after he cut his name on that tree, Boone, with a few companions, went to a new part of the country. The Indians called it Kentucky. There he saw buffalo, deer, bears, and wolves enough to satisfy the best hunter in America.

This region was a kind of No Man's Land, because, though many tribes of Indians roamed over it, none of them pretended to own it. These bands of Indians were always fighting and trying to drive each other out, so Kentucky was often called the "Dark and Bloody Ground." But, as much as the Indians hated each other, they hated the white men, or the "pale-faces," as they called them, still more.

Indian tricks; the owls. The hunters were on the lookout for these Indians, but the Indians practiced all kinds of tricks to get the hunters near enough to shoot them. Sometimes Boone would hear the gobble of a wild turkey. He would listen a moment, then he would say, "That is not a wild turkey, but an Indian, imitating that bird; but he won't fool me and get me to come near enough to put a bullet through my head."

One evening an old hunter, on his way to his cabin, heard what seemed to be two young owls calling to each other. But his keen ear noticed that there was something not quite natural in their calls, and what was stranger still, that the owls seemed to be on the ground instead of being perched on trees, as all well-behaved owls should be. He crept cautiously along through the bushes until he saw something ahead that looked like a stump. He didn't like the looks of the stump. He aimed his rifle at it and fired. The stump, or what had seemed to be one, fell over backward with a groan. He had killed an Indian, who had been waiting to kill him.

Boone makes the "Wilderness Road," and builds the fort at Boonesboro. In 1775 Boone, with a party of thirty men, chopped a path through the forest from the mountains of eastern Tennessee to the Kentucky River, a distance of about two hundred miles. This was the first path in that part of the country leading to the great west. It was called the "Wilderness Road." Over that road, which thousands of emigrants travelled afterward, Boone took his family, with other settlers, to the Kentucky River. There they built a fort called Boonesboro. That fort was a great protection to the early settlers in Kentucky. In fact, it is hard to see how the state could have grown up without it. So, in one way, we can say with truth that Daniel Boone, the hunter, fighter, and road-maker, was a state-builder as well.

Boone's daughter is stolen by Indians; how he found her. One day Boone's young daughter was out, with two other girls, in a canoe on the river. Suddenly, some Indians pounced on them and carried them off. One of the girls, as she went along, broke off twigs from the bushes, so that her friends might be able to follow her track through the woods. An Indian caught her doing it, and told her that he would kill her if she did not stop. Then she slyly tore off small bits of her dress, and dropped a piece from time to time.

A Picture of Boonesboro, Kentucky, drawn from Descriptions of the Fort

Boone and his men followed the Indians like blood-hounds. They picked up the bits of dress, and so easily found which way the men had gone. They came up to the Indians just as they were sitting down around a fire to eat their supper. Creeping toward them behind the trees as softly as a cat creeps up behind a mouse, Boone and his men aimed their rifles and fired. Two of the Indians fell dead, the rest ran for their lives, and the girls were carried back in safety to the fort.

Boone is captured by Indians; they adopt him as a son. Later, Boone himself was caught and carried off by the Indians. They respected his courage so much that they would not kill him, but decided to adopt him; that is, take him into the tribe as one of their own people, or make an Indian of him.

They pulled out all his hair except one long lock, called the "scalp-lock," which they left to grow in Indian fashion. The squaws and girls braided bright feathers in this lock, so that Boone looked quite silly. Then the Indians took him down to a river. There they stripped him, and scrubbed him with all their might, to get his white blood out, as they said. Next they painted his face in stripes with red and yellow clay, so that he looked, to their minds, handsomer than he had ever looked before. When all had been done, and they were satisfied with the appearance of their new Indian, they sat down to a great feast, and had fun.

Boone escapes, but the Indians find him again; what a handful of tobacco dust did. After a time Boone managed to escape, but the Indians were so fond of him that they could not rest until they found him again. One day he was at work in a type of shed, drying some tobacco leaves. He heard a slight noise, and turning round, saw four Indians with their guns pointed at him. "Now, Boone," said they, "we got you. You no get away this time." "How are you?" said Boone pleasantly; "glad to see you; just wait a minute till I get you some of my tobacco." He gathered two large handfuls of the leaves; they were as dry as powder and crumbled to dust in his hands. Coming forward, as if to give the welcome present to the Indians, he suddenly sprang on them and filled their eyes, mouths, and noses with the stinging tobacco dust. The Indians were half choked and nearly blinded. While they were dancing about, coughing, sneezing, and rubbing their eyes, Boone slipped out of the shed and ran to a place of safety. The Indians were as mad as they could be, yet they could hardly help laughing at Boone's trick; for cunning as the Indians were, he was more cunning still.

Boone's old age; he moves to Missouri; he begs for a piece of land; his grave. Boone lived to be a very old man. He had owned a good deal of land in the west, but he had lost possession of it. When Kentucky began to fill with people and the animals were killed off, Boone moved across the Mississippi into Missouri. He said that he went because he wanted "more elbow room" and a chance to hunt buffalo again.

He now begged the state of Kentucky to give him a small piece of land, where, as he said, he could "lay his bones." The people of that state helped him to get nearly a thousand acres, but he appears to have soon lost control of it. If this is true, then this brave old hunter, who had opened the way for such a large number of emigrants to get farms in the west, died without owning a piece of ground big enough for a grave. He is buried in Frankfort, Kentucky, within sight of the river on which he built his fort at Boonesboro.

Summary. Daniel Boone, a famous hunter from North Carolina, opened up a road through the forest, from the mountains of eastern Tennessee to the Kentucky River. It was called the "Wilderness Road," and over it thousands of emigrants went into Kentucky to settle. Boone, with others, built the fort at Boonesboro, Kentucky, and went there to live. That fort protected the settlers against the Indians, and so helped that part of the country to grow until it became the state of Kentucky.

Comprehension Questions

1. What did Boone cut on a beech tree?
2. Why was the Wilderness Road important?
3. What purpose did the fort at Boonesboro serve?
4. Tell the story of the tobacco dust.
5. What did Kentucky get for him?
6. Where is Daniel Boone buried?

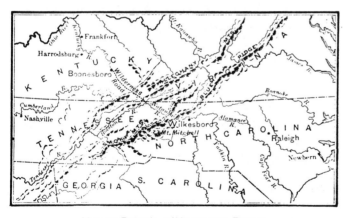

MAP OF BOONE'S "WILDERNESS ROAD"

DANIEL BOONE.

Chapter Eighteen
General James Robertson and
Governor John Sevier

(Born 1742-Died 1814; Born 1745-Died 1815)

Who James Robertson was; Governor Tryon; the battle of Alamance. When Daniel Boone first went to Kentucky (1769), he had a friend named James Robertson in North Carolina, who was, like himself, a mighty hunter. The British governor of North Carolina at that time was William Tryon. He lived in a palace built with money that he had forced the people to give him. The people disliked him because of his greed and cruelty, so they nicknamed him the "Great Wolf of North Carolina."

Eventually, many of the settlers vowed that they would not give the governor another penny. When he sent tax-collectors to get money, they drove them away. They flogged one of the governor's friends with a raw-hide until he had to run for his life.

The governor then collected some soldiers and marched against the people in the west. A battle was fought near the Alamance River. The governor had the most men, and cannon besides, so he gained the day. He took seven of the people prisoners and hanged them. They all died bravely, as men do who die for liberty.

James Robertson leaves North Carolina and goes west. After the battle of Alamance, James Robertson and his family decided they would not live any longer where Governor Tryon ruled. They resolved to go across the mountains into the western wilderness. Sixteen other families joined the Robertsons and went with them. It was a long, hard journey. They had to climb rocks and find their way through deep, tangled woods. The men went ahead with their axes and their guns; then the older children followed, driving the cows; last of all came the women with the little children, with beds, pots, and kettles packed on the backs of horses.

The emigrants settle on the Watauga River in Tennessee. When the little party had crossed the mountains into what is now the state of Tennessee, they found a delightful valley. Through this valley there ran a stream of clear, sparkling water called the Watauga River; the air of the valley was sweet with the smell of wild crab apples.

On the banks of that stream, the emigrants built their new homes. Their houses were simply rough log huts, but they were clean and comfortable. When the settlers put up these cabins, they chopped down every tree near them that was big enough for an Indian to hide behind. They knew that they might have to fight the red men; but they would rather do that than be robbed by tax-collectors. In the wilderness, Governor Tryon could not reach them. They were free-- free as the deer and the squirrels were. That one thought made them happy.

John Sevier goes to settle at Watauga; what he and Robertson did. The year after this little settlement was made, John Sevier went from Virginia to Watauga, as it was called. He and Robertson soon became best friends, for one brave man can always see something to respect and like in another brave man. Robertson and Sevier hunted together and worked together.

After a while, they called a meeting of the settlers and agreed on some excellent laws, so that everything in the log village might be done decently and in order; for, although these people lived in the woods, they did not want to live like savages or wild beasts. In time, President Washington gave James Robertson the rank of General in honor of what he had done for his country.

Out of this settlement on the Watauga River grew the state of Tennessee. Many years ago a small monument was erected to Sevier in the cemetery at Nashville, a city founded by his friend Robertson. Also, a noble monument to Sevier's memory has been erected in Knoxville, formerly the capital of the state of which he became the first governor.

Summary. James Robertson, of North Carolina, and John Sevier, of Virginia, emigrated across the mountains to the western wilderness. Their settlement on the Watauga River, was the first in the area that developed into the state of Tennessee, of which John Sevier became the first governor.

Comprehension Questions

1. What friend did Boone have in North Carolina?
2. Where did Robertson and others go?
3. Why did they like to be there?
4. What state grew out of the Watauga settlement?
5. What did Sevier become?
6. Where are his two monuments?

Chapter Nineteen
General Rufus Putnam

(Born 1738 - Died 1824)

What General Putnam did for Washington, and what the British said of Putnam's work. When the British had possession of Boston at the beginning of the War for American Independence, Washington asked Rufus Putnam, who was a great builder of forts, to help him drive them out. Putnam began to work, one dark, stormy night, and built a fort on some high land overlooking Boston harbor.

When the British commander woke up the next morning, he saw the American cannon pointed at his ships. He was so astonished that he could hardly believe his eyes. "Why," said he, "the rebels have done more in one night than my whole army could have done in a week." Another officer, who had command of the British vessels, said, "If the Americans hold that fort, I cannot keep a ship in the harbor."

Well, we know what happened. Our men did hold that fort, and the British had to leave Boston. Next to General Washington, General Rufus Putnam was the man who made them go; for not many officers in the American army could build such a fort as he could.

General Putnam builds the *Mayflower*; goes down the Ohio River and makes the first settlement in Ohio. After the war was over, General Putnam started, with a group of people from New England, to make a settlement on the Ohio River. In the spring of 1788, he and his emigrants built a boat at a place on a branch of the Ohio River just above Pittsburgh. They named this boat the *Mayflower*, because they were Pilgrims going west to make their home there.

At that time, there was not a European settler in what is now the state of Ohio. Most of that country was covered with thick woods. There were no roads through those woods; and there was not an automobile or a railroad in America or for that matter, in the whole world. If you look on the map and follow down the Ohio River from Pittsburgh, you will come to the place where the Muskingum River flows into it. There the *Mayflower* stopped, and the emigrants landed and began to build their settlement.

What the settlers named their town; the first Fourth of July celebration; what Washington said about the settlers. During the Revolutionary War, the beautiful Queen Mary of France was our firm friend, and she was very kind and helpful to Dr. Franklin when he went to France for us. Many of the emigrants to Ohio had fought in the Revolution, and so the company of settlers decided to name the town Marietta, in honor of the queen.

When the Marietta settlers celebrated the Fourth of July, Major Denny, who commanded a fort just across the river, came to visit them. He said, "These people appear to be the happiest folks in the world." President Washington said that he knew many of them and that he believed they were just the kind of men to succeed. He was right; for these people, with those who came later to build the city of Cincinnati, were the ones who laid the foundation of the great and rich state of Ohio.

Fights with the Indians; how the settlers held their town; Indian Rock; the "Miami Slaughter House." The people of Marietta had hardly begun to feel at home in their little settlement before a terrible Indian war broke out. The village of Marietta had a high fence built around it, and if a man walked outside that fence, he went at the risk of his life. The Indians were always hiding in the woods, ready to kill any settler they saw. When the settlers worked in the cornfield, they had to carry their guns as well as their hoes; and one man always stood on top of a high stump in the middle of the field, to keep a sharp lookout.

On the Ohio River, below Marietta, there is a lofty rock that is still called Indian Rock. It was given this name because the Indians used to climb to the top and watch for emigrants coming down the river in boats. When they saw a boat, they would fire a shower of bullets at it, and hopefully leave it full of dead and wounded men to drift down the stream. In the western part of Ohio, on the Miami River, the Indians killed so many people that the settlers called that part of the country by the terrible name of the "Miami Slaughter House."

What General Wayne did. But President Washington sent a man to Ohio who made the Indians beg for peace. This man was General Wayne; he had fought in the Revolution, and fought so furiously that he was called "Mad Anthony Wayne." The Indians said that he never slept. They named him "Black Snake," because that is the quickest and boldest snake there is in the woods, and in a fight with any other creature of his kind he is pretty sure to win the day. General Wayne won, and the Indians agreed to move off and give up a very large part of Ohio to the settlers. After that, there was not much trouble, and new emigrants moved in by the thousands.

Summary. In 1788 General Rufus Putnam, with a company of emigrants, settled Marietta, Ohio. The town was named in honor of Queen Mary of France, who had helped us during the Revolution. It was the first town built in what is now the state of Ohio. After General Wayne had conquered the Indians, that part of the country rapidly increased in population.

Comprehension Questions

1. What did General Rufus Putnam do for Washington?
2. Where did General Putnam go in 1788?
3. What did the Indians call General Wayne?
4. Why did the settlers call their town Marietta?
5. What did General Wayne do?
6. How many emigrants moved into Ohio after the fighting was over?

PUTNAM SUMMONED TO WAR.

Chapter Twenty
General George Rogers Clark

(Born 1752 - Died 1818)

The British in the west; their forts; hiring Indians to fight the settlers. While Washington was fighting the battles of the Revolution in the east, the British in the west were not sitting still. They had many forts in the Wilderness, as the country west of the Allegheny Mountains was then called. One of these forts was at Detroit, in what is now Michigan; another was at Vincennes, in what is now Indiana; a third fort was at Kaskaskia, in what is now Illinois.

Colonel Hamilton, the British commander at Detroit, was determined to drive the American settlers out of the west. During the beginning of the Revolution, the Americans resolved to hire the Indians to fight for them; but the British found that they could hire them better than the Americans could, and so they obtained their help. Many of the Indian warriors did their work in a terribly cruel way. Generally, they did not come out and do battle openly; but they crept up secretly, by night, and attacked the farmers' homes. They killed and scalped the settlers in the west, burned their log cabins, and carried off the women and children as prisoners. The greater part of the people in England hated this sort of war. They begged the king not to hire the Indians to do these horrible deeds of murder and destruction. Unfortunately, King George III was very set in his way, and he had fully made up his mind to conquer the "American rebels," as he called them, even if he had to hire Indians to murder innocent people.

George Rogers Clark gets help from Virginia and starts to attack Fort Kaskaskia. Daniel Boone had a friend in Virginia named George Rogers Clark, who believed that he could take the British forts in the west and drive out the British from that part of the country. Virginia then owned most of the Wilderness territory. For this reason, Clark went to Patrick Henry, governor of Virginia, and asked for help. The governor liked the plan, and let Clark have money to hire men to go with him to try to take Fort Kaskaskia.

Clark started in the spring of 1778 with about a hundred and fifty men. They built boats on the banks of the Allegheny River just above Pittsburgh, and floated down the Ohio River, a distance of over nine hundred miles. They went ashore in what is now the state of Illinois, and marched toward Fort Kaskaskia.

The march to Fort Kaskaskia; how a dance ended. It was a hundred miles to the fort, and half of the way the men had to find their way through thick woods, full of underbrush, briers, and vines. The British, thinking that the fort was perfectly safe from attack, had left it in the care of a French officer. Clark and his soldiers reached Kaskaskia at night. They found no one to stop them. The soldiers in the fort were having a dance, and the Americans could hear the merry music of a violin and the laughing voices of girls.

Clark left his men just outside the fort, and finding a door open, he walked in. He reached the room where the fun was happening, and stopping there, he stood leaning against the doorpost, looking on. The room was lighted with torches; the light of one of the torches happened to fall full on Clark's face. An Indian sitting on the floor caught sight of him; he sprang to his feet and gave a terrible war-whoop. The dancers stopped as though they had been shot; the women screamed; the men ran to the door to get their guns. Clark did not move, but said quietly, "Go on; only remember you are dancing under Virginia, and not under Great Britain." The next moment the Americans rushed in, and Clark and his "Long Knives," as the Indians called his men, had full control of the fort.

PATRICK HENRY.

GEORGE ROGERS CLARK.

How Fort Vincennes was taken; how the British got it back; what Francis Vigo did. Clark wanted next to march against Fort Vincennes, but he did not have enough men. There was a French Catholic priest at Kaskaskia, and Clark's kindness to him had made him his friend. He said, "I will go to Vincennes for you, and I will tell the French, who hold the fort for the British, that the Americans are their real friends, and that, in this war, they are in the right." He went to Vincennes. The French listened to him and then pulled down the British flag and ran up the American flag in its place.

The next year the British, led by Colonel Hamilton of Detroit, took the fort back. When Clark heard of this he said, "Either I must take Hamilton, or Hamilton will take me." Just then Francis Vigo, a trader from St. Louis, came to see Clark at Kaskaskia. Hamilton had held Vigo as a prisoner, so he knew all about Fort Vincennes. Vigo said to Clark, "Hamilton has only about eighty soldiers; you can take the fort, and I will lend you all the money you need to pay your men what you owe them."

Clark's march to Fort Vincennes; the "Drowned Lands." Clark, with about two hundred men, started for Vincennes. The distance was nearly a hundred and fifty miles. The first week everything went pretty well. It was in the month of February; the weather was cold and it rained a great deal, but the men did not mind that. They would get wet during the day but at night they built roaring log fires, gathered round them, roasted their buffalo meat or venison, smoked their pipes, told jolly stories, and sang lively songs.

The next week they came to a branch of the Wabash River. Then they found that the constant rains had raised the streams so that they had overflowed their banks; the whole country was under water three or four feet deep. This flooded country was called the "Drowned Lands." By the time Clark and his men had crossed these lands, they were nearly drowned themselves.

Wading on to victory. For about a week the Americans had to wade in ice-cold water, sometimes waist deep and sometimes nearly up to their chins. While wading, the men were obliged to hold their guns and powder horns above their heads to keep them dry. Now and then a man would stub his toe against a root or a stone and would go sprawling headfirst into the water. When he came up, puffing and blowing from such a dive, he was lucky if he still had his gun. For two days no one could get anything to eat; but hungry, wet, and cold, they kept moving slowly on.

The last part of the march was the worst of all. They were now near the fort, but they still had to wade through a sheet of water four miles across. Clark took the lead and plunged in. The rest, shivering, followed. A few looked as though their strength and courage had given out. Clark saw this, and calling to Captain Bowman, one of the bravest of his officers, he ordered him to kill the first man who refused to go forward.

Finally, with frozen hands and cold feet, all made it across. Some of the men were so weak and blue with cold that they could not take another step. They fell flat on their faces in the mud. These men were so nearly dead that no fire seemed to warm them. Clark ordered two strong men to lift each of these poor fellows up and run them up and down until they began to get warm. By doing this he saved everyone.

Clark takes the fort; what we gained by his victory; his grave. After a long and desperate fight, Clark took Fort Vincennes and raised the Stars and Stripes over it in triumph. The British never took it back. Most of the Indians were now glad to make peace, and promised to behave themselves.

With Clark's victory, the Americans now controlled the whole western wilderness up to Detroit. When the Revolutionary War came to an end, the British did not want to give us any part of America beyond the thirteen states on the Atlantic coast. But we said, the whole west, clear to the Mississippi, is ours. We fought for it, we took it, we hoisted our flag over its forts, and we mean to keep it. We did keep it.

There is a grass-grown grave in a burial ground in Louisville, Kentucky, which has a small headstone marked with the letters G. R. C., and nothing more. That is the grave of General George Rogers Clark, the man who did more than anyone else to expand the United States westward. Clark died feeling lonely and in great poverty. In 1895, a fine monument was erected in Indianapolis to his memory.

Summary. During the Revolutionary War, George Rogers Clark, of Virginia, with a small number of men, captured Fort Kaskaskia in Illinois, and Fort Vincennes in Indiana. Clark drove out the British from that part of the country. When peace was made we kept the west (the country beyond the Allegheny Mountains as far as the Mississippi River), as a part of the United States. Had it not been for Clark and Governor Patrick Henry, we might not have gained this territory.

Comprehension Questions

1. Did the British army have any forts in the western wilderness?
2. Who was the governor of Virginia in 1778?
3 Was Fort Kaskaskia located in the state of Michigan?
4. In what year was a monument erected for Clark in Indianapolis?
5 Was Fort Vincennes located in the state of Illinois?
6. Was Daniel Boone a friend of George Rogers Clark?

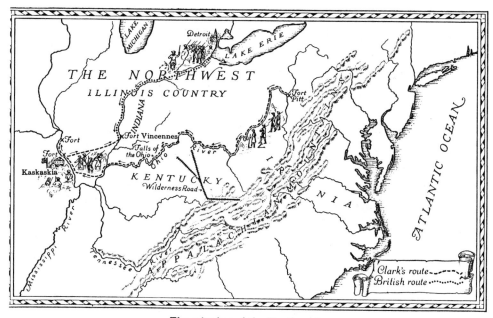

The winning of the Northwest

Chapter Twenty-One
James Madison

(Born 1751 - Died 1836)

James Madison's early years; his concern for religious liberty; his early political career. Many of the greatest men of the early days of American history came from Virginia. One of the most important was James Madison. He was born at Port Conway, Virginia, and was raised at Montpelier, his father's plantation.

He was initially educated at home by his grandmother, mother, and local tutors. At age eleven, he went off to a boarding school for five years. After returning home, he spent three more years studying with the pastor of his local church. In 1769 James Madison went to Princeton to study at the College of New Jersey (now known as Princeton University). After completing his college education in 1772, he returned home for further study in preparation for the ministry.

While Madison went into law and politics instead of the ministry, he never lost his concern for religious matters, especially as they concerned the law. Even though an Episcopalian, he defended local Baptists against minor acts of persecution from the legal and religious establishment of Virginia. He also supported religious liberty issues in the Virginia Convention of 1776 and the Virginia legislature in 1786.

Madison's political career began in 1775 with his election to the Orange County Committee of Safety. Between that election and the Constitutional Convention of 1787, he served in many responsible positions: the Virginia constitutional convention in 1776, the Virginia legislature, Virginia state government, the Continental Congress, and delegate to both the Mount Vernon Conference in 1785 and the Annapolis Convention of 1786.

Why the Articles of Confederation needed to be replaced; the "Father of the Constitution." Soon after the establishment of American independence it became evident to many that the government under the Articles of Confederation was not strong enough to hold the states together in peace. It was very plain that, unless some remedy could be found, the Union would go to pieces, and that instead of one republic there would be thirteen.

CARPENTERS' HALL, PHILADELPHIA
Where the Convention met which made the Constitution for the United States.

One of those who saw this need was James Madison. His participation in the Continental Congress showed him that there was a great need for a change in our government. He became a strong supporter of improving our government and did what he could to encourage efforts at reform.

All felt the need of union, but the states were so jealous of their own rights that it was doubtful whether they could be induced to give any additional powers to the national government. At that time the enforcement of any law passed by Congress was left entirely to the states. Therefore, the authority of the central government was very limited.

An effort was made in 1786 to get the states to send delegates to a convention in Annapolis, Maryland, to revise the Articles of Confederation. However, only five states responded to the call. One of the few to attend this convention was James Madison. A second effort was more successful. All the states except Rhode Island sent delegates to the convention which met in Philadelphia on the 14th of May, 1787. George Washington, of Virginia, was chosen president of the convention.

The assembling of the convention to revise the Articles of Confederation was due to the earnest efforts of three men — James Madison and George Washington, of Virginia, and Alexander Hamilton, of New York. The formation and adoption of the Constitution was due to James Madison more than to any other one man. His experience in state and national government made him invaluable in the work of the Convention. He was the author of many of its chief features, and has been called the "Father of the Constitution."

Details about the Constitution; the branches of government; amending the Constitution. Some of the delegates to the convention wished to establish a strong national government. But the majority would not even allow the word "national" to appear in the new constitution. They were willing to greatly enlarge the powers of the Federal Government, but they were determined to adhere to the idea of a confederation.

JAMES MADISON.

After four months of careful labor the new plan of union, called the Constitution of the United States, was ready to be offered to the people of the several states. Under this plan the states gave to the Federal Government much larger powers than it had possessed before; but each state reserved to itself the right to manage its domestic affairs and to pass any law which did not interfere with the rights of other states or of the Federal Government.

Under the first union, Congress exercised all the powers given to the government. Under the new plan, the government was to consist of three branches: the Legislative, which is to make the laws; the Judicial, which is to explain the laws; and the Executive, which is to see that the laws were carried out.

The law-making power is vested in Congress, which consists of two houses, the Senate and the House of Representatives. The number of representatives allowed to each state depends upon the population of the state. These representatives are elected by the people and hold office for two year terms. Two senators are allowed to each state, are elected by the people from each state, and hold office for six year terms. Congress is allowed to control all matters that pertain to the general interest of all the states. Its main job is to make laws for the nation.

Congress can also affect the Executive and Judicial branches through its confirmation and impeachment powers. The President, Vice-President, and all civil officers (including federal judges) can be removed from office by Congress through the impeachment process. The Senate has the responsibility to confirm the appointments by the President to all important offices in the Executive branch and the appointment of all federal judges.

The Judicial branch consists of one Supreme Court and of such inferior courts as may be established by Congress. The Supreme Court is made up of the Chief Justice and eight associate justices. If the justices on the Supreme Court declare that any law of Congress or of any of the states does not agree with the Constitution, then such law becomes at once null and void.

The Executive branch consists of the President, the Vice-President, and the federal bureaucracy. As chief executive, the President is responsible to execute the laws passed by Congress and administers the vast bureaucracy, the most important of which is the Executive Office of the President and the cabinet departments. The President is also the commander-in-chief of the armed forces of the United States and diplomatic leader of the nation. The President can attempt to stop Congress from passing a new law by vetoing it. A veto, however, can be overridden by a two-thirds vote in each house of Congress.

The cabinet consists of a group of important advisors to the President who also head important executive departments. Congress establishes the cabinet departments and the Senate must confirm the appointment of those whom the President has appointed to head these various departments. The Cabinet currently consists of the Secretaries of State, Defense, Agriculture, Veterans Affairs, the Treasury, Education, Energy, Health and Human Services, Housing and Urban Development, Commerce, Interior, Labor, and Transportation; the Attorney-General, who heads the Department of Justice, is also a Cabinet member.

The Vice-President has a limited formal role in the American government. The most important role of the Vice-President is to take the place of the President upon his death or disability. The Vice-President also serves as the President of the Senate, but has no vote in the Senate unless there is a tie vote. Other duties may be assigned to him by the President.

The Constitution can be amended by the consent of three-fourths of the states. However, no amendment can be made that would deprive any state without its own consent of its equal vote in the Senate.

Ratification of the Constitution. Under the Articles of Confederation no change could be made without the consent of all the states. The preamble to the Constitution, as at first adopted by the convention, mentioned each state by name. However, it became evident that there would be great difficulty in getting all the states to accept the new Constitution. Therefore, it was determined by the convention that the consent of nine states should suffice for its establishment between the states who ratified it. As it was uncertain which of the states would ratify the Constitution and thus constitute the new Union, the preamble was altered so as to read: "We the people of the United States...."

JAMES MADISON.

The seventh and last article of the Constitution as submitted by the convention reads: "The ratification of the conventions of nine states shall be sufficient for the establishment of this Constitution between the states so ratifying the same." Thus no state would be, without its own consent, bound by the new Constitution. Only those states which actually ratified the Constitution would be part of the new government.

Patrick Henry and others were concerned that the new Constitution, with a preamble that included the phrase "We the people...," meant a consolidated government instead of a confederation. For this reason, Patrick Henry earnestly opposed its ratification by Virginia. But in answer to his objection, Mr. Madison said: "Who are parties to it [the Constitution]? The people, but not the people as composing one great body, but the people as composing thirteen sovereignties. Were it a consolidated government, the assent of a majority of the people would be sufficient for its establishment, and as a majority have adopted it already, the remaining states would be bound by the act of the majority, even if they reprobated it; but, sir, no state is bound by it, as it is, without its own consent."

In response to the opposition to ratification of the Constitution in the state of New York, James Madison, Alexander Hamilton, and John Jay wrote a famous series of articles, known as *The Federalist,* in favor of the Constitution. Madison also took an active role in the debate over the Constitution in the Virginia ratification convention.

After much opposition, eleven states ratified the Constitution. The method was the same in each state. Delegates were chosen to meet in convention and decide the question according to the wish of the people who had elected them. The seventy thousand people of the little state of Delaware had precisely the same weight—one vote—in the

James Madison

ratification of the Constitution, as the more than seven hundred thousand of Virginia, or the four hundred thousand of Pennsylvania.

By the 26th of July, 1788, the conventions of eleven states had ratified the Constitution. The following table gives the names of the eleven states so ratifying it, and the dates of their ratification:

    Delaware, December 7, 1787
    Pennsylvania, December 12, 1787
    New Jersey, December 18, 1787
    Georgia, January 2, 1788
    Connecticut, January 9, 1788
    Massachusetts, February 6, 1788
    Maryland, April 28, 1788
    South Carolina, May 23, 1788
    New Hampshire, June 21, 1788
    Virginia, June 26, 1788
    New York, June 26, 1788

Virginia accompanied her ratification with the assertion of the right of the people to resume the powers granted under the Constitution, whenever the same should be used for their injury or oppression. As each state ratified the Constitution separately, the word "people" here meant the people of that particular state, who were then ratifying the Constitution in behalf of that state. The natural inference would be that, if the people of Virginia had that right, the people of each of the other ratifying states had the same right. New York's convention made a declaration similar to that of Virginia.

North Carolina and Rhode Island had not ratified. Steps were immediately taken for the establishment of the new government by the eleven ratifying states. In all of these eleven states, except New York, the necessary elections were held. George Washington of Virginia received every electoral vote cast for the office of President, and John Adams of Massachusetts was elected Vice-President by a majority of the electoral votes. On the 30th of April, 1789, in the city of New York, the inauguration took place amid imposing ceremonies. Under the guidance of the beloved Washington, whom all Americans of every section have ever delighted to honor as the "Father of his Country," the United States entered upon a brilliant career.

The new Union formed the most perfect model of a confederated republic, as both Washington and Hamilton styled it, that the wisdom of man ever devised. There were, as we have seen, only eleven states in the new republic. North Carolina and Rhode Island had thus far refused to adopt the Constitution. But there was no claim on the part of the eleven states that had formed the more perfect union to control the action of the other two. Their accession to the Union was desired, but their right to do as they pleased in this matter was never questioned. There was no inclination to violate the very principle for which they had contended in the war for independence by attempting to coerce any state which did not see fit to unite with them.

In September 1789, while Rhode Island was still holding aloof from the new Union, President Washington received and sent in to the Senate of the United States a letter from the General Assembly of Rhode Island, addressed to "the President, the Senate, and the House of Representatives of the eleven United States of America in Congress assembled." This letter is interesting, because it shows the relationship then existing between Rhode Island and the United States. It was a request that trade and commerce might be free and open between that state and the United States.

On November 21, 1789, North Carolina, after becoming satisfied that the most important of the amendments and "Declaration of Rights" that North Carolina and other states had proposed would be adopted, agreed to "adopt and ratify" the Constitution. On May 29th, 1790, Rhode Island gave its long-withheld assent to the Constitution, after becoming fully convinced that certain proposed amendments would be adopted.

When Washington announced to Congress that North Carolina had ratified the Constitution of 1787, he expressed his gratification at the accession of that state. On June 1st, 1790, he announced by special message the like accession of the state of Rhode Island, and congratulated Congress on the happy event which "united under the General Government all the states which were originally confederated."

The Bill of Rights; the Tenth Amendment. During the fight over ratification of the Constitution, it became clear that many people believed that the Constitution needed to include a list of rights. Many states ratified the Constitution with the understanding that a bill of rights would be added later. Some states even sent proposed lists of rights to Congress for its consideration.

In response, James Madison took the lead in drawing up a list of proposed amendments to the Constitution. Twelve amendments were submitted to the states in September 1789. Ten of these amendments were ratified in December 1791 and became known as the Bill of Rights.

Many important rights are listed in the Bill of Rights. Examples of some of these well-known rights are: freedom of religion, freedom of the press, freedom of speech, the right to bear arms, and the right to a speedy trial by jury. One of the least understood of the amendments is the Tenth Amendment, which specifically limits the powers of the United States government and is a safeguard to state authority. The Tenth Amendment states: "The powers not delegated to the United States by the Constitution, nor prohibited by it to the states, are reserved to the states respectively, or to the people."

Samuel Adams, of Massachusetts, said of the Tenth Amendment: "It is consonant with the second article in the present Confederation,[1] that each state retains its sovereignty, freedom, and independence, and every power, jurisdiction, and right, which is not by this Confederation expressly delegated to the United States in Congress assembled." Thus we see, our founding fathers, while anxious to form a more perfect union, guarded carefully the sovereignty of the states. President Washington referred to our country as a "nation of nations."

James Madison continues his public service to the country; he becomes President of the United States; Madison's impact lasts long after his death. Following the ratification of the Constitution, Madison served as a Representative from Virginia in the House of Representatives from 1789 through 1797. While in Congress, he was largely responsible for the writing and passage of the Bill of Rights. During his time in Congress, he married Dolley Payne Todd. After four years of private life, Madison became Secretary of State under President Thomas Jefferson. As Secretary of State, he helped to arrange for the purchase of the Louisiana Territory.

In 1809, Madison became the fourth President of the United States and served two terms, retiring in 1817. President Madison led the United States in its second war with Britain during the War of 1812. As president, he authorized the seizure of West Florida from Spain, supported the chartering of the second Bank of the United States, and encouraged Congress to pass a new protective tariff law.

WAR OF 1812
SHOWING STATES
ADMITTED TO 1812

SCALE OF MILES
0 50 100 150 200 250 300

Madison continued his public service after leaving office. He became a member of the board of the University of Virginia and served as its Rector from 1826 to 1834. He served as a delegate to the Virginia Constitutional Convention in 1829 and was called upon to give advice during various political controversies. He also edited his *Notes of Debates in the Federal Convention of 1787*, which was published after his death. Madison died on June 28, 1836, having provided his country with long and faithful service.

Even long after his death, Madison continues to affect our government. One of the two amendments Madison suggested that the states ratify, but which were not made part of the Bill of Rights, has become the Twenty-seventh Amendment of the Constitution. This amendment, which was originally proposed to the states by Congress in 1789, finally was made part of the Constitution in 1992, after Michigan became the thirty-eighth state to ratify the amendment. This new amendment prohibits Congress from introducing and voting through salary increases for itself within a single congressional term.

Summary. A good deal of the credit for the formation and adoption of our beloved Constitution and Bill of Rights belongs to James Madison. On several occasions, Madison was the only leader who continued to press for the passage of the key constitutional amendments known as the Bill of Rights. His faithfulness to the people gained him the respect and honor of all Americans past and present. He truly deserves the title of "Father of the Constitution."

Comprehension Questions

1. Where did James Madison receive his early education?
2. When did Madison begin his political career?
3. How many branches of government make up our Federal Government?
4. Who wrote the articles entitled *The Federalist*?
5. What state was the last to ratify the Constitution?
6. How did the Tenth Amendment promote the role of the states in our system of government?

Chapter Twenty-Two
James McGready

(Born 1758 - Died 1817)

James McGready; his role in the Second Great Awakening; how "camp meetings" developed; circuit riders. By the end of the Revolutionary War, the influence of Biblical Christianity upon American culture began to fade away. For example, by 1782 only two students out of the entire student body of the College of New Jersey confessed to be Christians. The people's interest in godliness declined throughout the country, especially on the great western frontier, where established churches were few in number. Frontiersmen were often sadly lacking in terms of basic morality and Biblical understanding.

However, God did not leave America in such a sad state of affairs. At the end of the 1790s and beginning of the 1800s, America experienced a new era of widespread spiritual revival, which was to have a major impact upon the nation's future. Certainly not all Americans became Christians, but few were unaffected by the new surge of Christianity. Under the influence of the Holy Spirit, many Americans were converted and came to accept the Bible as the inspired Word of God. The broad truths of the Bible thoroughly influenced America in the first half of the nineteenth century. Just as reverence for the Bible had played such a key role in the founding of America, it was to play a key role in the maturing of the nation. This new revival was commonly called the Second Great Awakening.

Many preachers from various Christian denominations were instrumental in re-kindling the fire of social and theological reformation in the early nineteenth century. However, few preachers had as much influence during this period as James McGready, who was a fiery and tough Presbyterian preacher. Rev. McGready had the reputation for preaching in a bold and uncompromising way the eternal truths of God and the necessity of repentance and conversion. His style, although at times crude, was well received by the simple country people who often attended his revival meetings.

Methodist Information

In 1796, James McGready became the pastor of three Presbyterian churches in notoriously immoral Logan County,

Kentucky. Here, under his preaching, the great western revival began.

McGready was joined by several Presbyterian and Methodist preachers and, by 1800, the success of the outdoor revival meetings he led was amazing. During that year, a massive revival meeting at Red River, Kentucky, drew thousands of people from hundreds of miles in every direction to hear the gospel of Jesus Christ. Great numbers of people were converted to the Christian faith at that time.

The crowds became so large, and the events so lengthy, that people began to bring food and tents with them so they could stay at the revival meetings for several days at a time. This was the beginning of the "camp meetings," which were to become a common practice in American society for many decades.

Later in 1811, Rev. McGready was sent to southern Indiana as a pioneer preacher. In Indiana he continued to use camp meetings effectively. He remarked in 1816 that he felt the same powerful work of God in Indiana that he had felt in Kentucky in 1800.

During this same period, similar revivals were taking place in the eastern part of the United States. Many of these revivals were under the leadership of Francis Asbury, a powerful Methodist bishop who encouraged men to travel from town to town on horseback to preach to the people. The Methodists, with their "circuit-riding" preachers, were so well received that the Methodist denomination experienced significant growth in New England and particularly in the Middle States. Baltimore, Maryland, became the headquarters of the Methodist churches in America.

The impact of the Second Great Awakening. As revival spread, church membership increased and public morality generally improved. Previous declines in true Christianity were also reversed at many of the great colleges of New England, such as Yale. In 1802 Timothy Dwight, president of Yale College, led a revival among the students that resulted in the conversion of one-third of the student body. Similar revivals swept across schools and colleges throughout the eastern part of the United States.

A spiritually—thirsty America responded to the dynamic preaching of leaders like James McGready and Francis Asbury. The positive effects of this period of spiritual awakening did not go unnoticed by people who visited America during the early nineteenth century. The famous French author and historian Alexis de Tocqueville visited America in the early 1830s and published his famous book *Democracy in America* in 1835 which helped the world understand the true source of America's success as a nation during that period. In his book, this keen social observer and gifted author wrote:

There is no country in the world where the Christian religion retains a greater influence over the souls of men than in America; and there can be no greater proof of its utility and of its conformity to human nature than that its influence is powerfully felt over the most enlightened and free nation of the earth. The secret to America's greatness is its moral goodness. If America ever ceases to be good it will cease to be great.

Summary. James McGready, a famous preacher of the late 1790s and early 1800s, helped to start a great spiritual awakening in the western part of the United States. Outdoor revival meetings became so popular that people would travel far distances to attend for several days. These events became known as "camp meetings," because people flocked to hear the gospel of Jesus Christ at these meetings and would bring tents and camp outside for several days. Horse-riding preachers traveled throughout the East and the frontier to preach the Word of God and they became known as "circuit-riders."

Comprehension Questions

1. When did the Second Great Awakening begin?
2. In what state did Rev. McGready begin his revival meetings?
3. Who was Francis Asbury?
. Who were the people known as "circuit-riders"?
5. Who was Alexis de Tocqueville?
6. What was the key to America's greatness during this period?

Chapter Twenty-Three
Eli Whitney

(Born 1765 - Died 1825)

The name cut on a door. Near Westboro, Massachusetts, there was an old farmhouse that was built before the Revolutionary War. Close to the house was a small wooden building; on the door you could read a boy's name, just as he cut it with his pocket knife more than a hundred years ago. Here is the door with the name. If the boy had added the date of his birth, he would have cut the figures 1765; but, just as he was about to try, his father appeared and said sharply: Eli, don't be cutting that door. No, sir, said Eli, with respect; and shutting his knife up with a snap, he hurried off to do his chores.

What Eli Whitney used to do in his father's little workshop; the fiddle. Eli Whitney's father used that little wooden building as a workshop, where he mended chairs and did many other small jobs. Eli liked to go to that workshop and make little things for himself, such as toy guns and windmills; for it was as natural for him to use tools as it was to whistle.

Once, when Eli's father was gone from home for several days, the boy was very busy all the while in the little shop. When Mr. Whitney came back, he asked his housekeeper, "What has Eli been doing?" "Oh," she replied, "he has been making a fiddle." His father shook his head, and said that he was afraid Eli would never succeed in the world. But Eli's fiddle, though it was rough looking, was well-made. It had music in it, and the neighbors liked to hear it. Somehow it seemed to say, through all the tunes played on it, "Whatever is worth doing, is worth doing well."

Eli Whitney begins making nails; he goes to college. When Eli was fifteen, he began making nails. We have machines today which will make more than a hundred nails a minute; but Eli made his, one by one, by pounding them out of a long, slender bar of red-hot iron. Whitney's hand-made nails were not handsome, but they were strong and tough, and as the Revolutionary War was then happening, he could sell all he could make.

After the war was over, the demand for nails declined. Then Whitney threw down his hammer and said, "I am going to college." He had no money; he worked his way through Yale College, partly by teaching and partly by doing little jobs with his tools. A carpenter who saw him at work one day noticed how neatly and skillfully he used his tools, and said, "There was one good mechanic spoiled when you went to college."

Whitney goes to Georgia; he stays with Mrs. Greene; the embroidery frame. When the young man had finished his course of study, he went to Georgia to find a job teaching. On the way to Savannah he became acquainted with Mrs. Greene, the widow of the famous General Greene of Rhode Island. General Greene had done such excellent fighting in the south during the Revolution that, after the war was over, the state of Georgia gave him a large piece of land near Savannah.

GEN. NATHANIEL GREENE.

Mrs. Greene invited young Whitney to stay and work at her house. As he had been disappointed in not finding a place to teach, he was very glad to accept her kind invitation. While he was there, he made her an embroidery frame. It was much better than the old one that she had been using, and she thought the maker of it was wonderfully skillful.

A talk about raising cotton, and about cotton seeds.
Not long after this, a number of cotton planters were at Mrs.
Greene's house. In speaking about raising cotton, they said
that the man who could invent a machine for stripping off
the cotton seeds from the plant would make his fortune.

What is called raw cotton or cotton wool, as it grows in the
field, has a great number of little green seeds clinging to it.
Before the cotton wool can be spun into thread and woven
into cloth, those seeds must be pulled off.

The Spinning-Wheel.

At that time, the Southern planters had their black slaves do
most of this work. When they had finished their day's labor
of gathering the cotton in the cotton field, the men, women,
and children would sit down and pick off the seeds, which
stuck so tight that getting them off was no easy task.

After the planters had talked awhile about this work, Mrs. Greene said, "If you want a machine to do it, you should apply to my young friend, Mr. Whitney; he can make anything." "But," said Mr. Whitney, "I have never seen a cotton plant or a cotton seed in my life," for it was not then the time of year to see it growing in the fields.

Whitney gets some cotton wool; he invents the cotton-gin; what that machine did. After the planters had gone, Eli Whitney went to Savannah and hunted about until he found, in some store or warehouse, a little cotton wool with the seeds left on it. He took this back with him and began to work to make a machine that would strip off the seeds.

THE COTTON GIN [1] (OR COTTON MACHINE)

He said to himself, if I fasten some upright pieces of wire in a board, and set the wires very close together, like the teeth of a comb, and then pull the cotton wool through the wires with my fingers, the seeds, being too large to come through, will be torn off and left behind. He tried it, and found that the cotton wool came through without any seeds on it. Now, said he, If I should make a wheel, and cover it with short steel teeth, shaped like hooks, these teeth would pull the cotton wool through the wires better than my fingers do, and much faster as well.

He made such a wheel, which was turned by a crank, and it did the work perfectly. So, in the year 1793, he had invented the machine the planters wanted.

Before that time it used to take a plantation worker all day to clean a single pound of cotton of its seeds, by picking them off one by one; now Eli Whitney's cotton-gin, as he called his machine, would clean a thousand pounds in a day. This new invention and many others like it, helped American workers produce things cheaper and better than ever before.

Price of common cloth today; what makes it so cheap; "King Cotton." Today nothing is much cheaper than common cotton cloth. You can buy it for very little money per yard; but before Whitney invented his cotton-gin it sold for a great deal of money per yard. Two hundred years ago the planters in the south raised very little cotton, for few people could afford to wear it; but after this wonderful machine was made, the planters kept making their fields bigger and bigger. Eventually, they raised so much more of this plant than of any other crop that they said, "Cotton is king." It was Eli Whitney who built the throne for that king. Although he did not make a fortune from his machine, he received a lot of money for its use in some southern states.

Later, Mr. Whitney built a gun factory near New Haven, Connecticut, at a place now called Whitneyville. At that factory he made thousands of the muskets that we used in our second war with England in 1812--the famous war that gave us the stirring song called *the Star Spangled Banner*, and secured our independence on the sea as the War for Independence did on the land.

Summary. About two hundred years ago (1793), Eli Whitney of Westboro, Massachusetts, invented the cotton-gin, a machine for pulling off the green seeds from cotton wool, so that it may be easily woven into cloth. That machine made thousands of cotton planters and cotton manufacturers rich, and it made cotton cloth so inexpensive that everybody could afford to use it.

Comprehension Questions

1. What was the name of the lady that Eli Whitney met when he went to Savannah?
2. What name did Eli Whitney give to his invention that pulled the seeds out of cotton?
3. What was the name of the college that Whitney attended?
4. What did Mr. Whitney build at Whitneyville, Connecticut?

ELI WHITNEY, INVENTOR

Eli Whitney

Our Nation's National Anthem
The Star-Spangled Banner
by Francis Scott Key

Oh, say, can you see, by the dawn's early light,
What so proudly we hailed at the twilight's last gleaming?
Whose broad stripes and bright stars, through the perilous fight,
O'er the ramparts we watched were so gallantly streaming!
And the rocket's red glare, the bombs bursting in air,
Gave proof through the night that our flag was still there.
O say does that star-spangled banner yet wave
O'er the land of the free and the home of the brave!

On the shore, dimly seen through the mists of the deep,
Where the foe's haughty host in dread silence reposes,
What is that which the breeze, o'er the towering steep,
As it fitfully blows, half conceals, half discloses?
Now it catches the gleam of the morning's first beam,
In full glory reflected now shines on the stream.
'Tis the star-spangled banner; Oh, long may it wave
O'er the land of the free and the home of the brave!

Oh, thus be it ever, when freemen shall stand
Between their loved homes and the war's desolation!
Blest with victory and peace, may the heaven-rescued land
Praise the Power that hath made and preserved us a nation.
Then conquer we must, when our cause it is just,
And this be our motto: "In God is our trust,"
And the star-spangled banner in triumph shall wave
O'er the land of the free and the home of the brave!

Chapter Twenty-Four
Thomas Jefferson

(Born 1743 - Died 1826)

How much cotton New Orleans sends to Europe; Eli Whitney's work; who it was that bought New Orleans and Louisiana for us. Today the city of New Orleans, near the mouth of the Mississippi River, sends more cotton to England and Europe than any other city in America.

"THE SIGNING OF THE DECLARATION OF INDEPENDENCE." (FROM JOHN TRUMBULL'S PAINTING.)

Before Eli Whitney invented his machine, we sent hardly a bale of cotton abroad. Now we send so much in one year that the bales can be counted by millions. If they were laid end to end, in a straight line, they would reach clear across the

American continent from San Francisco to New York, and then across the ocean from New York to Liverpool, England, and about three thousand miles further. Eli Whitney did more than any other man to build up this great trade. But at the time when he invented his cotton-gin, we did not own New Orleans, or for that matter, any part of Louisiana or of the country west of the Mississippi River. The man who bought New Orleans and Louisiana for us was Thomas Jefferson.

Who Thomas Jefferson was; Monticello. Thomas Jefferson was the son of a rich planter who lived near Charlottesville in Virginia. When his father died, he came into possession of a plantation of nearly two thousand acres of land, with forty or fifty slaves on it.

COTTON IN THE FIELD

MONTICELLO, THE HOME OF JEFFERSON.

There was a high hill on the plantation, to which Jefferson gave the Italian name of Monticello, or the little mountain. Here he built a fine house. From it, he could see the mountains and valleys of the Blue Ridge for an immense distance. No man in America had a more beautiful home, or enjoyed it more, than Thomas Jefferson.

Jefferson's slaves thought that no one could be better than their leader. He was always kind to them, and they were ready to do anything for him. Yet, Jefferson hoped and prayed that the time would come when every slave in the country might be set free.

Thomas Jefferson hears Patrick Henry speak at Richmond. Jefferson was educated to be a lawyer. He was not a good public speaker himself, but he liked to hear men who were good speakers. Just before the beginning of the Revolutionary War (1775), the people of Virginia sent men to Richmond to hold a meeting in old St. John's Church. They met to see what should be done about defending those rights which the king of England had refused to grant the Americans.

Liberty Bell, Independence Hall, Philadelphia.
(It was cracked in 1835, while tolling for the death of Chief Justice Marshall.)

" 'WE MUST *fight!* ' "

One of the speakers at that meeting was a famous Virginian named Patrick Henry. When he stood up to speak he looked very pale, but his eyes shone like coals of fire. He made a great speech. He said, "We must fight! I repeat it, sir, we must fight!" The other Virginians agreed with Patrick Henry; and George Washington and Thomas Jefferson, along with other noted men who were present at the meeting, began at once to prepare to fight.

Thomas Jefferson writes part of the Declaration of Independence; how it was sent through the country. Shortly after this the great war began. About a year after the first battle was fought, the Continental Congress asked Thomas Jefferson, Benjamin Franklin, and some others to write the Declaration of Independence. Mr. Jefferson was called the "Pen of the Revolution", for he could write as well as Patrick Henry could speak.

The Declaration was printed, and was then carried by men mounted on fast horses all over the United States. When men heard it, they rang the church bells and sent up cheer after cheer. General Washington had the Declaration read to all the soldiers in his army; and if powder had not been so scarce, they would have fired off every gun for joy.

Jefferson is chosen President of the United States; what he said about New Orleans. Several years after the war was over, Jefferson was elected President of the United States; while he was President (1801-1809) he did something for the country that will never be forgotten.

Louisiana, the city of New Orleans, and the lower part of the Mississippi River, all belonged to the French. At that time, the United States reached west only as far as the Mississippi River. Because New Orleans stands near the mouth of that river, the French could say, if they chose, which vessels could go out to sea, and which could come in. So far as that part of America was concerned, we were like a man who owns a house while another man owns one of the main doors to it. The man who has the door could say to the owner of the house, I shall stand here on the steps, and you must pay me so many dollars every time you go out and every time you want to go into your house.

Jefferson saw that as long as the French held the door of New Orleans, we would not be free to send our cotton down the river and across the ocean to Europe. He said we must have that door, no matter how much it cost.

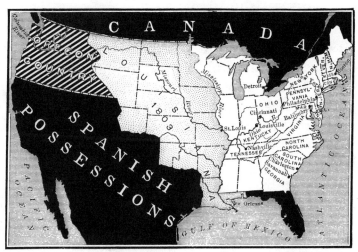

THE UNITED STATES IN 1803, AFTER THE PURCHASE OF LOUISIANA

Jefferson buys New Orleans and Louisiana for the United States. Robert R. Livingston, one of the signers of the Declaration of Independence, was in France at that time, and Jefferson sent him instructions to try to buy New

Orleans for the United States. Napoleon Bonaparte then ruled France. He said, I want money with which to buy warships so that I can fight England; I will sell not only New Orleans, but all Louisiana besides, for fifteen million dollars. That was cheap enough, and so in 1803 President Jefferson bought it.

If you look on the map you will see that Louisiana then was not simply a good-sized state, as it is now, but a huge territory reaching all the way to the Rocky Mountains. It was larger than the whole United States east of the Mississippi River. So, through President Jefferson's purchase, we added so much land that we now had more than twice as much as we had before. We also had the whole Mississippi River, New Orleans, and what is now the great city of St. Louis as well.

Death of Jefferson; the words cut on his gravestone. Jefferson lived to be an old man. He died at Monticello on the Fourth of July, 1826, just fifty years, to a day, after he had signed the Declaration of Independence. John Adams, who had been President just before Jefferson, died a few hours later. So America lost two of her great men on the same day.

THOMAS JEFFERSON.

JOHN ADAMS.

Jefferson was buried at Monticello. He asked to have these words, with some others, cut on his gravestone: Here Was Buried Thomas Jefferson, Author of the Declaration of American Independence.

Summary. Thomas Jefferson of Virginia wrote most of the Declaration of Independence. After he became President of the United States, he bought Louisiana for us. The purchase of Louisiana, with New Orleans, gave us the right to send our ships to sea via the Mississippi River, which now also belonged to us. Louisiana added so much land that it more than doubled the size of the United States.

Comprehension Questions

1. Did we own New Orleans or Louisiana when Whitney invented his cotton-gin?
2. Who bought them for us?
3. What elected office did Thomas Jefferson hold from 1801-1809?
4. For what profession was Jefferson educated?
5. How did Patrick Henry help the people become free?
6. What important paper did Thomas Jefferson help to write?
7. How much did the United States pay to France for the Louisiana territory?

Chapter Twenty-Five
Robert Fulton

(Born 1765 - Died 1815)

The Louisiana country; a small family in a big house; settlements in the west; the country beyond the Mississippi River. Even before we bought the great Louisiana country, we had more land than we then knew what to do with. After we had bought it, it seemed to some people as though we would be unable to use what we had bought for more than a hundred years. Such people thought that we were like a man with a small family who lives in a house much too large for him; but who, not contented with that, buys his neighbor's house, which is bigger still, and adds that to his own.

ROBERT FULTON.

If a traveller in those days went across the Allegheny Mountains to the west, he found some small settlements in Ohio, Kentucky, and Tennessee, but hardly anything else. The region which is now covered by the great states of Indiana, Illinois, Michigan, and Wisconsin was then a wilderness; and this was true also of what are now the states of Alabama and Mississippi.

If the same traveller, pushing westward on foot or on horseback (for there were no automobiles) crossed the Mississippi River, he could hardly find a settler outside what was then the little town of St. Louis. The country stretched west for more than a thousand miles, with nothing in it but wild beasts and Indians. In much of it there were no trees, no houses, no human beings. If you shouted as hard as you could in that solitary land, the only reply you would hear would be the echo of your own voice.

Emigration to the west, and the man who helped that emigration. But during the 1800s, that great empty land in the west filled with people. Thousands upon thousands of emigrants entered the Louisiana Territory. They built towns and cities and railroads and telephone lines. What made such a wonderful change? Well, one man helped to do a great deal toward it. His name was Robert Fulton. He saw how difficult it was for people to travel west, for if emigrants wanted to travel with their families in wagons, they had to chop roads through the forests. That was slow, hard work. Fulton found a way that was quick, easy, and cheap. Let us see who he was, and how he found that way.

Robert Fulton's boyhood; the old scow; what Robert did for his mother. Robert Fulton was the son of a poor Irish farmer in Pennsylvania. He did not care much for books, but liked to draw pictures with pencils, which he hammered out of pieces of lead.

ROBERT FULTON'S PADDLE-WHEEL SCOW

FLATBOAT

Like most boys, he was fond of fishing. He used to go out in an old scow, or flat-bottomed boat, on a river near his home. He and another boy would push the scow along with poles. But Robert said, "There is an easier way to make this boat move. I can put a pair of paddle-wheels on her, and then we can sit comfortably on the seat and turn the wheels by a crank." He tried it, and found that he was right. The boys now had a boat that suited them exactly.

When Robert was seventeen, he went to Philadelphia. His father was dead. Robert earned his living and helped his mother and sisters by painting pictures. He stayed in Philadelphia until he was twenty-one. By that time he had saved up enough money to buy a small farm for his mother, so that she might have a home of her own.

Fulton goes to England and to France; his iron bridges; his diving-boat, and what he did with it in France. Soon after buying the farm for his mother, young Fulton went to England and then to France. He stayed in those countries twenty years. In England, Fulton built some famous iron bridges, but he was more interested in boats than in anything else.

While he was in France, he made what he called a diving-boat. It would go underwater almost as well as it would on top, so that, wherever a big fish could go, Fulton could follow him. His object in building such a boat was to make war in a new way. When a swordfish attacks a whale, he dives under him and stabs the monster with his sword. Fulton said, "If an enemy's warship should come into the harbor to cause trouble, I can get into my diving-boat, slip under the ship, fasten a torpedo to it, and blow the ship sky high."

Napoleon Bonaparte liked nothing more than war, so he let Fulton have an old vessel to see if he could blow it up. He tried it, and everything happened as he expected: nothing was left of the vessel but the pieces.

What Fulton did in England with his diving-boat; what he said about America. Then Fulton went back to England and tried to do the same thing there. He went out in his diving-boat and fastened a torpedo under a vessel; when the torpedo exploded, the vessel, as he said, went up like a "bag of feathers," flying in all directions.

The English people paid Fulton seventy-five thousand dollars for showing them what he could do in this way. Then they offered to give him a great deal more, enough to make him a very rich man, if he would promise never to let any other country know just how he blew vessels up. But Fulton said, "I am an American; and if America should ever want to use my diving-boat in war, she shall have it first."

Fulton makes his first steamboat. While Fulton was doing these things with his diving-boat, he was always thinking of the paddle-wheel scow he used to fish in when a boy. "I turned those paddle-wheels by a crank," he said, "but what is to keep me from putting a steam engine into such a boat, so it can turn the crank for me?" That would be a steamboat. Such boats had already been tried, but for one reason or another, they had mostly failed. Robert R. Livingston was still in France, and he helped Fulton build his first steamboat. It was put on a river there; it barely moved.

Robert Fulton and Mr. Livingston go to New York City and build a steamboat; the trip up the Hudson River. But Robert Fulton and Mr. Livingston both believed that a steamboat could be built that would go, and that would keep going. So they went to New York City, and built one there.

In the summer of 1807, a great crowd gathered to see the boat start on her voyage up the Hudson River. They joked and laughed as crowds will at anything new. They called Fulton and Livingston fools. But when Fulton, standing on the deck of his steamboat, waved his hand, and the wheels began to turn, and the vessel began to move up the river, the crowd became silent with astonishment. Now it was Fulton's turn to laugh, and in such a case the man who laughs last has a right to laugh loudest.

FULTON'S STEAMBOAT. (THE CLERMONT.)

The "Clermont."

Up the river Fulton kept going. He passed the Palisades, the Highlands, and still he continued. Eventually, he reached Albany, a hundred and fifty miles from New York City.

Nobody had ever seen such a sight as that boat moving up the river without the help of oars or sails, but from that time people saw it every day. When Fulton came back to New York in his steamboat, everybody wanted to shake hands with him. The crowd, instead of shouting jeers, now whispered among themselves that Fulton was truly a very great man.

The first steamboat in the west; the Big Shake. Four years later Fulton built a steamboat for the west. In the autumn of 1811 it started from Pittsburgh to go down the Ohio River, and then down the Mississippi to New Orleans. The people of the west had never seen a steamboat before, and when the Indians saw the smoke puffing out, they called it the "Big Fire Canoe."

STEAM-TUG WITH LUMBER-RAFT.

On the way down the river, there was a terrible earthquake. In some places it changed the course of the Ohio, so that where there had been dry land there was now deep water, and where there had been deep water there was now dry land. One evening the captain of the "Big Fire Canoe" fastened his vessel to a large tree on the end of an island. In the morning the people on the steamboat looked out, but could not tell where they were. The island was gone; the earthquake had carried it away. The Indians called the earthquake the "Big Shake"; it was a good name, for it kept on shaking that part of the country and doing all sorts of damage for weeks.

The "Big Fire Canoe" on the Mississippi; the fight between steam and the Great River; what steamboats did; Robert Fulton's grave. When the steamboat reached the Mississippi, the settlers on that river said that the boat would never be able to go back, because the current was so strong. At one place a crowd had gathered to see her as she turned against the current, in order to come up to the landing-place. An old man stood watching the boat. It looked as if, in spite of all the captain could do, she would be carried down stream, but at last steam conquered, and the boat came up to the shore. Then the old man could hold in no longer: he threw up his ragged straw hat and shouted, 'Hooray! hooray! the old Mississippi's just met her master this time!'

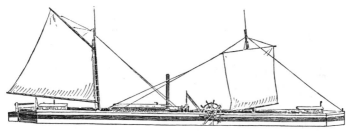

Model of the Clermont

Soon steamboats began to run regularly on the Mississippi; and after a few years they began to move up and down the Great Lakes and the Missouri River. Emigrants could now go to the west and the far west quickly and easily; they had to thank Robert Fulton for that.

Robert Fulton lies buried in New York, in the shadow of the tower of Trinity Church. There is no monument or mark over his grave; but every time we think of the great growth of our beloved country we will remember this great inventor.

Summary. In 1807 Robert Fulton of Pennsylvania built the first steamboat that ran on the Hudson River, and four years later he built the first one that navigated the rivers of the west. His boats helped to fill the whole western country with settlers.

Comprehension Questions

1. List the names of three states that were once a part of the great western wilderness.
2. What man helped Robert Fulton build the first successful steamboat?
3. In what countries did Robert Fulton build his diving-boat?
4. What did the Indians call Fulton's steamboat?
5. Where was Mr. Fulton buried?
6. How did the steamboat help people during this time?

Chapter Twenty-Six
General William Henry Harrison

(Born 1773 - Died 1841)

War with the Indians; how the Indians felt about being forced to leave their homes; the story of the log. During the year 1811, in which the first steamboat went west, a great battle was fought with the Indians. The battleground was on the Tippecanoe River, in what is now the state of Indiana.

The Indians fought because they were tired of being pushed farther west. They wanted to keep the west for themselves.

One day a military officer came to the wigwam of an old Indian chief to tell him that he and his tribe must go still farther west. The chief said, "General, let's sit down on this log and talk it over." So they both sat down. After they had talked a short time, the chief said, "Please move a little farther that way; I haven't room enough." The officer moved along. In a few minutes the chief asked him to move again, and he did so. Presently the chief gave him a push and said, "Do move farther on, won't you?" "I can't," said the general. "Why not?" asked the chief. "Because I've come to the end of the log," replied the officer. "Well, said the Indian, now you see how it is with us. You settlers have kept pushing us until you have pushed us clear to the end of our country, and yet you come now and say move on, move on."

What Tecumseh and his brother, the "Prophet," tried to do. A famous Indian warrior named Tecumseh determined to bring the different Indian tribes together, and drive out the European settlers from the west.

Tecumseh had a brother called the "Prophet," who pretended he could tell what would happen in the future. He said, the white traders come here, give the Indians whiskey, get them drunk, and then cheat them out of their lands. Once we owned this whole country; now, if an Indian strips a little bark from a tree to shelter him when it rains, a settler steps up with a gun in his hand and says, "That's my tree, let it alone".

Then the "Prophet" said to the Indian warriors, "'Stop drinking fire-water,' and you will have strength to kill off the 'pale-faces' and get your land back. When you have killed them off, I will bless the earth. I will make pumpkins grow to be as big as wigwams, and the corn shall be so large that one ear will be enough for a dinner for a dozen hungry

Indians." The Indians liked to hear these things; they wanted to taste those pumpkins and that corn, and so they prepared to fight.

Who William Henry Harrison was; the march to Tippecanoe; the "Prophet's" sacred beans; the battle of Tippecanoe. At this time, William Henry Harrison was governor of the Indiana territory. He had fought under General Wayne in his war with the Indians in Ohio. Everybody knew Governor Harrison's courage, and the Indians all respected him; but he tried in vain to prevent the Indians from going to war. The "Prophet" urged them on in the north, and Tecumseh had gone south to persuade the Indians there to join the northern tribes.

WILLIAM HENRY HARRISON.

Governor Harrison saw that a battle must soon be fought, so he started with his soldiers to meet the Indians. He marched to the Tippecanoe River, and there he stopped.

William Henry Harrison

While Harrison's men were asleep in the woods, the "Prophet" told the Indians not to wait, but to attack the soldiers immediately. In his hand he held up a string of beans. These beans, said he to the Indians, are sacred. Come and touch them, and you are safe; no white man's bullet can hit you. The Indians hurried up in crowds to touch the wonderful beans.

Now, said the "Prophet," let each one take his hatchet in one hand and his gun in the other, and creep through the tall grass until he gets to the edge of the woods. The soldiers lie there fast asleep; when you get close to them, spring up and go for them, like a wild-cat for a rabbit.

The Indians started to do this, but a soldier on guard saw the tall grass moving as though a great snake was gliding through it. He fired his gun at the moving grass; up sprang the whole band of Indians, and with a terrible yell, they rushed forward In a moment the battle began.

Harrison won the victory. He not only killed many of the Indians, but he marched against their village, set fire to it, and burned it to ashes.

After that, the Indians in that part of the country would not listen to the "Prophet." They called him a liar; his beans had not saved them.

The battle of Tippecanoe did much good, because it prevented the Indian tribes from uniting and beginning a great war all through the west. Governor Harrison received high praise for what he had done, and was made a general in the United States army.

Tecumseh takes the "Prophet" by the hair; the War of 1812; General Harrison's battle in Canada; President Harrison. When Tecumseh came back from the south, he was terribly angry with his brother for fighting before he was ready to have him begin. He seized the "Prophet" by his long hair, and shook him as a big dog shakes a rat. Tecumseh then left the United States and went to Canada to help the British, who were preparing to fight us.

A BATTLE AT SEA IN THE WAR OF 1812

The next year (1812) we began our second war with England. It is called the War of 1812. One of the major reasons we fought was that the British would not leave our merchant ships alone. They stopped them at sea and took thousands of our sailors from them. The British then forced the men to serve in their warships in their battles against the French.

During the War of 1812, the British burned the Capitol at Washington, but a grander building rose from its ashes. General Harrison fought a battle in Canada in which he defeated the British and killed Tecumseh, who was fighting on the side of the English.

Many years after this battle, the people of the west said, we must have the "Hero of Tippecanoe" for President of the United States. They went to vote for him, with songs and shouts, and he was elected. A month after he went to Washington, President Harrison died (1841), and the whole country was filled with sorrow.

Summary. In 1811 General Harrison gained a great victory over the Indians at Tippecanoe, in Indiana. By that victory he saved the west from a terrible Indian war. In the War of 1812, with England, General Harrison beat the British in a battle in Canada, and killed Tecumseh, the Indian chief who had caused us so much trouble. Many years later General Harrison was elected President of the United States.

Comprehension Questions

1. What state was the battle of Tippecanoe fought in?
2. Who was the famous Indian warrior who had a brother called "The Prophet"?
3. What countries fought during the War of 1812?
4. Did the British burn the capitol building in Washington during the war?
5. What year did President Harrison die?

Chapter Twenty-Seven
General Andrew Jackson

(Born 1767 - Died 1845)

Andrew Jackson and the War of 1812; his birthplace; his school; wrestling-matches; firing off the gun. The greatest land battle of our second war with England, the War of 1812, was fought by General Andrew Jackson.

He was the son of a poor emigrant who came from the North of Ireland and settled in North Carolina. When Thomas Jefferson wrote the Declaration of Independence in 1776, Andrew was nine years old, and his father had long been dead. He was a tall, slender, freckled-faced, barefooted boy, with eyes full of fun; the neighbors called him "Little Andy."

He went to school in a log hut in the pine woods; but he learned more things from what he saw in the woods than from the books he studied in school.

He was not a very strong boy, and in wrestling, some of his companions could pin him three times out of four; but though they could get him down without much trouble, it was quite another thing to keep him down. No sooner was he laid flat on his back, than he bounded up like a steel spring, and stood ready to try again.

He had a violent temper, and when, as the boys said, "Andy was mad all over," not many cared to face him. Once some of his playmates secretly loaded an old gun almost to the muzzle, and then dared him to fire it. They wanted to see what he would say when it kicked him over. Andrew fired the gun. It knocked him sprawling; he jumped up with eyes blazing with anger, and shaking his fist, cried out, "If one of you boys laughs, I'll punch him." He looked as though he meant exactly what he said, and the boys thought that maybe it would be just as well to wait and laugh some other day. Little Andrew Jackson did not as yet have the love of Christ ruling his heart. However, when Mr. Jackson was older, he came to know the Lord and was saved from his sins.

Tarleton's attack on the Americans; how Andrew helped his mother. When Andrew was thirteen, he learned the horrors of war. The country was then fighting the battles of the Revolution. A British officer named Tarleton came suddenly upon some American soldiers near the place where young Jackson lived. Tarleton had so many men that the Americans saw that it was useless to try to fight, and they made no attempt to do so. The British should have taken them all prisoners, but instead of that, they attacked them furiously, and killed them with their swords.

More than a hundred of our men were left dead, and a still larger number were so horribly wounded that they could not be moved any distance. Such an attack was not war, for war means a fair, stand-up fight; it was murder. When the people in England heard what Tarleton had done, many cried shame!

There was a little log meeting-house near Andrew's home, and it was turned into a hospital for the wounded men. Mrs. Jackson, with other kind-hearted women, did all she could for the poor fellows who lay there groaning and helpless. Andrew carried food and water to them. He had forgotten many of the lessons he had learned at school, but here was something he would never forget.

Andrew's hatred of the "red coats"; Tarleton's soldiers meet their match. From that time, when young Jackson went to the blacksmith's shop to get a garden tool fixed, he was sure to come back with a rude spear, or with some other weapon. Andrew Jackson longed for the day when he could fight against the cruel "red coats."

Tarleton said that no people in America hated the British as much as those who lived in that part of the country where Andrew Jackson had his home. The reason was that no other British officer was so cruel as "Butcher Tarleton," as he was called. Once, however, his men met their match. They were robbing a farm of its pigs and chickens and corn and hay. When they finished carrying things off, they were going to burn down the farm house; but one of the "red coats" in his haste, ran against a big hive of bees and upset it. The bees swarmed out in a fury and stung the soldiers so terribly that finally the robbers were glad to drop everything and run. If Andrew could have seen that battle, he would have laughed until he cried.

Dangerous state of the country; the roving bands. Andrew knew that he and his mother lived in constant danger. Some of the people in the state of North Carolina were for the king, and some were for liberty. Bands of armed men, belonging sometimes to one side, and sometimes to the other, went roving about the country. When they met a farmer, they would stop him and ask, "Which side are you for?" If he did not answer to their liking, the leader of the party would cry out, Hang him up! In an instant one of the group would cut down a long piece of wild grapevine, twist it into a noose, and throw it over the man's head; the next moment he would be dangling from the limb of a tree. Sometimes the gangs would let him down again while he was still alive; sometimes they would ride on and leave him hanging there.

Playing at battle; what Tarleton heard about himself. Even the children saw and heard so much of the war that was going on that they played at war, and fought battles with red and white corn: red for the British and white for the Americans.

At the battle of Cowpens, Colonel William Washington fought on the American side, and Tarleton was badly beaten and had to run. Not long afterward he happened to see some boys squatting on the ground, with a pile of corn instead of marbles. They were playing the battle of Cowpens. A red kernel stood for Tarleton, and a white one for Colonel Washington. The boys shoved the corn this way and that; sometimes the red would win, sometimes the white. At last the white kernel gained the victory, and the boys shouted, "Hurrah for Washington -- Tarleton runs!"

Tarleton had been quietly looking on without their knowing it. When he saw how the game ended, he turned angrily away. He had seen enough of "the little rebels," as he called them.

Andrew is taken prisoner by the British; "Here, boy, clean those boots"; the two scars. Not long after our victory at Cowpens, Andrew Jackson was taken prisoner by the British. The officer in command of the soldiers had just taken off his boots, splashed with mud. Pointing to them, he said to Andrew, "Here, boy, clean those boots." Andrew replied, "Sir, I am a prisoner of war, and it is not my job to clean boots." The officer, in great anger, whipped out his sword and hit the boy. It cut a gash on his head and another on his hand. Andrew Jackson lived to be an old man, but the marks of that blow never disappeared: he carried the scars to his grave.

JACKSON AND THE OFFICER'S BOOTS

The prisoners in the yard of Camden jail, seeing a battle through a knot-hole. Andrew was sent, with other prisoners, to Camden, South Carolina, and locked up in the jail. In this jail, many became sick and died of small pox.

One day some of the prisoners heard that General Greene, the greatest American general in the Revolution, next to Washington, was coming to fight the British at Camden. Andrew's heart leaped for joy, for he knew that if General Greene would win he would let all the prisoners go free.

General Greene with his little army was on a hill in sight of the jail; but there was a high board fence around the jail yard, and the prisoners could not see them. With the help of an old razor, Andrew managed to dig out a knot from one of the boards. Through that knot hole he watched the battle of Hobkirk's Hill.

Our men were beaten in the fight, and Andrew saw their horses with empty saddles running wildly about. Then the boy turned away, sick at heart. Soon after that he was seized with the small pox, and would have died if his mother had not been able to get him set free.

Mrs. Jackson goes to visit the American prisoners at Charleston; Andrew loses his best friend; what he said of her. In the summer Mrs. Jackson made a journey on horseback to Charleston, a hundred and sixty miles away. She went to carry some little comforts to the poor American prisoners, who were starving and dying of disease in the crowded and filthy British prison-ships in the harbor. While visiting these sick men, she caught the fever that many of them had. Two weeks later she was in her grave, and Andrew, then a lad of fourteen, stood alone in the world.

Years afterward, when he had risen to be a noted man, people would sometimes praise him because he was never afraid to say and do what he believed to be right. Jackson would answer, "That I learned from my good old mother. She taught me to trust in God and do what the Bible says is right."

Andrew begins to learn a trade; he studies law and goes west; Judge Jackson; General Jackson. Andrew began to study law. After he became a lawyer he went across the mountains to Nashville, Tennessee. There he was made a judge. There were plenty of rough men in that part of the country who meant to have their own way in all things, but they soon found that they must respect and obey Judge Jackson. They could frighten other judges, but it was no use to try to frighten him. Seeing what sort of stuff Jackson was made of, they thought that they would like to have such a man to lead them in battle. And so Judge Andrew Jackson became General Andrew Jackson. When trouble came with the Indians, Jackson proved to be the very man they needed.

ANDREW JACKSON.

Tecumseh and the Indians of Alabama; Tecumseh threatens to stamp his foot on the ground; the earthquake; war begins. We have already seen how the Indian chief Tecumseh went south to stir up the tribes to make war on the settlers in the west. In Alabama he told the Indians that if they fought, they would gain a great victory. "I see," said Tecumseh, "that you don't believe what I say, and that you don't mean to fight. Well, I am now going north to Detroit. When I get there I shall stamp my foot on the ground, and shake down every wigwam you have." It happened that, shortly after Tecumseh had gone north, a sharp shock of earthquake was felt in Alabama, and the wigwams were shaken down by it. When the terrified Indians felt their houses falling to pieces, they ran out of them shouting, "Tecumseh has come to Detroit!"

INDIANS ATTACKING OVERLAND STAGE

These Indians now believed all that Tecumseh had said. They began to attack the settlers, and they killed a large number of them.

**Jackson conquers the Indians; the "Holy Ground";
Weathersford and Jackson; feeding the starving.**
General Jackson marched against the Indians and beat them
in battle. The Indians that escaped fled to a place they
called the "Holy Ground." They believed that if a white man
dared to set his foot on that ground he would be struck dead,
as if by a flash of lightning. General Jackson and his men
marched onto the "Holy Ground," and the Indians soon found
that, unless they made peace, they would be the ones who
would be struck dead by his bullets.

GENERAL JACKSON AND THE INDIAN CHIEF

Not long after this, a noted leader of the Indians, named
Weathersford, rode boldly up to Jackson's tent. "Kill him!
kill him!" cried Jackson's men but the general asked
Weathersford into his tent. "You can kill me if you want to,"
said he to Jackson, "But I came to tell you that the Indian
women and children are starving in the woods, and to ask
you to help them, for they never did you any harm." General
Jackson sent Weathersford away in safety, and ordered that

corn should be given to feed the starving women and children. That act showed that he was as merciful as he was brave. Jackson had learned how to fulfill the teaching of Jesus Christ to "love your enemies."

The British send warships to take New Orleans; the great battle and the great victory. These things happened during our second war with England, called the War of 1812. About a year after Jackson's victory over the Indians, the British sent an army in ships to take New Orleans. General Jackson now went to New Orleans to prevent the enemy from capturing the city.

BATTLE OF NEW ORLEANS

About four miles below the city, which stands on the Mississippi River, there was a broad, deep ditch, running from the river into a swamp. Jackson saw that the British would have to cross that ditch when they marched against the city. For that reason he built a high wall on the upper side of the ditch, and placed cannon along the top of the bank.

Early on Sunday morning, January 8, 1815, the British sent a rocket whizzing up into the sky; a few minutes afterward they sent up a second one. It was the signal that they were about to march to attack Jackson's men.

Just before the fight began, General Jackson walked along among his men, who were getting ready to defend the ditch. He said to them, "Stand to your guns; see that every shot hits; give it to them, boys!" The "boys" did give it to them. The British soldiers were brave men. They had been in many terrible battles, and they were not afraid to die. They fought hard. They tried again and again to cross that ditch and climb the bank, but they could not do it. The fire of our guns cut them down just as a mower cuts down the tall grass. In less than half an hour the great battle was over. Jackson had won the victory and saved New Orleans. We lost only eight killed; the enemy lost over two thousand. We have never had another battle since that time with England. Hopefully we shall never have another, for two great nations, like England and America, that speak the same language should be firm and true friends.

We buy Florida; General Jackson made President of the United States; the first railroad. After the battle of New Orleans, General Jackson conquered the Indians in Florida, and in 1819 we bought that territory from Spain. This new land made the United States much larger on the south. This was our second great land purchase.

Ten years after we bought Florida, General Jackson became President of the United States. He had fought his way up. Here are the four steps: first the boy, "Andy Jackson"; then "Judge Jackson"; then "General Jackson"; last of all, "President Jackson."

General Andrew Jackson

Shortly after he became President of the nation, the first steam railroad in the United States was built (1830). From that time, railroad tracks kept creeping farther and farther west. The Indians had frightened the settlers with their terrible war-whoop. Now it was their turn to be frightened, for the locomotive whistle could beat their wildest yell. They saw that these people were coming as fast as steam could carry them, and that they were determined to get possession of the whole land. The greater part of the Indians moved across the Mississippi; but the settlers kept following them and the buffalo farther and farther across the country, toward the Pacific Ocean. The railroad followed the path of the settlers as they moved westward.

Summary. Andrew Jackson of North Carolina, but later a citizen of Tennessee, gained a great victory over the Indians in Alabama and also in Florida. In 1815, in our second war with England, General Jackson beat the British at New Orleans, and so prevented their getting possession of that city. A few years later we bought Florida from Spain.

After General Jackson became President of the United States, the first steam railroad was built in this country. Railroads helped to settle the west and build up states beyond the Mississippi River.

Comprehension Questions

1. Who hit Andrew Jackson with a sword when he was a prisoner?
2. Was the man named Weathersford a famous British general?
3. Who won the battle of New Orleans?
4. In what year did America buy the territory of Florida?
5. In what year did the first steam powered railroad appear?
6. How did the railroads help the western part of the United States develop?

An Early Railroad Train

Chapter Twenty-Eight
Professor Samuel Morse

(Born 1791 - Died 1872)

How they sent the news of the completion of the Erie Canal to New York City; Franklin and Morse. The Erie Canal, in the state of New York, connects the Hudson River at Albany with Lake Erie at Buffalo. It is the greatest work of the kind in America, and was completed many years ago. When the water was let into the canal from the lake, the news was flashed from Buffalo to New York City by a row of cannon, about five miles apart, which were fired as rapidly as possible, one after the other. The first cannon was fired at Buffalo at ten o'clock in the morning; the last was fired at New York at half-past eleven. In an hour and a half, the

PROFESSOR S. F. B. MORSE, THE INVENTOR OF THE ELECTRO-MAGNETIC TELEGRAPH.

sound had travelled over five hundred miles. Everybody said that was very quick work; but an inventor who lived in the mid-1800s discovered a way to send messages like this in less than a minute. The man who found out how to do this was Samuel F. B. Morse.

We have seen how Benjamin Franklin discovered with his kite that lightning and electricity are the same. Samuel Morse was born in Charlestown, Massachusetts, about a mile from Franklin's birthplace, the year after that great man died. He began his work where Franklin left off. He said to himself, Dr. Franklin found out what lightning is; I will find out how to harness it and make it carry news and deliver messages.

Morse becomes a painter; what he thought might be done about sending messages. When Samuel Morse was a little boy, he liked to draw pictures, particularly faces. After he became a man, he learned to paint. At one time, he lived in France with several other American artists. One day they were talking about how long it took to get letters from America, and they were wishing the time could be shortened. Somebody spoke of how cannon had been used when the Erie Canal was opened. Morse was familiar with all that. He had been educated at Yale College, and he knew that the sound of a gun will travel a mile while you are counting five. But, quick as that is, he wanted to find something better and quicker still. He said, Why not try lightning or electricity? The speed of light will go more than a thousand miles while you are counting one.

What a telegraph is; a wire telegraph; Professor Morse invents the electric telegraph. Some time after that, Mr. Morse set sail for America. On the way across the Atlantic he was constantly talking about electricity and how

Professor Samuel Morse

PROFESSOR MORSE AT WORK MAKING
HIS TELEGRAPH

ONE KIND OF TELEGRAPH

a telegraph--that is, a machine which would write at a distance--might be invented. He thought about this so much that he could not sleep nights. At last, he believed that he knew how he could make such a machine.

Suppose you take a straight and stiff piece of wire as long as your desk and fasten it in the middle so that the ends will swing easily. Next, tie a pencil tight to each end; then put a sheet of paper under the point of each pencil. Now, if you make a mark with the pencil nearest you, you will find that the pencil at the other end of the wire will make the same kind of mark. Such a wire would be a type of telegraph, because it would make marks or signs at a distance. Mr. Morse said: I will have a wire a mile long, with a pencil, or something sharp-pointed like a pencil, fastened to the farther end; the wire itself shall not move at all, but the pencil will, for I will make electricity run along the wire and move it. Mr. Morse was then a professor or teacher in the University of New York. He put up such a wire in one of the rooms of the building, sent the electricity through it, and found that it made the pencil mark just as he wanted. Mr. Morse knew that he had invented the electric telegraph; for if he could do this over a mile of wire, then what was to stop him from doing it over a hundred or even a thousand miles?

How Professor Morse lived while he was making his telegraph. But all this was not done in a day, for this invention cost years of patient labor. At first, Mr. Morse lived in a little room alone. There he worked, ate when he could get something to eat, and slept if he wasn't too tired to sleep. Later he had a room in the university. While he was there he painted pictures to get money enough to buy food; there, too (1839), he took the first photograph ever made in America. Yet, with all his hard work, there were times when he had to go hungry. Once he told a young man that if he did not get some money he would be dead in a week--dead of starvation.

Professor Morse gets help with his telegraph; what Alfred Vail did. But better times were coming. A young man named Alfred Vail happened to see Professor Morse's telegraph. He believed it would be successful. He persuaded his father, Judge Vail, to lend him two thousand dollars, and he became Professor Morse's partner in the work. Mr. Vail was an excellent mechanic, and he made many improvements in the telegraph. He then made a model of it at his own expense, and took it to Washington and got a patent for it in Professor Morse's name. The invention was now safe in one way, for no one else had the right to make a telegraph like his. Yet, though he had this help, Professor Morse did not get rich very fast, for a few years later he said, "I have not a cent in the world; I am as poor as a church mouse."

Professor Morse asks Congress to help him build a telegraph line; what Congress thought. Professor Morse now asked Congress to let him have thirty thousand dollars to build a telegraph line from Washington to Baltimore. He felt sure that business men would be glad to send messages by telegraph, and to pay him for his work. But many members of Congress laughed at it, and said they might as well give Professor Morse the money to build "a railroad to the moon."

The original instrument, preserved in Washington, on which the first message ("What hath God wrought") was sent in 1844. The first line ran from Baltimore to Washington

Samuel F. B. Morse and the Telegraph

Week after week went by, and the last day that Congress would sit was reached, but still no money had been granted.

Then came the last night of the last day (March 3, 1843). Professor Morse stayed in the Senate Chamber of Congress until after ten o'clock; then, tired and disappointed, he went back to his hotel, thinking that he must give up trying to build his telegraph line.

Miss Annie Ellsworth brings good news. The next morning Annie G. Ellsworth met him as he was coming down to breakfast. She was the daughter of his friend who had charge of the Patent Office in Washington. She came forward with a smile, grasped his hand, and said that she had good news for him, that Congress had decided to let him have the money. "Surely you must be mistaken," said the professor, "for I waited last night until nearly midnight, and came away because nothing had been done." "But," said the young lady, my father stayed until it was past midnight, and a few minutes before the clock struck twelve, Congress voted the money; it was the very last thing that was done."

Professor Morse was then a gray-haired man over fifty. He had worked hard for years, and had received little for his labor. This was his first great success. He never said whether he laughed or cried at this time: perhaps he felt a little like doing both. Hopefully, he remembered to send up a prayer of thanks to Almighty God.

The first telegraph line built; the first message sent; the telegraph and the telephone now. When Professor Morse did speak, he said to Miss Ellsworth, "Now, Annie, when my line is built from Washington to Baltimore, you shall send the first message over it." In the spring of 1844, the line was completed, and Miss Ellsworth, by Professor Morse, sent these words over it (they are words taken from the Bible): "What hath God wrought!"

Professor Samuel Morse

PROFESSOR MORSE SENDING THE FIRST TELEGRAM

For nearly a year after that, the telegraph was free to all who wished to use it; then a small charge was made, a very short message costing only one cent. On the first of April, 1845, a man came into the office and bought a cent's worth of telegraphing. That was all the money that was taken in that day for the use of forty miles of wire. A few years later there were nearly a million miles of telegraph wire in the United States. This is almost enough to reach thirty-six times around the earth. Americans could telegraph not only across America, but across the Atlantic Ocean, and even to China, by a line laid under the sea. Professor Morse's invention made it possible to write by electricity; but now, with the telephone, a man in New York or Boston can talk with someone in Chicago, St. Louis, or in most other cities; and the man listening at the other end of the wire can hear every word he says, and can talk with him freely. Professor Morse did not live to see this wonderful invention, which, in many ways, is an improvement over his telegraph.

Summary. Professor Morse invented the electric telegraph. He received much help from Alfred Vail. In 1844, Professor Morse and Mr. Vail built the first line of telegraph in the world. It extended from Washington to Baltimore. The telegraph makes it possible for us to send a written message thousands of miles in a moment. The telephone, which was invented after Professor Morse's death by Professor Alexander Graham Bell, allows us to talk with people who are many hundreds of miles away and hear what they say in reply.

Comprehension Questions

1. Tell how they sent the news of the completion of the Erie Canal.
2. What is a telegraph?
3. What did Mr. Morse ask Congress to do?
4. What was the first message sent by telegraph in 1844?
5. Why is the telephone an improvement over the old telegraph?
6. Who invented the telephone?

Chapter Twenty-Nine
General Sam Houston

(Born 1793 - Died 1863)

Sam Houston and the Indians; Houston goes to live with the Indians. When General Jackson beat the Indians in Alabama, a young man named Sam Houston fought under Jackson and was badly wounded. It was thought that the brave fellow would surely die, but God's grace carried him through, and he lived to do many great things for the southwest part of the United States.

Although Houston fought the Indians as an adult, he was very fond of them as a boy, and spent much of his time with them in the woods of Tennessee.

Long after he became a man, his love for wilderness living came back to him. While Houston was governor of Tennessee (1829) he suddenly made up his mind to leave his home and his friends, go across the Mississippi River, and start a new life with an Indian tribe in that part of the country. The chief, who had known him as a boy, gave him a hearty welcome. "Rest with us," he said. "My wigwam is yours." Houston stayed with the tribe three years.

Houston goes to Texas; what he said he would do; the murders at Alamo; the flag with one star; what Houston did; Texas added to the United States; our war with Mexico. At the end of that time he said to a friend, "I am going to Texas, and in that new country I will make a man of myself." Texas then belonged to Mexico; and President Andrew Jackson had tried in vain to buy it as

Jefferson bought Louisiana. Houston said, "I will make it part of the United States." About twenty thousand Americans had already moved into Texas, and they felt that the Mexican rulers treated them harshly because they came from the United States.

Campaigns of the Mexican War

War broke out between Texas and Mexico, and General Sam Houston led the Texan soldiers in their fight for independence. He had many noted American pioneers and hunters in his little army: one of them was the brave Colonel Travis of Alabama; another was Colonel Bowie of

Louisiana, the inventor of the "bowie knife"; still another was Colonel David Crockett of Tennessee, whose motto is a good one for every young American: "Be sure you're right, then -- go ahead." Travis, Bowie, and Crockett, with a small force, held Fort Alamo, an old Spanish church in San Antonio. The Mexicans fought against the fort with a large army of men and killed every man in it.

Not long after that, General Houston fought a great battle near the place where the city called by his name now stands. The Mexicans had more than two men to every one of Houston's; but the Americans and Texans went into battle shouting the terrible cry "Remember the Alamo!" and the Mexicans fled before them. Texas then became an independent state, and elected General Houston president. The people of Texas raised a flag having on it a single star. For this reason, the state is sometimes called the "Lone Star State."

Texas was not contented to stand alone; she begged the United States to add her to its great and growing family of states. This was done in 1845. As we shall presently see, a war soon broke out (1846) between the United States and Mexico, and when that war ended we added a great deal more land in the west.

General Sam Houston in the great war between the North and South; what he said. We have noted the actions which General Sam Houston took in getting new country to add to the United States. He lived in Texas for many years after that. When the great war broke out between the North and the South in 1861, General Houston was governor of the state. He withdrew from office, and went home to his log cabin in Huntsville. He refused to take any part in the war, for he loved the Union -- that is, the whole country, North and South together -- and he said to his wife, "My heart is broken." Before the War Between the States ended, he was laid in his grave.

Summary. General Sam Houston of Tennessee led the people of Texas in their war against Mexico. The Texans gained the victory, and made their country an independent state with General Houston as its president. After a time, Texas was added to the United States. We then had a war with Mexico, and added a great deal more land in the west. General Houston died during the war between the North and the South in the 1860s.

Comprehension Questions

1. What was David Crockett's motto?
2. What happened at Fort Alamo?
3. When was Texas added to the United States?
4. Did General Houston like the war between the North and the South?
5. What do people sometimes call the state of Texas after they look at the Texas flag?
6. When did General Houston die?

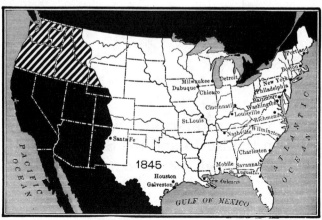

Map showing the extent of the United States after we added Texas in 1845.

Chapter Thirty
Captain Robert Gray

(Born 1755 - Died 1806)

Captain Gray goes to the Pacific coast to buy furs; he is first to take the Stars and Stripes around the globe. Not long after the war of the Revolution had ended, some merchants from Boston sent out two vessels to Vancouver Island, on the northwest coast of America. The names of the vessels were the *Columbia* and the *Lady Washington*, and they sailed down the long coast of North and South America and then round Cape Horn into the Pacific. Captain Robert Gray went out as commander of one of these vessels. He was born in Rhode Island and had fought in one of our warships in the Revolution.

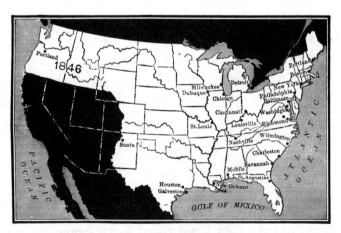

Map showing the extent of the United States after we added the
Oregon Country in 1846

Captain Gray was sent out by the Boston merchants to buy furs from the Indians on the Pacific coast. He had no difficulty in getting all he wanted, for the Indians were glad to sell them for very little. In one case a chief traded two hundred sea-otter skins,(used for making ladies' coats) worth thousands of dollars, for an old iron chisel. After getting a valuable cargo of furs, Captain Gray sailed in the *Columbia* for China, where he bought a quantity of tea. He then went down the coast of Asia and Africa, and round the Cape of Good Hope into the Atlantic. He kept sailing west until he reached Boston in the summer of 1790. He had been gone about three years; and he was the first man who carried the American flag clear around the globe.

Captain Gray's second voyage to the Pacific coast; he enters a great river and names it the Columbia; the United States claims the Oregon Country; we get Oregon in 1846. Captain Gray did not stay long at Boston, for he sailed again that autumn in the *Columbia* for the Pacific coast, to buy more furs. He stayed on that coast a long time. In the spring of 1792, he entered a great river and sailed on it a distance of nearly thirty miles. He seems to have been the first white man who had ever entered it. He named the vast stream the Columbia River, from the name of his vessel. It is the largest American river that empties into the Pacific Ocean south of Alaska.

Captain Gray returned to Boston and told the people about his voyage of exploration; this led Congress to claim the country through which the Columbia flows as part of the United States.

After Captain Gray had been dead forty years, we came into possession, in 1846, of the large territory then called the Oregon Country. It was through what he had done that we held our first claim to that country, which now forms the states of Oregon, Washington, and Idaho, and parts of Wyoming and Montana.

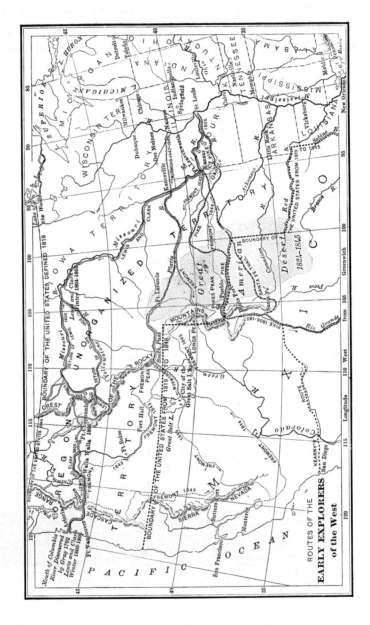

Summary. In 1790, Captain Robert Gray of Rhode Island first carried the American flag around the world. In 1792, he entered and named the Columbia River. Because he did that, the United States claimed the country, known as the Oregon Country, through which that river runs. In 1846 we added the Oregon Country to our possession; it now forms the three great states of Oregon, Washington, and Idaho.

Comprehension Questions

1. What was the name of the sailing vessel commanded by Captain Gray that took three years to sail from Boston to the Pacific coast, to China, and finally back to Boston?
2. What items did Captain Gray buy from the Indians on the Pacific coast?
3. Where was Captain Robert Gray born?
4. What name did Captain Gray give to the large river he found in the Oregon territory?
5. In what year did the United States come into possession of the Oregon territory?
6. In what year did Captain Gray die?

CAPTAIN GRAY TAKING POSSESSION OF OREGON

Chapter Thirty-One
Captain Sutter

(Born 1803 - Died 1880)

Captain Sutter and his fort; how the captain lived.
At the time when Professor Morse sent his first message by
telegraph from Washington to Baltimore (1844), Captain J.
A. Sutter, an emigrant from Switzerland, was living near the
Sacramento River in California. California then belonged to
Mexico. The governor of that part of the country had given
Captain Sutter a large piece of land. The captain had built a
fort at a point where a stream which he named the American
River joins the Sacramento River. People then called the
place Sutter's Fort, but today it is known as Sacramento,
the capital of the great and rich state of California.

In his fort Captain Sutter lived like a king. He owned land
enough to make a thousand fair-sized farms. He had twelve
thousand head of cattle, more than ten thousand sheep, and
over two thousand horses and mules. Hundreds of laborers
worked for him in his wheatfields, and fifty well-armed
soldiers guarded his fort. Many Americans had built houses
near the fort. They thought that the time was coming when
all that country would become part of the United States.

**Captain Sutter builds a sawmill at Coloma; a man
finds some sparkling dust.** About forty miles up the
American River was a place the Mexicans called Coloma, or
the beautiful valley. There was a good waterfall there and
plenty of big trees to saw into boards, so Captain Sutter sent
a man named Marshall to build a sawmill at that place. The

captain needed a sawmill to produce lumber to build with, and to fence his fields.

Sutter's mil

Marshall began to work, and before the end of January 1848, he had built a dam across the river and had finished half of the sawmill. One day as he was walking along the bank of a ditch, which had been dug near the mill to carry off the water, he saw some bright yellow specks shining in the dirt. He gathered a little of the sparkling dust, washed it clean, and carried it to the house. That evening after the men had come in from their work on the mill, Marshall said to them, "Boys, I believe I've found a gold mine." They laughed, and one of them said, "I reckon not; no such luck."

Marshall takes the shining dust to Captain Sutter; what he did with it, and how he felt about the discovery. A few days after that, Marshall went down to the fort to see Captain Sutter. "Are you alone?" he asked when he saw the captain. "Yes," he answered. "Well, would you please do me a favor and lock the door; I've something I want to show you." The captain locked the door, and Marshall took a little bag out of his pocket, opened it, and poured some glittering dust on a paper he had spread out. "See here," said he, "I believe this is gold; but the people at the mill laugh at me and call me crazy."

Captain Sutter examined it carefully. He weighed it; he pounded it flat; he poured some strong acid on it. There are three very interesting things about gold. In the first place, it is very heavy, heavier even than lead. Next, gold is very tough. If you hammer a piece of iron long enough, it will break to pieces; but you can hammer a piece of gold until it is thinner than the thinnest tissue paper. Last of all, if you pour strong acids on gold they will have no more effect on it than an acid like vinegar has on a piece of glass.

For these and other reasons most people think that gold is a very valuable metal; and the more they see of it, especially if it is their own, the better they are pleased with it.

Well, the shining dust stood all these tests. It was very heavy, it was very tough, and the sharp acid did not hurt it. Captain Sutter and Marshall both felt sure that it was gold.

But, strange to say, the captain was not pleased. He wished to build up an American settlement and have it called by his name. Captain Sutter did not care about a gold mine.   He did not need riches for he had everything he wanted without it. He was afraid, too that if gold should be found in any quantity, thousands of people would rush in; they would dig up his land, and probably take it all away from him. We shall see very soon whether he was right or not.

War with Mexico; Mexico lets us have California and New Mexico; "Gold! gold! gold!" ; what happened at Coloma; how California was settled; what happened to Captain Sutter and to Marshall. While these things were happening we had been at war with Mexico for two years (1846-1848), because Texas and Mexico could not agree about the western boundary line of the new state. Texas wanted to push that line as far west as possible, so as to have more land; Mexico wanted to push it as far east as possible, so as to give up as little land as possible. This dispute soon brought on a war between the United States and Mexico. Soon after gold was discovered at Coloma, the war ended

(1848); and we obtained not only all the land the people of Texas had asked for, but a great deal more; for we obtained the great territory of California and New Mexico, out of which several states have since been made.

WASHING GOLD OUT OF THE DIRT

Map showing the extent of the United States in 1848, after Mexico let us have California and New Mexico

In May 1848, a man came to San Francisco holding up a bottle full of gold dust in one hand and swinging his hat with the other. As he walked through the streets he shouted with all his might, "Gold! gold! gold! from the American River."

Then the rush for Coloma began. Every man had a shovel and pick-axe. In a short time, the beautiful valley was dug so full of holes that it looked like an empty honeycomb. The next year a hundred thousand people poured into California from all parts of the United States. The discovery of gold filled that part of the country with emigrants years before they would have gone if no gold had been found there.

Captain Sutter lost all his property. He would have died poor if the people of California had not given him money to live on. Marshall was still more to be pitied. He received nothing for his discovery. Years after he had found the shining dust, someone wrote to him and asked him for his photograph. He refused to send it. He said, "My likeness...is, in fact, all I have that I can call my own; I want something for myself."

How we bought more land; our growth since the Revolution. Long before Captain Sutter died, the United States bought from Mexico another great piece of land (1853), marked on the map by the name of the Gadsden Purchase. Many years later (1867), we bought the territory of Alaska from Russia. Alaska became a state in 1959.

The Revolutionary War ended slightly over two hundred years ago. If you look on the map on the following page, you will see how we have grown during that time. Then we had only thirteen states. They stretched along the Atlantic, and with the country west of them, extended as far as the Mississippi River. If you add up the additions we have made of new territory on the North American continent, you will see that, beginning with Louisiana in 1803 and ending with Alaska in 1867, they number seven in all. Our wonderful country, with its fifty states, now stretches from the Atlantic Ocean to the Pacific Ocean. We also control a few islands far away.

Crossing the plains

Summary. In January 1848, gold was discovered at Captain Sutter's sawmill at Coloma, California. Soon after that, Mexico let us have California and New Mexico, and they were added to the United States. Thousands of people, from all parts of the country, hurried to California to dig gold; and so that state grew more rapidly in population than any other new part of the United States ever had.

Comprehension Questions

1. What country was Captain Sutter born in?
2. What city is now the capitol of California?
3. Who owned the territory of California in 1844?
4. What country went to war with the United States during the years 1846-1848?
5. What valuable item did Mr. Marshall find near Coloma, California?
6. Why did so many American families move out to California during the 1840s?

Chapter Thirty-Two
Abraham Lincoln

(Born 1809 - Died 1865)

The tall man from Illinois making his first speech in Congress; how he wrote his name; what the people called him. Not many days before gold was found at Sutter's sawmill in California (1848), a tall, awkward-looking man from Illinois was making his first speech in Congress. At that time he generally wrote his name "A. Lincoln" but after he had become President of the United States, he often wrote it out in full: Abraham Lincoln. The plain country people of Illinois, who knew all about him, liked best to call him by the title they had first given him: "Honest Abe Lincoln," or for short, "Honest Abe." Let us see how he received that name.

This map shows the extent of the United States in 1853 after we had added the land called the Gadsden Purchase, bought from Mexico; the land is marked on the map, 1853.

The Lincoln family moves to Indiana; "Abe" helps his father build a new home; what it was like. Abraham Lincoln was born on February 12, 1809, in a log cabin on a lonely little farm in Kentucky. When "Abe," as he was called, was seven years old, his father, Thomas Lincoln, moved to Indiana. There they built a new home in the woods. That new home was not as good or as comfortable as some of the barns that cows sleep in. It was simply a hut made of rough logs and limbs of trees. It had no door and no windows. One side of it was left entirely open; and if a traveling Indian or a bear wanted to walk in for dinner, there was nothing whatsoever to stop him. In winter "Abe's" mother often hung up some buffalo skins before this wide entrance to keep out the cold; but in summer the skins were taken down, so that living in such a cabin was not much better than living outdoors.

"A Cabin in Kentucky"

The new log cabin with four sides to it; how the furniture was made; "Abe's" bed in the loft. The Lincoln family stayed in that shed for about a year, while they were building a new log cabin that had four sides to it. They also made a new set of furniture for the new house. To make a table, "Abe's" father split a large log in two, smoothed off the flat side, bored holes in the under side, and drove in four stout sticks for legs. They had no chairs, for it would have been too much trouble to make the backs; but they had three-legged stools, which Thomas Lincoln made with an axe just as he did the table. Perhaps "Abe" helped him push in the legs.

In one corner of the loft of this cabin, the boy had a big bag of dry leaves for his bed. Whenever he felt like having a new bed, all that he had to do was to go out in the woods and gather more leaves.

OLD FORT DEARBORN, CHICAGO

He worked around the cabin during the day, helping his father and mother. For his supper he had a piece of cornbread. After he had eaten it, he climbed up to his loft in the dark, by a ladder of wooden pins driven into the logs. Five minutes after that, he was fast asleep on his bed of sweet-smelling leaves, and was dreaming of hunting, or of building big bonfires out of sticks.

Death of "Abe's" mother; the lonely grave in the woods; what Abraham Lincoln said of his mother after he had grown to be a man; what "Abe's" new mother said about him. "Abe's" mother was not strong; and before they had been in their new log cabin a year, she became sick and died. She was buried on the farm. "Abe" often went out and sat by her lonely grave in the forest and cried. It was the first great sorrow that had ever touched the boy's heart.

After he had grown to be a man, he said with eyes full of tears, to a friend with whom he was talking: "God bless my mother; all that I am or ever hope to be I owe to her."

After a year, Thomas Lincoln married again. The new wife that he brought home was a kind-hearted and excellent woman. She did all she could to make the poor, ragged, barefooted boy happy. After he had grown up and become famous, she said: "Abe never gave me a bad word or look, and never refused to do anything I asked him. Abe was the best boy I ever saw."

The school in the woods; the new teacher; reading by the open fire; how "Abe" used the fire-shovel. There was a log schoolhouse in the wood quite a distance off, and there "Abe" went for a short time. At the school he learned to read and write a little, but after a while he found a new teacher that was--himself. When the rest of the family had gone to bed, he would sit up and read his favorite books by the light of the great blazing logs heaped up on the open fire. He had not more than half a dozen books in all. They were *Robinson Crusoe, Pilgrim's Progress, Æsop's Fables, the Bible,* a *Life of Washington*, and a small *History of the United States.* The boy read these books over until he knew many of them by heart and could repeat whole pages from them.

Boyhood of Lincoln.

Part of his evenings he spent writing and doing math. Thomas Lincoln was so poor that he could seldom afford to buy paper and pens for his son, so the boy had to manage without them. He often took the back of the broad wooden fire-shovel to write on and a piece of charcoal for a pencil. When he had covered the shovel with words or with sums in arithmetic, he would shave it clean and begin again. If "Abe's" father complained that the shovel was getting thin, the boy would go out into the woods, cut down a tree, and make a new one; for while the woods lasted, fire-shovels and furniture were cheap.

What Lincoln could do at seventeen; what he was at nineteen; his strength. By the time the lad was seventeen he could write well, do hard examples in long division, and spell better than anyone else in his area. Sometimes he wrote a little piece of his own about something which interested him; when he read it to the neighbors, they would say, "The world can't beat it."

At nineteen, Abraham Lincoln had reached his full height. He stood nearly six feet four inches, barefooted. He was a good-natured giant. No one in the neighborhood could strike an axe as deep into a tree as he could, and few, if any, were equal to him in strength. It takes a powerful man to put a barrel of flour into a wagon without help, and there is not one in a hundred who can lift a barrel of cider off the ground. But, it is said that young Lincoln could stoop down, lift a barrel onto his knees, and drink from the bung-hole.

Young Lincoln makes a voyage to New Orleans; how he handled the robbers. At this time, a neighbor hired Abraham Lincoln to travel with his son to New Orleans. The two young men were to take a flatboat, loaded with corn and other produce, down the Ohio River and the Mississippi. It was a voyage of about eighteen hundred miles, and it would take three or four weeks.

LINCOLN ON THE FLATBOAT

Young Lincoln was greatly pleased with the thought of making such a trip. He had never been any distance away from home, and, as he told his father, he felt that he wanted to see something more of the world. His father made no objection, but as he told his son good-bye he said, "Take care that in trying to see the world you don't see the bottom of the Mississippi."

The two young men managed to get the boat through safely. But one night a gang of robbers came on board, intending to steal part of their cargo. Lincoln soon showed the robbers he could handle a club as well as he could an axe. The rascals, bruised and bleeding, were glad to get off with their lives.

The Lincolns move to Illinois; what Abraham did; hunting frolics; how Abraham chopped; how he bought his clothes. Not long after young Lincoln's return, his father moved to Illinois. It was a two weeks' journey through the woods with ox-teams. Abraham helped his father build a comfortable log cabin; then he and a man named John Hanks split walnut rails and fenced in fifteen acres of land for a cornfield.

THE LOG CABIN IN ILLINOIS WHICH LINCOLN
HELPED HIS FATHER BUILD

That part of the country had but few settlers, and it was still full of wild beasts. When the men became tired of work and wanted some fun, they had a grand wolf hunt. First, a tall pole was put up in a clearing; next, the hunters in the woods formed a big circle ten miles around. Then they began to move nearer and nearer together, beating the bushes and yelling with all their might. The frightened deer and other wild creatures within the circle of hunters were driven to the pole in the clearing; there they were shot down.

Young Lincoln was not much of a hunter, but he always tried to do his part. Yet, after all, he liked the axe better than he did the rifle. He would start off before light in the morning and walk to his work in the woods, five or six miles away. There he would chop steadily all day. The neighbors knew when they hired him that he wouldn't sit down on the first log he came to and fall asleep. Once when he needed a new pair of trousers, he made a bargain for them with a Mrs. Nancy Miller. She agreed to make him a certain number of yards of cloth, and dye it brown with walnut bark. For every yard she made, Lincoln agreed to split four hundred good fence-rails for her. In this way, he made his axe pay for his clothes.

Lincoln decides to work at a store; the gang of foolish teens in New Salem; Jack Armstrong and "Tall Abe." The year after young Lincoln came of age he decided to work at a grocery store in New Salem, Illinois. There was a gang of foolish teens in that neighborhood who made it a point to pick a fight with every stranger. Sometimes they beat him black and blue; sometimes they amused themselves with rolling him down a hill. The leader of this gang was a fellow named Jack Armstrong. He made up his mind that he would try his hand on "Tall Abe," as Lincoln was called. He attacked Lincoln, and he was so astonished at what happened to him that he never wanted to try it again. From that time on, Abraham Lincoln had no better friends than young Armstrong and the Armstrong family.

Lincoln's faithfulness in little things; the six cents; "Honest Abe." Through his work in the store, Lincoln soon won everybody's respect and confidence. He was faithful in little things, and in that way he made himself able to deal with large ones.

Once a woman made a mistake in paying for something she had bought, and gave the young man six cents too much. He did not notice it then, but after his customer had gone, he realized she had overpaid him. That night after the store was closed, Lincoln walked to the woman's house, some five or six miles out of the village, and paid her back the six cents. It was such things as this that caused people to call him "Honest Abe."

The Black Hawk War; the Indian's handful of dry leaves; what Lincoln did in the war. The next year Lincoln went to fight the Indians in what was called the Black Hawk War. The people in that part of the country had been expecting the war. Some time before, an Indian had walked up to a settler's cabin and said, "Too much white man." He then threw a handful of dry leaves into the air, to show how he and his warriors were coming to scatter the white men. He never came, but a noted chief named Black Hawk, who had been a friend of Tecumseh's, made an attempt to drive out the settlers and get back the lands that certain Indians had sold them.

Lincoln said that the only battles he fought in this war were with the mosquitoes. He did not kill a single Indian, but he saved the life of one old warrior.

Lincoln becomes postmaster and surveyor; how he studied law; what the people thought of him as a lawyer. After Lincoln returned from the war, he was made postmaster of New Salem. He also found time to do some surveying and to begin the study of law. On hot summer mornings he might be seen lying on his back, on the grass, under a big tree, reading a law book; as the shade moved around, Lincoln would move with it, so that, by sundown, he had travelled nearly around the tree.

When he began to practice law, everybody who knew him had confidence in him. Other men might be admired because they were smart, but Lincoln was respected because he was honest. When he said a thing, people knew that it was because he believed it. They also knew that he could not be hired to say what he did not believe. That gave him great influence.

The Armstrong murder trial; how Lincoln saved young Armstrong from being hanged. But Lincoln was as keen as he was truthful and honest -- or maybe it would be better to say he was keen because he was truthful and honest. A man was killed in a fight near where Lincoln had lived, and one of Jack Armstrong's brothers was arrested for the murder. Everybody thought that he was guilty, and felt sure that he would be hanged. Lincoln made some inquiry about the case, and became convinced that Armstrong had not killed the man.

Mrs. Armstrong was too poor to hire a lawyer to defend her son, but Lincoln wrote to her that he would gladly defend him for nothing.

When the day of the trial came, the chief witness testified that he saw young Armstrong strike the man dead. Lincoln questioned him closely. He asked him when it was that he saw the murder committed. The witness said it was in the evening, at a certain hour, and that he saw it all clearly because there was a bright moon. "Are you sure?" asked Lincoln. "Yes," replied the witness. "Do you swear to it?" "I do," answered the witness. Then Lincoln took an almanac out of his pocket, turned to the day of the month on which the murder had been committed, and said to the court: "The almanac shows that there was no moon shining at the time at which the witness says he saw the murder." The jury was convinced that the witness had not spoken the truth; they declared the prisoner "Not guilty," and he was immediately set free.

Lincoln was a man who always paid his debts. Mrs. Armstrong had been very kind to him when he was poor and friendless. Now he had paid that debt.

Lincoln and the pig. Some men have hearts big enough to be kind to their fellow men when they are in trouble, but not to a dumb animal. Lincoln's heart was big enough for both.

LINCOLN AND THE PIG

One morning just after he had bought a new suit of clothes, he started to drive to the courthouse, many miles away. On the way, he saw a pig that was making desperate efforts to climb out of a deep mud-hole. The creature would get part way up the slippery bank, and then slide back again over his head in mire and water. Lincoln said to himself: I suppose that I should get out and help that pig; if he's left there, he'll smother in the mud. Then he remembered his fine new clothes. He felt that he really couldn't afford to spoil them for the sake of any pig, so he whipped up his horse and drove on. But the pig was in his mind, and he could think of nothing else. After he had gone about two miles, he said to himself, I've no right to leave that poor creature there to die in the mud, and what is more, I won't leave him. Turning his horse, he drove back to the spot. He carried half a dozen fence-rails to the edge of the hole, and placed them so that he could reach into the mud without falling in himself. Then, he bent down, seized the pig firmly by the forelegs and pulled him up onto the solid ground, where he was safe. The pig grunted out his best thanks, and Lincoln, plastered with mud, but with a light heart, drove on to the courthouse in his carriage.

Lincoln is elected to the state legislature; he goes to Springfield to live; he is elected to Congress. Many people in Illinois thought that they would like to see such a man in the state legislature, helping to make their laws. They knew they could trust him. They elected him; and as he was too poor at that time to pay for a train ride, he walked from New Salem, a distance of over a hundred miles, to Vandalia, which was then the capital of the state.

Lincoln was elected to the legislature four times He later moved to Springfield, Illinois, and made that place his home for the rest of his life.

Abraham Lincoln

GREETING LINCOLN; AN INCIDENT OF
THE LINCOLN-DOUGLAS DEBATE.

The next time the people elected him to office, they sent him to Washington to help make laws in Congress, not for his state only, but for the whole country. He had come a long way up since the time when he worked with John Hanks fencing the cornfield around his father's cabin; but he was going higher still: he was going to the top.

The meeting for choosing a candidate for President of the United States; the two fence-rails; the Chicago meeting; Abraham Lincoln elected President of the United States. In the spring of 1860 a great convention, or meeting, was held in Illinois. Lincoln was present at that convention. The object of the people who had gathered there was to choose a candidate that they would like to see elected President of the United States. Several speeches had already been made when Lincoln's old friend, John Hanks, and one of his neighbors brought in two old fence-rails and a banner with these words painted on it: Abraham Lincoln-- The rail candidate for the Presidency in 1860.

> ABRAHAM LINCOLN,
> THE RAIL CANDIDATE FOR THE PRESIDENCY
> IN 1860.
> TWO RAILS FROM A LOT OF 3000
> MADE IN 1830
> BY JOHN HANKS AND ABE LINCOLN.

DAVIS.

The rails were received with cheer after cheer; and Lincoln was chosen candidate. About a week after that a much greater meeting was held in Chicago, and he was chosen there in the same way. The next November, Abraham Lincoln, "the Illinois rail-splitter," was elected President of the United States. He had little time to rejoice, however, because our nation was experiencing numerous political problems at this time.

The great war between the North and the South; why a large part of the people of the South wished to leave the Union. In less than six weeks after Lincoln became President, in the spring of 1861, a terrible war broke out between the North and the South. This war is often called the Civil War. A civil war means that people who live in the same country are fighting with each other.

The Southern states felt that they would not receive fair treatment if Lincoln was their president, so they decided to establish an independent government, called the Confederate States of America, and made Jefferson Davis its president. The Confederate state leaders sincerely believed that the federal government did not possess the constitutional authority to force any state to stay in the Union against its will. These leaders often reminded their opponents that the Declaration of Independence clearly sets forth the principal that governments can only rule if they have the consent of the governed. The main reason why so many of the people of the South wished to withdraw from the United States was that they had begun to view the U. S. Constitution and the role of the federal government in a very different manner from the Northern politicians. In short, the South felt that the principle of states' rights was being destroyed by those in the federal government who wanted to see the power of the central government grow significantly.

Confederate Flag.
(The Stars and Bars.)

LEE

GENERAL LEE.

Another issue that divided our nation involved the problem of slavery. At the time of the Revolution, when we broke away from the rule of England, every one of the states held black slaves; but after eighty years a great change had taken place. The blacks in the North had become free, but those in the South still remained slaves. In the course of time, many Northern leaders began to pressure the Southern leaders to free the slaves. The Southern leaders thought that the Northern politicians were hypocrites because the Northern businessmen sold most of the slaves to the Southern farmers a few years earlier. Many of the people in the South, along with their leaders, were looking for a workable plan to move away from slavery, but radical forces in the North were not interested in any plan that would permit the South to gradually get rid of slavery.

But this was not all. The leaders in the Southern part of the United States also felt that they were losing their constitutional rights and economic prosperity. Northern leaders had passed several laws that the people in the South did not like. These laws made it hard for the southern people, especially the farmers, to make a good living. The South was losing its wealth and many Southern leaders felt that the Federal Government was making them poor. The Southern states were tired of arguing for their rights. Nevertheless, due to the fact that the South refused to publicly admit that slavery on the basis of race was morally wrong, they greatly weakened their position and gave their enemies an issue to rally around.

The states had become like two boys in a boat who want to go in opposite directions. One pulls one way with his oars, the other pulls another way, and so the boat does not move ahead.

For this reason, it happened that when Lincoln became President, most of the slave states resolved to leave the Union, and if necessary, to make war rather than be compelled to surrender their constitutional rights and state sovereignty.

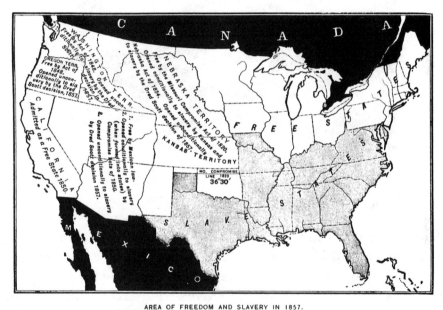

AREA OF FREEDOM AND SLAVERY IN 1857.

(Congress abolished slavery in the District of Columbia, April 16, 1862, and prohibited it in the Territories, June 10, 1862.)

The North and the South in the war; President Lincoln frees the slaves; General Grant and General Lee; peace is made. The North had the most fighting men and the most money; but the people of the South had the advantage of being able to stay at home and fight on their own ground. Also, the South had several skilled and brave generals such as General Thomas "Stonewall" Jackson, General Robert E. Lee, and General J.E.B. Stuart.

BATTLE OF GETTYSBURG.

The war lasted four years (1861-1865). Many terrible battles were fought, and thousands of brave men were killed on both sides. During the war President Lincoln made an important proclamation which gave the slaves their freedom in all the states that were fighting against the Union, and those in the other slave states received their freedom later. This historic presidential proclamation is known as the Emancipation Proclamation.

After a time, the command of all the armies of the North was given to General Grant. General Lee became the chief defender of the South. Although the Southern armies frequently won the various battles during the War, the South was slowly forced to retreat because they were consistently forced to fight against much larger Northern armies.

The last battles between these two great generals were fought around Richmond, Virginia. When the Southern soldiers saw that it was useless to attempt to fight longer, they laid down their weapons, and peace was made. The War Between the States did not solve the major problems that originally caused the war to break out. Time, however, and God's grace would help to heal our broken nation.

The success of the North preserves the Union and makes all slaves free; the North and the South shake hands; murder of President Lincoln. The success of the North in the war preserved the Union; and as all black laborers were now free, there was no longer any political dispute about slavery. The North and the South could now begin to pull in the same direction again.

The saddest thing at the close of the war was the murder of President Lincoln by a madman named John Wilkes Booth. Not only the people of the North, but many of those in the South, shed tears at his death. Lincoln loved all of America, just as any American should love his whole country.

Summary. Abraham Lincoln became a famous lawyer and politician in America during the 1850s in spite of the fact that he was reared in a very poor family. Lincoln became President of the United States in 1861, and six weeks later our nation was divided by a bloody war. The War Between the States lasted four years. In 1865, the Southern, or Confederate, army finally surrendered to the Northern, or Union, army. President Lincoln did everything in his power to preserve the Union, even to the extent of exceeding his limited Constitutional authority as President. He sincerely believed that God desired him to preserve the United States regardless of the cost. President Lincoln was murdered just a few days after the Union armies achieved victory in the War Between the States.

GRANT.

LEE.

STONEWALL JACKSON.

Comprehension Questions

1. What did Abraham Lincoln and John Hanks do?
2. Why did Lincoln get the name of "Honest Abe"?
3. Tell why so many people in the South wished to leave the Union.
4. How long did the Civil War last?
5. What did President Lincoln do for the slaves?
6. What was the saddest thing that happened at the close of the war?

Chapter Thirty-Three
Healing a Broken Nation

(1865 - 1901)

How the United States grew after the War Between the States. Shortly after the War Between the States was over, a difficult period of reconstruction began. Parts of the South suffered tremendous damage because the Northern armies that invaded the south often inflicted as much punishment as possible upon the Southern people. Many farms and some cities were destroyed during the final months of the war, and this left many people in the South homeless and hungry. To make matters worse, almost a quarter of the men of military age in the states of the old Confederacy were killed during the war.

Therefore, the people of the South were forced to patiently endure a long period of suffering and humiliation. It took several years before the South began to recover from all the death and destruction. After the time of reconstruction was over, the united North and South began to grow again and prospered as never before. In the South, many new and flourishing towns and cities were established. Mines of coal and iron were opened, hundreds of factories were built, and the railroads were rebuilt and expanded.

In the West, even greater changes took place. Cities and towns were established where there none before the Civil War, silver and gold mines were opened, and immense farms and cattle ranches were established which helped to provide food to feed America and the world. Several great railroad lines were built across the West to connect with railroads in the East. This connected the continent by rail from the Atlantic to the Pacific. Into that vast country beyond the Mississippi, millions of industrious people moved from all parts of the earth, and built homes for themselves and for their children.

Celebration of the discovery of America by Columbus. More than five hundred years have passed since Columbus crossed the ocean and discovered this new world which we call America. In 1893 we celebrated that discovery made by Columbus, not only in the schools throughout the country, but also with a great fair called the "World's Columbian Exposition" held in Chicago. There, on the low shores of Lake Michigan, on what was once a swamp, the people of the West had built a great city. They had built it where a United States government engineer had said that it was simply impossible to do such a thing. Large groups of people from every state in the Union visited the exposition, and many came from all parts of the globe to join us in Chicago.

MACHINERY HALL—CHICAGO EXPOSITION, 1893

Our Hundred Days' War with Spain. A little less than five years after the opening of the Columbian Exposition, we declared war against Spain. The Spanish - American War was the first time we had crossed swords with any European nation since General Jackson defeated the British army at the famous battle of New Orleans in the War of 1812.

When William McKinley became President in 1897, we had no expectation of fighting Spain. The contest came suddenly, and Cuba was the cause of it. Spain once owned not only all the large islands in the West Indies that Columbus had discovered, but held Mexico, Florida, and the greater part of that vast country west of the Mississippi, which now belongs to the United States. Piece by piece Spain lost control of all these great lands, until eventually, she had nothing left but the two islands of Cuba and Puerto Rico.

WILLIAM MCKINLEY.

The rebellion in Cuba. Many of the Cubans hated Spanish rule, and with good reason. They made several attempts to rid themselves of it and fought for ten years (1868-1878), but without success. Finally, in the spring of 1895, they took up arms again, and with the battle cry of "Independence or death!" they set to work in grim earnest to drive out the Spaniards. Spain was determined to crush the rebellion. She sent over thousands of soldiers to accomplish it. The desperate fight continued to go on year after year, until it looked as though the whole island, which Columbus said was the most beautiful he had ever seen, would be converted into a wilderness covered with graves and ruins. During the war great numbers of peaceful Cuban farmers were driven from their homes and starved to death; and many Americans who had bought sugar and tobacco plantations saw all their valuable property completely destroyed.

The destruction of the *Maine*. Cuba is about the size of the State of Pennsylvania. It is our nearest island neighbor on the south, and is very close to Key West, Florida. The people of the United States could not look on the war without sadness. While we were sending ship-loads of food to feed the starving Cubans, it was both natural and right that we should hope that the terrible war might be quickly brought to an end.

Our government first urged, and then demanded, that Spain try to make peace in the island. Spain did try, tried honestly so far as we can see, but failed. The Cuban revolutionaries had no faith in Spanish promises; they flatly refused to accept anything short of separation and independence. Spain was poor and proud; she replied that come what may, she would not give up Cuba.

While we were waiting to see what should be done, a terrible event happened. We had sent Captain Sigsbee in command of the battleship *Maine* to visit Havana. On the night of February 15, 1898, the *Maine* was blown up in the harbor at Havanna. Out of three hundred and fifty-three officers and men on board the vessel, two hundred and sixty-six were instantly killed, or were so badly hurt that they died soon after. We appointed a Court of Inquiry, composed of naval officers, to examine the wreck. After a long and careful investigation of all the facts, they reported that the *Maine* had been blown up by a mine planted in the harbor or placed under her hull. Whether the mine was exploded by accident or by design, or who did the evil deed, was more than the Court could say.

Declaration of war and the blockade of Cuba. President McKinley sent a special message to Congress in which he said, "The war in Cuba must stop." Soon afterward Congress decided that the people of Cuba "are, and of a right ought to be, free and independent." They also resolved that if Spain did not proceed at once to withdraw her soldiers from the island, we would take measures to make her do it. Spain refused to withdraw her army, and war was promptly declared by both nations.

The President then sent Captain Sampson with a fleet of warships to blockade Havana and other Cuban ports, so that the Spaniards should not get help from Spain to carry on the war. He next put Commodore Schley in command of a "flying squadron" of fast war vessels, so that he might stand ready to act when called upon.

Dewey's victory at Manila. In the Pacific, Spain owned the group of islands called the Philippines. Many of the people of those islands had long been discontented with their government, and when the Cubans rose in revolt against Spain, it stirred the people of the Philippines to begin a struggle for liberty. They, too, were fighting for independence.

President McKinley resolved to strike two blows at once. He decided that our army would hit Spain in Cuba and at the same time at Manila, the capital of the Philippines. Thankfully, by God's grace, the United States had a fleet of six ships under the command of Commodore Dewey stationed at Hong Kong, China. The Assistant Secretary of the Navy had the foresight to send orders to Commodore Dewey before the war started that if we fought with Spain, he should go immediately to Manila and "capture or destroy" the Spanish fleet which guarded that important port. The Spaniards there were brave men who were determined to hold Manila against all attack; they had forts to help them, and they had twice as many vessels as Commodore Dewey. On the other hand, our vessels were larger and better armed, and best of all, our men could fire straight, which was more than the Spaniards knew how to do.

Commodore Dewey carried out his orders very well. On May 1, 1898, he sent a letter to the President, saying that he had just fought a battle and had knocked every Spanish warship to pieces without losing a single man in the fight. The victorious Americans took good care of the wounded Spaniards.

The President immediately sent General Merritt from San Francisco with many soldiers to join Commodore Dewey. Congress voted the "Hero of Manila" a sword of honor, and the President, with the consent of the Senate of the United States, made him Rear Admiral, and later Admiral. This honor gave Dewey the highest rank to which he could be promoted in the navy.

Cervera "bottled up"; Hobson's brave deed. Spain had lost one fleet, but she still had another and a far more powerful one under the command of Admiral Cervera.

Where Cervera was we did not know. For all we knew he might be coming across the Atlantic to suddenly attack New York or Boston or some other city on the Atlantic coast. The President sent Commodore Schley with his "flying squadron" to find the Spanish fleet. After a long search, the Commodore found that the Spanish warships had secretly moved into the harbor of Santiago on the southeastern coast of Cuba.

BATTLE OF SANTIAGO

A day or two afterward Captain Sampson went to Santiago with several war vessels and took command of our combined fleet in front of that port. One of Captain Sampson's vessels was the famous battleship *Oregon*, which had come from San Francisco around South America, a voyage of about thirteen thousand miles, in order to join in the coming fight.

The entrance to the harbor of Santiago is by a long, narrow, crooked channel guarded by forts. We could not enter it without great risk of losing our ships. It was plain enough that we had "bottled up" Cervera's fleet, and so long as Cervera remained there he could do us no harm. But there was a chance, despite our watching the entrance to the harbor as a cat watches a mouse-hole, that the Spanish commander might slip out of his hiding place and, under cover of darkness or fog, escape our guns.

Captain Sampson believed that he saw a way by which he could effectually cork the bottle and make Cervera's escape impossible. By permission of Captain Sampson, Lieutenant Hobson proceeded to carry out his daring scheme. With the help of seven sailors, who were eager to go with him at the risk of almost certain death, Hobson ran the coal ship *Merrimac* into the narrow channel, and by exploding torpedoes sank the vessel part way across it. Then he and his men jumped into the water to save themselves as best they could. It was one of the bravest deeds ever done in war and will never be forgotten. The Spaniards captured Hobson and his men, but they treated them well, and after a time sent all of them back to us in exchange for Spanish prisoners of war.

Fighting near Santiago; the "Rough Riders"; Cervera caught. A few weeks later General Shafter landed a large number of American soldiers on the coast of Cuba near Santiago. The force included General Wheeler's cavalry, and among them were the "Rough Riders." The "Rough Riders" had been Western "cowboys"; Colonel Roosevelt was one of their leaders, and on horseback or on foot they were a match for anything, whether man or beast.

The Americans immediately set out to find the enemy. The Spaniards had hidden in the underbrush, where they could fire on us without being seen. They opened the battle, and as they used smokeless powder, it was difficult for our men

to tell where the bullets came from or how to reply to them.
But in the end, after pretty sharp fighting, we gained
possession of some high ground from which we could plainly
see Santiago, where Cervera's fleet lay hidden behind the
hills.

Colonel Roosevelt.

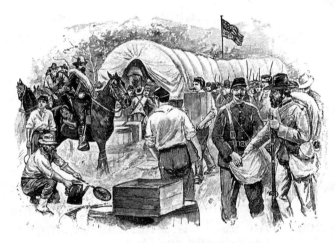

A week later our regular soldiers, with the "Rough Riders"
and other volunteers, stormed up the steep heights, drove
the Spaniards into Santiago, and forced them to take refuge
behind the earthworks which protected the town.

Meanwhile, Captain Sampson had gone to consult with
General Shafter. While he was absent, Commodore Schley
and the other commanders of the fleet maintained a sharp
lookout for Cervera, who was anxious to escape.

On Sunday morning, July 3, 1898, a great shout was sent up from the flagship *Brooklyn*, and another from Captain Evans's ship, the *Iowa*: "The Spaniards are coming out of the harbor!" It was true, for the sunken *Merrimac* had only half-corked the bottle after all, and Cervera was making a dash out, hoping to reach the broad Atlantic before we could hit him.

Then all was excitement. "Open fire!" shouted Schley. We did open fire. The Spanish admiral was a brave man; he did the best he could with his guns to answer us, but it was of no use. In less than three hours all of the enemy's ships were helpless, blazing wrecks. Cervera himself barely escaped with his life. He was rescued by the crew of the *Gloucester*; as he came on board that ship, Commander Wainwright said to him, "I congratulate you, sir, on having made a most gallant fight." When not long afterward one of our cruisers reached Portsmouth, New Hampshire, with Cervera and more than seven hundred other prisoners of war taken in the battle, the people sent up cheer after cheer for the Spanish Admiral who had treated Lieutenant Hobson and his men so kindly.

The end of the war; what the Red Cross Society did. Soon after this crushing defeat the Spaniards surrendered Santiago. Next, Puerto Rico surrendered to General Miles. By that time, Spain had given up the struggle and begged for peace. An armistice was signed between Spain and the United States on August 12, 1898, to stop the fighting until a peace treaty could be signed between the two countries. Our government immediately sent a letter to our forces at the Philippines ordering them to stop fighting. Before the message could get there, Rear Admiral Dewey and General Merritt had taken Manila.

The war was not without its bright side. That was the noble work done by the American Red Cross Society under Clara Barton. They labored on battlefields and in hospitals to help the wounded and the sick of both armies, and to soothe the last moments of the dying. Many a poor fellow who was called to lay down his life for the American cause, and many others who fell fighting for Spain, blessed the kind hands that did everything that human power could do to relieve their suffering. For the Red Cross helpers and nurses treated all alike. They did not ask under what flag a man served or what language he spoke; it was enough for them to know that he needed their aid. So, too, it is pleasant to find that the Spanish prisoners of war were so well treated by our people that when they sailed for Spain they cheered heartily for America and the Americans.

While the war was going on we peacefully annexed the Republic of Hawaii, also known as the Sandwich Islands, on July 7, 1898. Before the end of the contest with Spain our flag waved above those islands, as a sign that they had become part of the territory of the United States. Many years later, in 1960, Hawaii became America's fiftieth state.

The United States and Spain signed a peace treaty to end the war in December, 1898. Spain gave up its colony of Cuba and gave the islands of Guam and Puerto Rico to the United States. In addition, the United States bought the Philippines Islands from Spain for $20 million.

Many of our people desired to keep all of the islands we conquered from Spain. They believed that by so doing we would open new markets for our goods in the East and in China, and that by having possessions in various parts of the globe we make the United States a great world-power--the greatest, perhaps, that had ever existed in history. Some also thought that acquiring these territories would give American missionaries greater opportunities to spread the Gospel.

Many other Americans, who were equally patriotic and equally proud of their country, believed that it would be a mistake for us to keep all of these islands. They said that distant possessions would make us weaker instead of stronger; they would be likely to get us into quarrels with other nations, and we would have to spend large sums of the people's money to defend these new territories.

In spite of these disagreements, the treaty with Spain was ratified by the Senate on February 6, 1899. On New Year's Day, 1899, the Spanish colors were hauled down at Havana, and the stars and stripes took their place, as our sign of guardianship of Cuba. It should be remembered that Havana is the city in which Columbus was believed to be buried. By order of the Queen of Spain, his remains were sent back after the war (December 12, 1898) to Valladolid, his old home in Spain. Today the Spaniards have nothing left on this side of the Atlantic to call their own, not even the corpse of the great navigator who re-discovered the New World, unless by chance his body still rests in the old church in San Domingo.

What America did with the territories it acquired from Spain. We did not keep all of the territory gained from Spain. America never intended to make Cuba our own colony. The Teller Resolution, which Congress passed before we went to war with Spain, stated "that the United States disclaims any intention of control over said island except for the pacification thereof, and asserts its determination, when that is accomplished, to leave the government and the control of the island to its people." America followed through on this commitment by withdrawing from Cuba in 1902 after the first president of Cuba was installed in office.

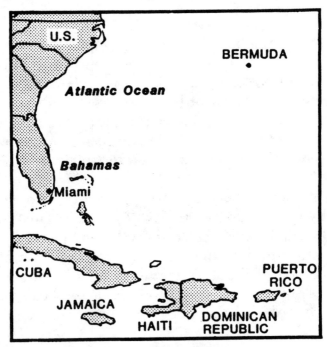

We remained in the Philippines for many years and, although we had to put down a revolt against American authority right after we assumed control over the territory, we soon set about to prepare the Philippines for independence. The Philippine Islands eventually became an independent republic in 1946, after we liberated these islands from Japanese occupation during the Second World War.

Puerto Rico and Guam still remain under American control. However, the residents of these islands were awarded American citizenship many years ago. They each have internal self-government, electing their own legislatures and governors, and each also has a non-voting representative in the U. S. Congress.

The murder of President McKinley. In the autumn of 1900, Major McKinley was re-elected President of the United States with Colonel Theodore Roosevelt as Vice President.

The next spring (1901) a grand exhibition, called the Pan-American Exposition, was opened at Buffalo, New York. In the autumn, President McKinley attended a public reception at the Exposition. On this occasion (September 6), great numbers of people came forward to shake hands with him. Among these was a young man who was the son of some emigrants that had come to the United States from Poland. At the moment the President was reaching out his hand to the young man, the latter shot him twice with a gun which he held hidden in a handkerchief. The President fell back fatally wounded and died about a week later (September 14). His last words to his friends were: "Good-bye, all; good-bye. It is God's way. His will be done."

PRESIDENT ROOSEVELT WRITING THE TELEGRAM WHICH WENT AROUND
THE WORLD

By law, Vice-President Roosevelt then became President. Five days later (September 19) the body of the dead President was laid in its last earthly resting place at his former home in Canton, Ohio. President Roosevelt appointed that day for mourning and prayer. It was solemnly kept, not only by all the people of the United States, but by great numbers of the people of Europe, who joined with us in our sorrow.

Throughout America, a great silence fell upon the people when the body of the murdered President was laid in the grave. In New York, and in many other of our chief cities, cars and steamboats ceased to run for a time; the ever-busy telegraph ceased to click its messages, and thousands of people stood reverently in the streets as though they felt that they were present at the burial-ground in Ohio. It was an occasion that no one who took part in it ever forgot.

Summary. America enjoyed peace for over thirty years after the civil war ended. However, in 1898, America declared war against Spain for the purpose of helping to free the people of Cuba from Spanish rule. Thankfully, this war only lasted several months. America was successful in freeing the people of Cuba from Spanish rule. The new century began with the tragic murder of President McKinley in September 1901. Vice-President Theodore Roosevelt assumed the office of President of the United States in 1901.

Comprehension Questions

1. How long has it been since Columbus discovered America?
2. Who were the "Rough Riders"?
3. What happened to Cervera's fleet?
4. What did the Red Cross do in Cuba?
5. What is said about the remains of Columbus?
6. What terrible event happened at Buffalo in the autumn of 1901?

William McKinley

Admiral Dewey

Chapter Thirty-Four
Theodore Roosevelt

(Born 1858 - Died 1919)

A Brief description of Theodore Roosevelt. President Theodore Roosevelt was the twenty-sixth president of the United States. He served from 1901 until the year 1909, and was largely responsible for strengthening America's military and establishing a system of national parks. Roosevelt was an avid hunter and loved the outdoors. He loved God's creation and used his presidential power to encourage the federal government to take an active role in conserving America's natural resources. President Roosevelt was a man of action. He loved to confront problems in a straight-forward manner. As a young boy, Theodore was often sick and in a weakened condition. However, his mother taught him to trust in God and work hard to overcome problems. As an older man, President Roosevelt would often credit his mother for giving him a strong character and godly convictions. Mr. Roosevelt was grateful for the Christian training that he received at home. He often said that "a thorough knowledge of the Bible is worth more than a college education."

Booker T. Washington shows black Americans the path to progress and success. One of the greatest Americans of the late 1800s and early 1900s was Booker T. Washington. This gentleman was born in 1856 into slavery on a Virginia plantation. After the Civil War, he worked in a coal mine while he attended night school to further his education. Washington worked his way through the Hampton Institute as a janitor, attended a seminary, and returned to Hampton as an instructor. A few years later, Mr. Washington began his greatest work in helping to found a college in Alabama known as the Tuskegee Institute. With tireless effort, he overcame the difficulties of poverty and racial bigotry to build a truly successful college with more than forty buildings and a large staff. Many gifted students graduated from this college.

Mr. Washington taught his students that the best way for black Americans to improve themselves economically and politically was by developing a better level of job and educational skills. He advised his fellow citizens to live peaceably within the system, to learn new skills, and to reform American society by working hard and honestly.

Unfortunately, Booker T. Washington's advice has been ignored by many black leaders during the twentieth century. Consequently, the economic level of black people in the United States has grown very slowly during the twentieth century. Mr. Washington was wise enough to realize that the best way for any American to obtain access to his legitimate civil or constitutional rights is by developing economic power through self-improvement, hard work, and persistence.

Booker T. Washington will long be remembered as a great role model for all Americans. His courageous outlook enabled him to overcome great adversity. His wisdom and leadership skills were a blessing to thousands of young men and women who desperately needed training, encouragement, and hope.

Booker T. Washington

Why we developed a strip of land on the Isthmus of Panama. While Mr. Theodore Roosevelt was President, the United States rented a strip of land on the Isthmus of

Panama. The strip is ten miles wide and it extends clear across the Isthmus from the Atlantic to the Pacific, a distance of nearly fifty miles. America paid millions of dollars for the right to use that narrow and crooked piece of land, which we have named the Panama Canal Zone, yet in itself it is worth very little. Very few of our farmers would give much of anything for it, because most of it is made up of rocks, hills, and swamps. Then again, very few Americans would want to stay long in a climate which is either terribly hot and dry or terribly hot and wet. People in Panama are baked one half of the year and stewed the other half.

Why, then, were we so eager to get possession of such a small amount of territory? It was because of our war with Spain, when the battleship *Oregon* had to sail around the whole continent of South America to get from California to Cuba, that we made up our minds to build a canal across the Isthmus of Panama. Then both our merchant ships and our warships could pass through both ways, from California to Cuba, or from Cuba to California.

Although the United States and other nations frequently sent warships through the Panama Canal during World Wars One and Two, the Canal has most often been used by non-military ships to transport commercial goods throughout the world.

The U.S. signed a controversial treaty in 1977 that began the process of transferring control of the Panama Canal Zone to the independent nation of Panama. Many Americans continue to express the concern that our nation's security has been weakened because the United States no longer has direct control over the Panama Canal.

The North Pole; World War I; the World's Fair; and American Inventions. While the laborers on the Isthmus were digging the canal and while Howard Taft was President, a remarkable feat was accomplished in the North. For many years, explorers had tried to make their way to the North Pole, but had always failed to get there. It was a hard journey over ice and snow, and not a few who started on it perished miserably from cold and starvation. But in the spring of 1909, Commander Robert E. Peary, of the United States Navy succeeded in getting to the Pole, and put up an American flag there to celebrate his success. Later Captain Amundsen of Norway discovered the South Pole; so we can then say we had seen both the top and the bottom of the world.

Woodrow Wilson

In the summer of 1914, after Mr. Wilson became President, a large war began in Europe. The people of the United States resolved not to take any part in it if they could avoid it, but to do everything they could to hasten the coming of peace. To show our good will toward all, we sent a ship to Europe loaded with Christmas presents for thousands of poor children whose fathers had left their homes to go and fight. After the great European war had raged for nearly three years, we were forced to join in. It happened this way: the German submarines had destroyed many English vessels; later they began to blow up American merchant ships trading with England. President Wilson warned the German government that this destruction must stop. It did not stop, and in the spring of 1917, we began sending men and vessels of war across the Atlantic to fight in defense of our lives and our rights upon the sea. This war became known as the First World War.

The fighting in World War I ended on November 11, 1918. The American army fought in Europe for slightly more than one year. During that time, the United States supplied France and Britain with the help they needed to defeat both Germany and Austria-Hungary.

Meanwhile, the people of San Francisco had opened a World's Fair (1915). It celebrated two things: first, Balboa's discovery of the Pacific, about four hundred years earlier; and second, Colonel Goethals' completion of the Panama Canal, which united the waters of the Atlantic and the Pacific.

The largest building in the Fair was Machinery Palace. There, and elsewhere, many labor-saving inventions made by Americans were exhibited. One of these inventions was a little machine which would add up a long column of figures in less than half the time that you or I could do it. Another interesting thing was a model of one of the big steam-shovels used in digging the Panama Canal. Those big shovels did more hard work in an hour than six hundred men could do with hand-shovels in that amount of time. A third invention was a press that could print more than a thousand newspapers in a minute, fold them, and pile them up. Looking at these things, we can understand why American machines are sold and used throughout the world. In this book you have read something about Whitney's cotton gin, Fulton's steamboat, and Morse's telegraph; the telephone too has been mentioned. There are, however, several other inventions which should be spoken of here.

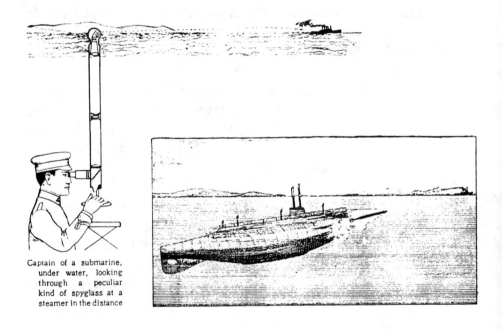

Captain of a submarine, under water, looking through a peculiar kind of spyglass at a steamer in the distance

Robert Fulton's "Diving-Boat." You have already seen that Fulton spent much work on this boat. He said he hoped the time would come when it would destroy so many warships that it would put an end to all fighting on the ocean. That was more than a hundred years ago. Within a short time many of these "Diving-Boats" had been built in Europe, Japan, and the United States. They are now called submarines, because they can travel beneath the surface of the sea. Some of them can travel thousands of miles at a time because they are nuclear-powered. When one of these vessels gets sight of an enemy ship, it sends out a torpedo to destroy it. The torpedo looks like a large fish. It moves swiftly under water toward the ship, and when it strikes, it explodes and tears a large hole in the ship, which soon sinks. The submarines did terrible work during World War I and World War II. But in times of peace, these "Diving-Boats" have often been used to explore parts of the ocean, to find the remains of wrecked vessels, and also to take very interesting movies of life under the sea.

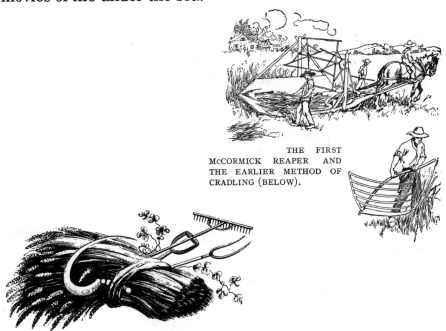

THE FIRST McCORMICK REAPER AND THE EARLIER METHOD OF CRADLING (BELOW).

A machine for cutting grain. Two hundred years ago wheat and other grain were cut by hand. A Virginia farmer said to himself, "Why can't I make a machine which my horses can pull and which will cut my wheat in less time than a dozen men can do it with sickles or cradles?" He built a machine, but it did not satisfy him, and he left it to rust to pieces where it stood.

His son, Cyrus H. McCormick, made up his mind that he would find out why his father's reaper would not work. Cyrus had learned to do one thing at a time, and to do the hardest thing first. Now the hardest thing in this case was to discover why the reaper, when it cut the wheat, would not throw it down straight, so that it could be easily bundled for the threshing machine, which separated the grain from the straw. By patient effort, young McCormick succeeded in making a reaper that would do what was wanted. This was in 1831. He had to wait nine years before anyone bought one of his new machines, and even then he found that he needed to improve it. He began to make some improvements; but not many farmers there could afford to buy it.

Finally a friend said to him, "Cyrus, why don't you go West with your reaper, where the land is level and where it is difficult for the farmers to hire men enough to cut all the grain that grows?" "Yes," answered Cyrus, "I will go West." He started at once, and for the first time in his life saw a prairie. It stretched out as far as the eye could see, and seemed as smooth as a barn floor. Then the thought came to him, "What must this country look like when it is covered with golden fields of wheat?" "Now," said he, "I see what I really made my machine for. I must come out here and build it, for every farmer will be sure to buy it."

He traveled on until he came to Lake Michigan. On the southern shore of the lake, he stopped at a town called Chicago. "Here," said Mr. McCormick, "I shall start my business, for this town will grow, and my business will grow with it." He made no mistake that time. He built reapers and found no difficulty in selling them. He kept making improvements in his work. He improved his reapers so that they would cut the grain rapidly and smoothly and then tie it up in bundles.

Having done all this; he took the last step. He made a new reaper, or Harvester, which would do all that the old one did, and would even thresh out the grain as well. This did everything that the Western farmer could ask, for it filled row after row of bags with the precious wheat that gives us "our daily bread."

Elias Howe invents the sewing machine. While Cyrus H. McCormick was busy in the West, a young man named Elias Howe was just as busy in his house in Cambridge, Massachusetts. When someone asked him what he was trying to make, he answered, "I am trying to make a machine that will sew cloth." His answer was met by a loud laugh. Mr. Howe paid no attention to the laugh, but kept quietly at work. By the end of the winter, he was able to put together a clumsy machine which he called his "Iron Needle-woman." This was in 1845.

Elias Howe's Sewing-machine, now
preserved in Washington

He hoped that in time his machine would be able to sew faster than any girl, but in the end people found that the "Iron Needle-woman" could sew faster than ten girls. The young man expected to sell his invention to the tailors, but they were afraid that if they bought the machines, the men they hired to do sewing by hand would refuse to use them for fear of losing their jobs, so they refused to have anything to do with him.

Then Mr. Howe traveled to London, England, thinking that maybe he could sell his invention in that city. There he was worse off than he was at home, for the tailors would try his machine, but would not pay for it. He decided that he must leave England and go back to America. He found that the only way he could get money enough to pay his passage across the ocean was to borrow it and leave his "Iron Needle-woman" as security. When he landed in New York he had less than a dollar in his pocket. He was discouraged. Then came a still harder experience. He learned that while he had been abroad someone had been making and selling his invention who had no lawful right to do so.

In fact, a man in western New York was travelling about, at that very time, showing this sewing machine to anyone who would pay twelve cents to see it.

Many ladies went to see it and bought fancy work done by this sewing machine. They carried the work home to show their friends what the wonderful "Iron Needle-woman" could do. Still very few believed that the machine would ever prove to be of any real use in a family.

Mr. Howe was too poor to go to court to protect his rights, but he at length found means to prevent others from taking his machine away from him. Then he became prosperous, and this man who once did not have a dollar in his pocket, began to complain that he hadn't enough pockets to hold all the dollars that poured in on him.

At the same time, several other inventors made various improvements to the sewing machine. Finally, one of them built a machine that would sew leather with a waxed thread. This opened a new field of work. Today, most of our clothing is made by sewing machines, and our boots and shoes are generally stitched together by them. The result is that now both clothing and footwear are far cheaper than when they were all made by hand.

How the telephone was invented. Long after the sewing machine had come into use, Professor Alexander G. Bell, of Boston, began to make experiments with the human voice. His friends thought that he was wasting his time, but he said, "Professor Morse made an electric wire write while I hope to do still better, for I believe I can make an electric wire talk."

After many disappointments, he succeeded in sending a faint sound over a wire that passed from one room to another. Next, he stretched one from the basement of a building in Boston up to the third floor. One day when he was at work he called down through this wire to his assistant, "Mr. Watson, come up here; I want you." Mr. Watson rushed upstairs greatly excited, crying out, "Mr. Bell, I can hear your words!" Then Mr. Bell knew that he had made the wire speak.

That was in the spring of 1876. In the summer, a World's Fair was held at Philadelphia to celebrate the remarkable things which had been done in the United States since the Declaration of Independence a hundred years before. Mr.

Bell took his Speaking Wire, or "Talking Telegraph," to exhibit at the Fair. Nobody seemed to pay much attention to it. But, one evening the Emperor of Brazil came in and said, "Professor Bell, I am delighted to meet you again; I want to see your new machine." Mr. Bell went to the end of the long hall and took up the mouthpiece of the wire while the Emperor, standing where Mr. Bell had left him, picked up the other end and put it to his ear. He listened a moment, and then, suddenly throwing his head back, he exclaimed: "Why, it talks!"

Yes, it did talk, and it has been talking ever since. At first, the telephone, as it was finally named, could only be used for very short distances. But now, after many years of improvement, it will talk all across the United States, from the Atlantic to the Pacific, and even around the world. Today a boy in New York can speak to a boy in San Francisco and hear what he says in reply. The telephone makes the two boys just as near to each other, so far as talking is concerned, as though they lived in the same house. This was done by using an electric wire over three thousand miles long. But people are now telephoning each other without using any wire at all, just as they can telegraph one another without one. In both cases, they send their messages along the electrical particles in the air. Special FAX machines, make it possible to transmit written images from one phone to another. Now people can even use the phone to send letters and other written documents to people all over the world.

Mr. Edison and his work. Thomas A. Edison began earning his living by selling newspapers on a railroad train in Michigan. He was then a boy of twelve. A few years later he began printing a small weekly paper of his own in the baggage car of the train. After he had grown to manhood, he invented (1877) the "record player" or phonograph. That machine makes a record of what is said to it and can repeat the words years afterward. It can also repeat music in the same way. Once people would have declared such a thing impossible, but Mr. Edison found a way of doing it. Now his phonograph has become so common that almost everyone has heard it talk or sing. Besides being used for amusement, it is used by businesses and by schools.

The Evolution of the Lamp

The colonists generally used candles, although the use of the whale-oil lamp came in about 1750, when many American ships began to hunt whales. There were over three hundred American ships hunting whales during the Revolution, and over seven hundred as late as 1846. Do you see that the whale-oil lamp was at first shaped to fit into a candlestick, and that the kerosene lamp was an improvement on the whale-oil lamp? The gas lamp was fed from a pipe that ran through the wall; the electric lamp gets its current from a wire likewise coming from the wall. What parts of each way of lighting a room came from the way used just before it? A series of gradual changes of this kind is called an evolution.

Next Mr. Edison invented (1879) the electric light, which we see in almost every house and store. The next year (1880) he built an electric car, which he used for a while at Menlo Park, New Jersey, where he then lived. That started people thinking how convenient it would be to have electric cars in which to travel. Now people are using cars though no longer primarily electric, to rush in all directions over the United States.

Later, Mr. Edison took up a small toy which showed a few pictures the size of postage stamps in motion. He greatly improved that toy, and out of it, in 1895, he produced the motion pictures we know so well.

The Flying Machine. Eight years after Edison began to astonish people with his marvelous pictures, two brothers, Orville and Wilbur Wright, of Dayton, Ohio, did something remarkable that no one had done before. The Wright brothers decided to learn to fly, but instead of making wings, they made a flying machine. It was simply a long, light frame of wood covered with cotton cloth which they called a "Glider." They would take it to the top of a hill, and when the wind blew strong and steadily, one of them would mount the glider and slide downhill on the air. It was good fun unless the wind happened to die and let the rider down with a bump. However, this was not flying as a bird flies, so the Wrights decided to do something different.

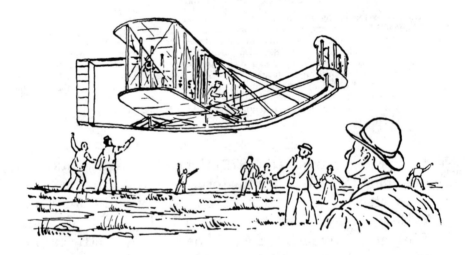

They made a very light engine, like the engine of an automobile, and fastened it on the glider. The engine drove an air-wheel that pushed the glider forward, somewhat as the paddle-wheels push a steamboat forward. They practiced awhile with this and at last, in 1903, their "Flying Machine" (for it was now more than a glider) flew against the wind, for fifty-nine seconds! They tried hard to stay in the air for a whole minute, but could not.

After a while they succeeded, one at a time, in staying up for several minutes. They nearly always had to fly in a straight line, for if they tried to turn corners, they were in great danger of crashing.

However, they were not the kind of men to quit. They were determined that their machine should turn and twist like a letter "S"; so they watched the hawks and gulls to see how they managed. These big birds spread their wings and fly swiftly round and round as though they enjoy the game. Finally, the two brothers found out how the birds did it, and the next year they made two circular flights of three miles each in their new airplaine.

In 1909, they went to Fort Myer, near Washington, to show some officers of the United States Government what they could do. The Government offered to give a prize of twenty-five thousand dollars to any man who could accomplish these three things:

1. He must fly a whole hour without coming down.
2. He must take a passenger with him in his flight.
3. He must fly at the rate of not less than forty miles an hour.

One of the Wrights did all these things, and better, too. He went up in his airplane, as it is now generally called, and flew with a passenger for more than an hour. Next, he flew at the rate of a little more than forty-two miles an hour. Thousands watched him as he glided like a bird through the sky and then landed on the grass as easily and gracefully as a bird lands.

The great crowd cheered and shouted like mad. The United States Government was entirely satisfied. It not only paid the Wright brothers twenty-five thousand dollars for their airplane, but it gave them five thousand dollars more, because they had made greater speed than was demanded. These two men, by years of patient and persistent effort, had won the victory. They had taught the world how to travel through the air. Some of their friends asked them if it was very hard work finding out how to do it. They answered, "Yes; it was." But, they also said, "After all, it is easier for a man to learn to fly than for a child to learn to walk."

Now airplanes are in use in many parts of the world. Seaplanes are also in use. They can skim over the surface of the sea at a great speed, and can then rise and fly if they like. Airplanes have been used to cross deserts, mountains, and regions covered with ice. They are also of very great use in war, and few armies now would feel like fighting without having their help. Modern airplanes are known as jets. These modern airplanes can fly at fast speeds while they carry hundreds of people all around the world. The invention of the airplane has even led to the use of planes that can fly into outer space. These special planes are known as "space shuttles."

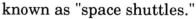

While the Wright brothers were growing up and while they were learning to travel through the air, two more remarkable machines came into use. One of these was the typewriter, which was exhibited at the World's Fair in Philadelphia in 1876, and which now writes business letters throughout the world. The other machine was the "Horseless Carriage," now called the automobile, which began to attract a good deal of attention about 1900. It did not move very rapidly at first, but now it enables people to move through the country at a rate of speed which beats even the railway trains of America. An automobile manufacturer named Henry Ford taught the world how to make cars quickly. He revolutionized automobile production during the early 1900s by introducing the concept of an "assembly line" for producing cars. His assembly line utilized "teams" of workers who each contributed certain parts to each car until it was ready to roll.

Summary. Commander Robert E. Peary was the first person to successfully lead a team of explorers to the North Pole. In 1914, a great war broke out in Europe. In 1917, America joined in the First World War. The United States came to the aid of France and Great Britain during World War I and helped to force Germany and Austria-Hungary to ask for peace. American inventors began to create wonderful new machines during the early 1900s. These inventors gave the world the telephone, airplane, sewing machine, submarine, reaper, typewriter, electric light, and the record player.

Comprehension Questions

1. Who built the Panama Canal?
2. In what year did the United States begin to fight in World War I?
3. What famous farm machine was invented by Cyrus McCormick?
4. Who invented the telephone?
5. Who invented the record player?
6. What machine did the Wright brothers invent?
7. Who was the twenty-sixth President of the United States?
8. Who founded the Tuskegee Institute?

Chapter Thirty-Five
New Leaders Change the World

(1917 - 1939)

The Russian Revolution; the rise of communism, the effect of communism. After World War I, new leaders came to power in many countries, which changed the way people lived in many parts of the world. The leaders in these countries actually came to dominate their governments as dictators. In other countries, leaders who changed their nations' political traditions were elected by their people.

Nicolai Lenin

New Leaders Change the World

Russia did not do well during the First World War. After some initial success, Russian armies were frequently defeated by the German and Austrian armies. At the same time, the Russian economy became steadily worse. Finally, many Russians could no longer support the Russian emperor (also known as the tsar), and strikes and uprisings occurred throughout the country. Finally, Tsar Nicholas II had to step down from his position on March 15, 1917, because he could no longer control the country.

A new, more democratic government took over but could do no better. Russia continued to do badly in the war and the economy continued to get worse. As disorder increased, a revolutionary Marxist group called Bolsheviks (now commonly called communists) led by Nicolai Lenin seized power in the Russian capital of Petrograd (now known as St. Petersburg) on November 7, 1917.

The Bolsheviks made peace with Germany and Austria in 1918, and attempted to gain complete control over Russia, but were only able to do so after winning a bloody civil war against anti-communist Russians. Many Russians were killed in the war, including the tsar and his family.

By 1921, the Communist Party won the Russian Civil War and gained complete control over most of the old Russian Empire, changing the name of Russia to the Union of Soviet Socialist Republics (also known as the Soviet Union). Lenin died in 1924 and one of his followers, Joseph Stalin, came to power in 1928. Both of these men claimed to act on the behalf of workers and peasants, but were tyrants who chose to win political power through murder and deceit. Many millions of the Soviet people were killed or imprisoned during the 1920s and 1930s for daring to speak out against the communist system of government or resisting communist policies.

Joseph Stalin was even worse than Lenin. The killing and imprisonment of Russians became even more common during his time as the ruler of the Soviet Union. He became so concerned to keep his own power that he even had many of the older supporters of Lenin put on trial and then imprisoned or executed to protect his own position.

From the beginning, the communists attempted to expand their influence and control throughout the world as they had opportunity to do so. Communist uprisings took place in Germany and Hungary right after World War I. In the 1920s, communists took power in Mongolia and were involved in a civil war against the Nationalists in China, which did not end until a communist victory in 1949.

People who are forced to live under communism do not enjoy the freedom to worship God according to the dictates of their own conscience. The government owns all property, as well as all the means of business and industry. In many respects, the people living under communist rule are like slaves. For example, under Joseph Stalin in 1928, the Soviet Union began a series of five-year economic plans, in which the communist government set goals and plans for the entire economy. The government forced the people to live as the government wished. The people did not even have the right to vote the leaders of their choice into power. They were only allowed to vote for communists as their rulers.

All freedom-loving people should work and pray so that the system of communism can be defeated around the world. By God's grace, most of the countries in Eastern Europe have been able to free themselves from communist rule in recent years. In addition, the communists in Russia lost control over their Union of Soviet Republics in 1991 and the Soviet Union was formally dissolved. The former Soviet Republics are now trying to establish democratic governments. Russia itself has also made political changes in recent years that may well mean the end of communism in Russia.

Joseph Stalin

Dictators come to power in Italy and Germany; Japan has its own military dictator; the road to World War II is opened. Dictatorship was not limited to Russia. Early in the 1920s, dictatorship came to Italy. In 1922, Benito Mussolini came to power as the dictator in Italy. Many claimed that Mussolini would make the economy of Italy work better. For example, some said that he made the trains run on time. However, economic improvements came at the expense of the Italian people's freedoms.

As the 1930s began to unfold, many countries throughout the world were experiencing economic trouble and violent revolution. During this time, people in Europe were turning to these powerful leaders could get them out of their economic trouble.

In 1933 the National Socialist (Nazi) party, led by Adolf Hitler, came to power in the country of Germany. Hitler promised the German people many things. However, after twelve years of rule he provided only war and death in Germany and the rest of Europe. Mussolini, like Hitler, did not give the people freedom and stability. Germany and Italy became friends with each other during the 1930s.

Adolf Hitler

Benito Mussolini

On the other side of the world, a series of military-dominated governments came to power in Japan during the 1930s, which led Japan into a policy of territorial expansion against neighboring countries in the 1930s and 1940s. The trend toward military governments in Japan culminated in the appointment of a strong Japanese military leader, General Hideki Tojo, who was appointed Minister of War in 1940 and Premier in 1941. It was General Tojo who led Japan into war with the United States.

The aggressiveness of these dictatorships led the world into another world war. In the 1930s, Japan attacked China, killing many people in their quest for land and power, and fought a border war with the Soviet Union. Italy conquered Albania and Ethiopia during this same decade. Germany also took over Austria, Czechoslovakia, and part of Lithuania during this time. Japan joined in friendship with Germany and Italy during the late 1930s. These countries tried to help each other during World War II.

The United States economy grows; Charles Lindbergh makes solo flight across the Atlantic; election of President Hoover; the Great Depression. By 1920, America had established itself as a great industrial power in the eyes of the world. The United States had developed into a busy and prosperous nation because it produced new and better products in its factories.

The airplane had gone through many changes and improvements in the few short years since it had been introduced to the world by the Wright brothers. A daring young pilot named Charles Lindbergh flew his single engine plane across the Atlantic Ocean in 1927. This was the first time any pilot had been able to fly from the United States to Europe. The plane Lindbergh flew was called the *Spirit of St. Louis*. This great event opened up a new era in world travel and further established America as a world leader.

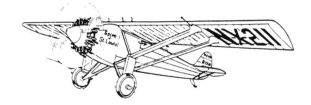

Herbert Hoover

In 1928, Herbert Hoover was elected President of the United States. The first year that Hoover was in office the United States was still growing strong and prosperous. However, in October 1929, the "good times" of the 1920s suddenly came to an end. A great depression had begun, because the stock market in the United States went down as fast as the confidence of the American people in the national economy. Millions of people lost their savings and thousands of people were without a job of any kind. God was teaching the American people important lessons regarding why it is foolish to live in debt and the uncertainty of riches. It would take many years for the United States' economy to recover from the depression. By God's grace, America did survive this difficult period of time. Sadly, however, most of the American people still refuse to follow the Biblical principle that states, "Owe no man anything..." (Romans 13:8a).

President Roosevelt begins to change the role of government in America; our republic is exchanged for a welfare state. While the rest of the world was changing, America changed presidents once again. In 1933 Franklin D. Roosevelt became our nation's thirty-second president. In an effort to combat the effects of the depression, President Roosevelt established his New Deal programs, which had the effect of changing the constitutional role of the United States government by greatly increasing the power of our central or federal government in Washington, D.C. Roosevelt thought that the only way for America to get out of her economic problems was through a government-planned economy.

Franklin D. Roosevelt

Our Constitution was designed to establish a government that would have only minor controls over the states and over the people themselves. President Roosevelt thought that the federal government should have more control over the states and over the people than the Constitution allowed. This thinking caused major changes in our economy. Under a republican form of government, the people themselves run the economy by freely trading items and services in exchange for money. However, Roosevelt helped to pass laws that would take away the people's freedom to control their own businesses and spend their own money. The people began to look to the government for security and began to rely on the government to provide them with jobs and food.

President Franklin Roosevelt was the first American president to officially promote policies that would begin to transform America from a free constitutional republic into a welfare state. The American people had to give up many of their liberties during this time of change. It is very important to remember that whenever people ask their government to give something, they must be willing for the government to take something in return. Governments can not create wealth, therefore they must obtain it from one part of society before they can give it away.

In spite of all of the New Deal programs President Roosevelt established, they contributed little to a permanent improvement in the American economy. Many people were still unemployed at the time of World War II, although some people were helped at the cost of a great change in our system of government. It was not until the war and the economic expansion after the war that America truly recovered from the Great Depression.

New Leaders Change the World

Summary. The 1920s and 1930s saw the rise of several dictatorships around the world. The communists gained complete control of Russia in 1921 and began a reign of terror which lasted until recently. Dictators also came to power in Italy, Germany, and Japan as people looked for strong leaders to bring an end to their troubles. These aggressive dictatorships brought the world to the brink of war by the end of the 1930s.

At first, America was doing very well. Its economy was the envy of much of the world and many did very well during the 1920s. In 1927 a young pilot named Charles Lindbergh flew from the United States to Europe. This was the first time any person flew from America to Europe. However, the United States' economy went into a depression in 1929. President Franklin D. Roosevelt greatly increased the size and power of our federal government after he was elected President in 1933.

Comprehension Questions

1. Who were the two most important leaders in Russia during the 1920s and 1930s?
2. Who made the first airplane flight from the United States to Europe?
3. During what year did the Great Depression begin in America?
4. Who was Hideki Tojo?
5. In what year did Adolf Hitler come to power in Germany?
6. Were the nations of Japan, Italy, and Germany friends during World War II?

Chapter Thirty-Six
Douglas MacArthur

(Born 1880 - Died 1964)

World War II begins in Europe; Japan attacks Pearl Harbor and America enters the war. World War II officially began on September 1, 1939, when Germany invaded Poland. The country of Poland was also later invaded by armies from the Soviet Union (Russia). Poland was quickly taken over by these two countries. On September 3, 1939, England and France declared war on Germany and the whole of Europe was soon at war.

German Stuka Dive Bomber - 1939

General Douglas MacArthur

In less than three months (April - June 1940), Germany conquered Denmark, Norway, Belgium, the Netherlands, Luxembourg, and France, and forced the British army off of the continent of Europe. German airplanes inflicted a lot of damage with bombing attacks on British cities. In 1941, Germany turned toward North Africa and Eastern Europe. Yugoslavia was defeated and German troops were sent to Hungary, Bulgaria, and Rumania. On June 22, 1941, Germany invaded the Soviet Union and was very successful at first. Still, America refused to enter the war at this time. It would take the country of Japan to force the United States into World War II.

America entered the war on December 7, 1941, after its naval and air forces stationed at Pearl Harbor in the Hawaiian Islands were attacked by Japanese airplanes. The attack resulted in the deaths of thousands of American sailors and soldiers and severe damage to our ships and airplanes at the base. In response, the Congress of the United States declared war against Japan on December 8, 1941. Germany and Italy then declared war on the United States on December 11, 1941. America was now a full-fledged participant in the war.

German and Italian successes; victory in Europe. German and Italian armed forces continued their winning ways for awhile. German submarines sank many American and British ships in the Atlantic Ocean. German armies conquered much of the Soviet Union in 1941 and 1942. German and Italian armies drove the British out of Greece and Crete and conquered much of Egypt in 1941 and 1942.

However, the success of the Germans and Italians soon ended. The British stopped the German and Italian armies in Egypt and their armies were driven out of North Africa after American and British forces invaded French North Africa. In the East, the Germans were defeated in late 1942 and early 1943 at the battle of Stalingrad. While much hard fighting remained in the East, the Soviets were able to drive the German armies from their territory. In 1943, the British and American navies were finally able to get the German submarines under control. The American and British air forces began a bombing campaign on German targets, which would continue and grow throughout the rest of the war. By September 1943, American and British forces were able to force Italy to surrender after capturing the island of Sicily and invading the Italian mainland.

Europe during World War II.

By the middle of 1944, Germany still held considerable territory but was in a dangerous position. The Soviets were advancing in the East and the Allies (the United States,

Great Britain, France, and Canada) were fighting in Italy and getting ready to attack the Germans in France. On June 6, 1944, British, Canadian, and American forces invaded northern France from England, on what is now known as "D-Day," and French and American troops attacked southern France on August 15, 1944. The Soviets also began massive offensives during the summer of 1944.

After much hard fighting, the Allied armies under the command of General Dwight D. Eisenhower had freed the people of Western Europe from Hitler's control and invaded Germany within several months after the D-Day invasion. The Soviets also invaded Germany and captured the German capital of Berlin on May 2, 1945. American and Soviet forces met each other on April 25, 1945, thus cutting Germany in two. Germany finally surrendered on May 8, 1945.

Shortly before the final defeat of Germany, the leaders of the United States, Italy, and Germany died. President Roosevelt died of a heart attack on April 12, 1945. On April 28, 1945, Mussolini was killed by Italians who were opposed to the Germans. Hitler killed himself on April 30, 1945, before he could be captured by the Soviets.

Each nation had brave and skillful commanders. Generals such as George S. Patton and Omar Bradley led the American armies to victory against the Germans and Italians. Britain's best known general was Bernard Montgomery.

Douglas MacArthur; he leads America to victory against Japan. A brave and gallant soldier named Douglas MacArthur was put in charge of the American armies who fought against Japan. General MacArthur, along with many other fine soldiers, fought bravely to free the world from power-hungry dictators whose only love was power and war.

Douglas MacArthur was born into an Army family in Arkansas. He went to school at home as a young boy and graduated with honors from the United States Military Academy at West Point a few years before the outbreak of World War I. He served bravely in France during World War I. After the war, he went on to become the Superintendent of the Military Academy and later the Chief of Staff of the Army.

General MacArthur kept his pledge: "I shall return."

MacArthur spent much time in the Philippines before the war with Japan. His father was stationed in the Philippines during his time in the Army. Douglas MacArthur commanded the Department of the Philippines from 1928 to

1930. After retiring from the Army in 1935, he moved to the Philippines to help with the establishment of the armed forces for this territory in preparation for its independence. When war seemed likely with Japan in 1941, he was called back into service with the United States Army to command the combined United States and Filipino armed forces in the Philippines.

After their attack on America at Pearl Harbor, the Japanese captured American, British, and Dutch possessions throughout the Pacific region during the following six months. American and Filipino forces in the Philippines surrendered on May 6, 1942. Before the end in the Philippines, General MacArthur was ordered by President Roosevelt to leave for Australia, which he did in March 1942. Just before leaving, MacArthur told the people of the Philippines, "I shall return."

American forces fought on land, sea, and air for over three years before the Japanese were finally forced to surrender. After arriving in Australia in 1942, General MacArthur was given command of Allied forces in the Southwest Pacific region. He led American and Australian forces into New Guinea and back to the Philippines, recapturing Manila, the capital of the Philippines, in February 1945. In recognition of his work in the war, MacArthur was given command of all United States Army forces in the Pacific in April 1945 and was appointed a five-star general.

The war with Japan dragged on until August 1945. American forces had driven the Japanese back in both the Central Pacific and the South Pacific regions. We bombed Japanese cities and were preparing to invade Japan if necessary. However, Japan did not stop fighting until we dropped atomic bombs on two Japanese cities on August 6 and 8, 1945 and the Soviet Union declared war on Japan and attacked Japanese forces in China and Korea. President Harry S. Truman, who had become president after Franklin Roosevelt died of a heart-attack, decided to drop these bombs on Japan after it seemed that both the Americans and Japanese would suffer terrible casualties if we invaded Japan. The age of nuclear energy and warfare had begun in a sad manner.

World War II officially ended on September 2, 1945, after Japan signed the surrender agreements on board the American battleship *U.S.S. Missouri.* General MacArthur was at the Japanese surrender, as well as representatives of the other victorious countries. He then went on to command the American occupation forces in Japan and was responsible for the reconstruction of Japan.

The world could at last rejoice in the fact that World War II was over. This war was the most destructive and horrible war that the world has ever known. Let us hope, by God's grace, that we will never have such a horrible war again.

The expansion of communism; the Cold War begins. After World War II was over, a new threat to the nations of the world arose. The forces of Communism in the Soviet Union (Russia) had taken over most of Eastern Europe and the northern part of Korea during World War II and did not want to give up their control of these countries. Communist governments were established in most of the areas that had been occupied by the armies of the Soviet Union during the Second World War. Communists completed their take-over of Eastern Europe with the overthrow of a democratic government in Czechoslovakia in 1948. Joseph Stalin, who was still the leader in the Soviet Union, was looking for more power in Europe and Asia. Communists in Greece and China were engaged in violent attacks against the governments of their countries. Yugoslavia and Albania were taken over by local communist forces.

Winston Churchill

Franklin D. Roosevelt

Joseph Stalin

Allied leaders at the end of World War II.

A type of "Cold War" began to develop. A cold war is mostly a war of words between countries who do not agree with each other, but sometimes includes military and economic support for threatened areas. In 1949 the countries of Western Europe, Canada, and the United States established a military alliance known as the North Atlantic Treaty Organization (NATO) to oppose Soviet moves in Europe. The United States would later establish alliances with countries around the world to help fight against the spread of communist forces. We also gave financial aid to many countries, especially in Europe, to help them recover from the damage of World War II.

The Cold War began to get more dangerous in the late 1940s and early 1950s. The Soviets blockaded the land routes to the city of Berlin in 1948 and, for several months, the British and American air forces had to send supplies to the city by air. The mainland of China was taken over by people who believed in communism in 1949 and the Nationalist government was forced to retreat to the island of Taiwan. In 1950 the communist forces of North Korea decided to invade the country of South Korea to bring the entire peninsula under communist control. This act led to the Korean War.

The United Nations; Douglas MacArthur and the Korean War. Many countries in the world were tired of war and tried to urge the communists to stop sending soldiers into South Korea. A new organization, called the United Nations (UN), had been developed just before the end of World War II by the victors of the war in the hope that nations could meet together on a regular basis and solve their problems without war. The communists, however, would not listen to the world's cry for peace as voiced through the United Nations. Therefore, the leaders of the world decided to send a special army to South Korea under the authority of the United Nations. General Douglas MacArthur was chosen as Supreme Commander of the United Nations' forces. Many of the soldiers who fought under MacArthur in Korea were American soldiers.

Douglas MacArthur

However, several countries of the world sent soldiers to help the people of South Korea remain free.

The Korean War lasted for three years. The North Koreans were very successful at first and almost captured the entire peninsula of Korea. However, their advance was finally halted and then defeated after General MacArthur led a successful landing of troops behind North Korean lines. United Nations troops went on to invade North Korea and almost captured the entire country before the communist government in China decided to send soldiers to help the North Koreans. The UN forces had to retreat from North Korea but were able to successfully defeat further Chinese and North Korean attempts to conquer South Korea.

The fighting finally ended after both sides signed a truce on March 5, 1953, but no final peace treaty was ever agreed upon. Regrettably, General MacArthur was not part of this peace because he had been relieved of duty by President Truman on April 11, 1951, due to disagreements on how the war should be fought. The world should always remember the brave soldiers from many countries who fought and died during this bloody war. This war could have been avoided if the communist leaders would have been willing to listen to the just concerns of the free world.

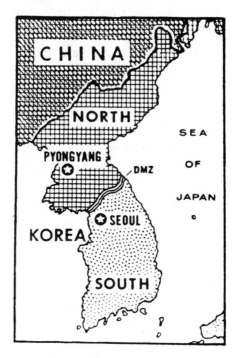

Defenses against Communism. The Korean War was a very real example of the fact that the followers of communism are determined to make the entire world their own. If they succeed in taking over one nation after another, the free nations will soon be outnumbered. If this happens, the communists will be able to "bury" us as they have

Douglas MacArthur

threatened to do. The United States and other free nations are in a contest with the communists for survival. As a leader of the free world, our nation must meet the communist challenge with all the resources at our command. Recent positive political changes in the Soviet Union and Eastern Europe during the late 1980s and early 1990s have encouraged the free nations of the earth. Communism can be defeated on a world-wide basis if free nations will continue to stand up for liberty.

As long as communists continue to threaten the world, we have no choice but to maintain strong military forces at home and abroad. Since we cannot afford to give communist nations the lead in military strength, we must continue to develop modern weapons for defense. Even more important, we must not let the communists get ahead of us in the rivalry for leadership of the world. To meet the growing power of communist nations like the People's Republic of China, we shall need to move forward in industry, in scientific research, and in education. If they get ahead of us in these fields, the communists could dominate the world. Thus, our way of life could be destroyed just as effectively as if we had been destroyed in war!

Although the United States must be prepared for possible attack, our government is also working for peace. The fears and tensions in the world might at any time explode into real war. And total war in this atomic age could destroy our way of life. Even a limited war could use up our resources and weaken our country. To lessen the danger of war, the United States is working for gradual reduction of nuclear weapons. However, until the world is rid of atheistic communist countries, our nation must stand on the policy of "peace through strength."

Summary. The Second World War began in September 1939, but the United States did not enter the war until December 7, 1941, after the Japanese attacked American forces at Pearl Harbor. By 1945 the United States armed forces had defeated the Japanese army and navy and helped to free Europe from the control of Adolf Hitler and Benito Mussolini. Although the war was won, trouble in the world did not end. Communism began to threaten the free world after World War II as a type of "Cold War" began to develop. The free nations of the world had to send soldiers to South Korea during the early 1950s to help stop the spread of communism. The "Cold War" continued to plague the world up until recently.

One of America's greatest soldiers during the 1940s and early 1950s was General MacArthur. He led large numbers of United States soldiers to victory against Japan during World War II and saved South Korea from being conquered by the communists during the early part of the Korean War. This military hero often reminded the American people that in war there is no substitute for victory.

Comprehension Questions

1. In what year did World War II begin?
2. When did the United States finally enter World War II?
3. What was the name of the soldier who commanded the United States' army in its fight against Japan?
4. How did President Franklin Roosevelt die?
5. Why did the Japanese finally stop fighting?
6. Did the United States send soldiers in 1950 to help the country of South Korea remain free?

Chapter Thirty-Seven
The United States Changes

(1953 - 1974)

Eisenhower is elected as our 34th President; a decade of growth and peace. In 1952, the American people elected former General Dwight D. Eisenhower as the thirty-fourth President of the United States. Eisenhower held the office of President for eight years. It was a period of relative peace, and the American people turned their attention to solving problems within their own land.

During President Eisenhower's time as president, the Cold War was quiet and stable enough that most American soldiers could remain at home. The death of Joseph Stalin in

1953 helped to calm world affairs. In spite of this relative peace, America did not withdraw from actively participating in the world. We kept soldiers in South Korea and Europe to protect these areas from attack. We made agreements with other countries around the world to help protect them against communist aggression and revolution. The people of East Germany, Poland, and Hungary tried to free themselves from communist oppression, but these uprisings were brutally defeated.

One of the greatest problems in our land at this time was racial bigotry. Many people in America who had black, brown, yellow, or red skin were denied the basic rights granted to all Americans under the Bill of Rights. President Eisenhower, along with the United States Congress, began to deal with this problem during the late 1950s. However, it would take several more years before the constitutional rights of all American citizens would be clearly protected.

Our federal government continued to grow steadily under President Eisenhower, although at a slower rate than during the administrations of Franklin Roosevelt and Harry Truman. Gradually, our government began to spend great sums of money in an effort to provide jobs, food, clothing, education, and housing for millions of people. One of the major programs started by President Eisenhower in 1956 was the Federal Highway Act. This act was responsible for starting the largest road building project in American history. These new roads were called interstate highways. The federal government felt that this was a good project for it would help to unite the entire country and would provide jobs for many Americans.

The number of states in our country continued to grow. In 1959, the states of Hawaii and Alaska were added to our union. Our nation now has a total of fifty states. The map below will help to show how our country has grown over the years.

John F. Kennedy is elected our 35th President; problems with Cuba; the murder of President Kennedy. In 1960, the American people elected John F. Kennedy as their new president. President Kennedy had to spend much time dealing with foreign problems. Trouble arose in Europe over the building of the Berlin Wall by the East German communists. Trouble also was building in Southeast Asia over attempts by communists to take over the nations in that area.

John F. Kennedy

President Kennedy's most dangerous problem was with the island of Cuba. This nation was taken over by the Communists in 1959, and a violent dictator named Fidel Castro came to power. We tried to work with Castro at first but soon came to understand the communistic character of his government. We tried to help free the Cuban people by landing anti-communist Cubans at the Bay of Pigs in Cuba in 1961. However, insufficient help was given to them and they were defeated by communist forces.

The Soviets began to send weapons of war to Cuba in 1962. The Cubans and Soviets claimed that these were just conventional weapons that all countries have but, in fact, they were also secretly sending nuclear weapons. Since Cuba is located just a few miles from the state of Florida, many people in America became concerned. Late in 1962, it was confirmed that Cuba had nuclear missiles that could destroy American cities. President Kennedy told the Soviets and the Cubans that all missiles and nuclear weapons must be removed from Cuba. To show that we meant business, we established a naval blockade around Cuba during October and November 1962 to keep the Soviets from bringing any more weapons into the country. The Cubans agreed to remove the missiles provided that America would not invade Cuba with American soldiers. The problem was settled without a war being fought.

To help poor and undeveloped countries, President Kennedy established the Peace Corps. The Peace Corps would send Americans to live in poor countries and help them to develop their economies and societies.

On November 22, 1963, President Kennedy was murdered by Lee Harvey Oswald. No one knows for sure why he killed the president because he was killed soon afterward himself, but, it is interesting to note that he had lived in the Soviet Union for a short period of time during the 1950s and had tried to get into Cuba after Castro had come to power. Vice-President Lyndon Johnson became president after the death of President Kennedy.

Johnson took the presidential oath in an hour of tragedy.

President Johnson expands the role of the federal government; the Vietnam War. Lyndon Johnson served as President of the United States from late 1963 until early 1969. During his time as president, the role of the federal government expanded greatly. Through his Great Society and War on Poverty programs, he attempted to solve many of the problems of the poor through extensive government spending. He also sought to support and defend the civil rights of Americans through the activities of the federal government. This was a period of difficulty between the races and riots broke out in several American cities. Tensions were particularly high after Dr. Martin Luther King, Jr. was killed in 1968. While many of these needs were real and some of these programs were helpful, they also greatly extended the influence of the government in the life of the nation and made the federal government's budget problems worse.

While President Johnson was trying to deal with problems at home, he also had problems around the world as well. We intervened in the Dominican Republic in 1964 when leftists threatened the stability of that country. In 1967 war broke out among Israel, Egypt, Syria, and Jordan. War was threatened in Korea in 1968 when North Korea captured the *U.S.S. Pueblo*, a United States Navy ship. Also in 1968, the Soviet Union and its allies invaded Czechoslovakia to stop a reform movement within that country. However, his greatest foreign problem was in Vietnam.

The United States had been involved in Vietnam since the end of World War II. In 1945 we sent a modest amount of weapons and other supplies to a group of Vietnamese nationalists, led by Ho Chi Minh, who were fighting the Japanese occupiers of this French colony. After the war ended, we came to realize the communistic nature of the leaders of this movement and began to support the French in their fight against this communist-led nationalist group. Despite much American aid, the French had to grant independence to Vietnam in 1954. Two countries emerged, a communist North Vietnam and a non-communist South Vietnam.

The United States Changes

Communist rebels in South Vietnam, supported by the communist government in North Vietnam, continued their fight to take over all of Vietnam. President Eisenhower sent supplies and some advisors to help the South Vietnamese people defend themselves. When John Kennedy became president, he sent even more help to South Vietnam.

Our nation's new president, Lyndon B. Johnson, decided to send large numbers of American combat soldiers to Vietnam during 1964 and 1965. At the start of this conflict, many Americans were in favor of sending troops to Vietnam. However, as the 1960s began to develop, the war became bigger and bloodier. The federal government was so afraid of starting another world war that it often would not let its soldiers wage full-scale war against the North Vietnamese. American soldiers were being killed every day, but it seemed as if the government did not want to win this conflict. Therefore, by 1969, the American people began to march in the streets and demand that we pull our soldiers out of Vietnam. The American people became divided on this issue and our country no longer had the will to support the Vietnam War in a unified way.

This was a sad time in American history. The enemies of freedom had managed to damage the noble spirit of America. Many people in the United States began to doubt their government leaders and question if our great country should stop trying to save the world from Communism. By 1973 the American government finally realized that it was foolish to keep our men in Vietnam if we did not have the will to win; therefore, a ceasefire was signed with the communists. Our armed forces were removed from Vietnam in 1973, and some of our American prisoners-of-war came home. The Vietnam War finally ended in 1975 as the Communist forces of North Vietnam took over the nation of South Vietnam. It took many years for the American people to regain the spirit of patriotism that they lost during the Vietnam War.

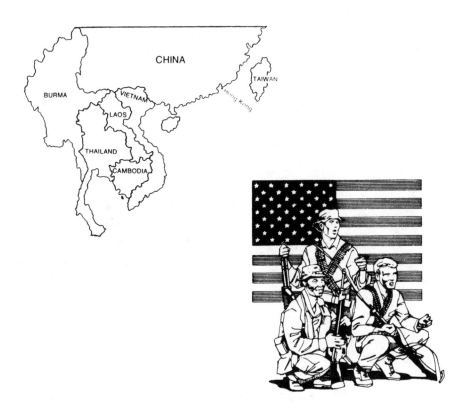

Richard Nixon is elected President; the Twenty-sixth Amendment; President Nixon resigns in dishonor. President Johnson decided not to run for reelection in 1968, and Richard Nixon defeated George Wallace and Hubert Humphrey to become the next president. President Nixon began the process of withdrawing American forces from Vietnam and sought to find an honorable peace to end the war. While he was president, a wonderful event took place in 1971 that helped young adults to become more involved with American government. A special addition or "amendment" to our beloved Constitution was passed by our Congress and ratified by the states. This is the Twenty-sixth Amendment, that says that anyone who is a citizen of the United States of age eighteen or older could vote in all of our country's elections. Before this amendment, citizens had to be at least 21 years old before they could vote. It is a great privilege and duty to help vote good and godly people into public office. All patriotic Americans who are old enough to vote should be responsible enough to vote as often as possible.

In 1972, shortly before the close of the Vietnam War, President Richard Nixon was re-elected as our nation's president. Nixon was under constant pressure from the American people to pull our soldiers out of Vietnam. Violent protests were common during the early 1970s, as Americans demanded an end to the war. Other citizens were marching in the streets to protest the fact that black Americans were not being given fair treatment. Adding to this confusion, the United States was going through an economic recession. The war between Israel, Egypt, and Syria in 1973, and the resulting oil embargo by many Arab countries against nations that had supported Israel made our economic problems worse.

President Nixon became involved in an immoral "cover-up" of what became known as the Watergate affair. In 1972 a few Nixon staff members burglarized the Democratic party headquarters in Washington, D.C. This led to a long and ugly investigation of Richard Nixon and his administration in 1973 and 1974. Sadly, Mr. Nixon lied to the American people regarding the actions of his staff. Finally, on August 19, 1974, Nixon decided to resign as President of the United States. Vice-President Gerald Ford took over the office of

President after Richard Nixon's resignation and became America's 38th President.

America's space program. During this era of history, American inventors and scientists developed many new products and services. They also improved on many earlier inventions. Color television sets became commonplace in many homes during the 1970s. Computers, calculators, stereos, and supersonic jets were just a few of the high-technology items that were invented during the middle of the twentieth century.

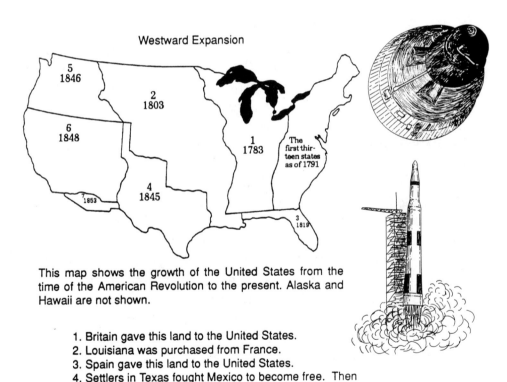

Westward Expansion

5
1846

2
1803

6
1848

1
1783

The first thir-teen states as of 1791

7
1853

4
1845

3
1819

This map shows the growth of the United States from the time of the American Revolution to the present. Alaska and Hawaii are not shown.

1. Britain gave this land to the United States.
2. Louisiana was purchased from France.
3. Spain gave this land to the United States.
4. Settlers in Texas fought Mexico to become free. Then they joined the United States.
5. Settlers in Oregon wanted to belong to the United States instead of Britain.
6. This land was won in the Mexican War.
7. This land was bought from Mexico.

The United States Changes

One of the greatest successes of our scientists was our space program. During the 1950s scientists in America and other nations began to experiment with rockets that could travel into outer space. The Soviets launched two satellites into orbit around the earth during 1957, which they called Sputnik I and Sputnik II. This event encouraged the United States to speed up its own space program. The United States government had already selected Werner Von Braun a former German scientist, to organize America's space and rocket programs. By 1958, the United States had also launched a satellite into space.

In the early 1960s we began to send men into space. In 1961 Alan Shepard, Jr., became the first American to go into space. John Glenn became the first American to orbit the earth on February 20, 1962. We also sent our first communications satellites into space in 1962.

Perhaps the brightest and best achievement of our nation in the late 1960s was our success in landing a man on the moon. In 1969 millions of Americans watched astronauts Neil Armstrong and Edwin Aldrin walk on the moon for the first time. No other nation has ever been able to send men to the moon and return them safely to earth. America's space program has continued to grow over the years. In 1981 the United States developed a special reusable spacecraft known as the space shuttle. This craft can carry several astronauts into outer space and return to earth in much the same manner as a regular airplane. Therefore, the space shuttle can be used over and over again.

Summary. A period of relative peace and prosperity began during the administration of Dwight Eisenhower. John F. Kennedy, who was elected President of the United States in 1960, stopped the flow of nuclear missiles into

Cuba during 1962. He was murdered in late 1963 and Vice-President Johnson took over as President. President Johnson decided to vastly increase the number of American soldiers in South Vietnam during the mid-1960s to help South Vietnam defend itself against communist rebels and soldiers from North Vietnam. The American people could not unite behind this war effort and the United States' army left Vietnam in 1973. The Communists in North Vietnam took over South Vietnam in 1975.

The territories of Alaska and Hawaii became states in 1959. America now has fifty states. America's space program gave the American people considerable joy and excitement in 1969, when it placed a man on the moon. The number of people who could vote grew after the Twenty-sixth Amendment became part of our Constitution. The role of the federal government continued to grow in the life of our country during this time and the freedoms of American people declined.

Comprehension Questions

1. Who was elected as the thirty-fifth president of the United States?
2. Why did America enter the Vietnam War?
3. During what year was Alaska added to the United States?
4. Who took over as dictator of Cuba in 1959?
5. During what year did the Vietnam War end?
6. When did American astronauts first land on the moon?
7. What was the reason for the Twenty-sixth Amendment of the United States Constitution?
8. Why did President Nixon have to resign from office?

Chapter Thirty-Eight
In Recent Years

(1974 - 2003)

America enters a period of decline; President Ford; President Carter. When Gerald Ford became President of the United States on August 9, 1974, he became the first unelected President in our history. He was originally appointed Vice President after Richard Nixon's first Vice President, Spiro Agnew, had to resign from office due to crimes unrelated to the Watergate affair. Therefore, Gerald Ford was not elected as either Vice President or President. President Ford had a difficult time as president and was only able to complete the time of Richard Nixon's second term of office. The economy continued to do poorly and the foreign situation was difficult. Communists took over the countries of South Vietnam, Cambodia, and Laos and made inroads in Africa after the collapse of the Portuguese empire in Africa. Communists also took over the country of Ethiopia in 1974 when army officers overthrew the government of the Ethiopian emperor. President Ford gave Richard Nixon a pardon for any crimes he may have committed during the Watergate affair but many people believed that Nixon should not have been given this pardon.

In 1976 the American people elected a new President. James (Jimmy) Carter defeated President Ford and became our nation's thirty-ninth President. Jimmy Carter, a former governor of Georgia, was the first person from the deep South to be elected president since 1848. Many people were initially attracted to President Carter because of his religious background as a member of a Baptist church in his hometown; he seemed to be personally honest and have a nice family. He expressed a great concern for civil rights in America and human rights around the world. However, over time, his popularity declined. The economy continued to do poorly and there were several difficult foreign problems. He was unable to move our nation in a positive, forward direction.

America's image as a world power suffered greatly during the late 1970s. Many nations around the world lost respect for the United States. Communist influence continued to grow in the world, particularly in Africa and Central America. The Soviet Union invaded the country of Afghanistan with a large number of troops in late 1979 to support the communist government of that country in its fight against anticommunist Afghans.

A Muslim revolution in the oil-rich nation of Iran occurred in 1978, which caused a further large increase in oil prices and made our economic problems still worse. In 1979, a large group of American citizens in our embassy in Iran were kidnapped by radical Muslim terrorists and President Carter provided poor leadership during this crisis.

President Carter was very active in relations with different countries. Some of his activity was considered very helpful, while other things were more controversial. He signed a nuclear arms agreement with the Soviet Union, although it was never ratified by the Senate because of the Soviet invasion of Afghanistan. He established normal relations with the Communist government on mainland China while breaking relations with the Nationalist Chinese government on the island of Taiwan. The United States signed a treaty with the nation of Panama, in which we agreed to return control of the Panama Canal Zone to the Panamanians in 1999. While these actions proved to be of concern to many, Carter's most popular and positive foreign work was his help in getting the nations of Israel and Egypt to sign a peace treaty in 1979.

The 1970s were a difficult time for the United States. Communism made significant gains around the world, and we were humiliated in Vietnam. The constitutional crisis of the Watergate affair brought our government institutions into question. The economy did very poorly, worsened by large increases in oil prices. Our country sank to new lows during the Carter years. Our nation was humbled by Almighty God.

Ronald Reagan   **George H. W. Bush**

The spirit of America revives; Ronald Reagan and George Bush. The American people began to look for a new president in 1980. Our nation decided to elect a president who could motivate the American people to return to the values that made our country great. The people chose Ronald Reagan as their new president. Ronald Reagan told the American people that they should not look to big government to save them; they were told to look to God for help and strength.

In his inaugural address, President Reagan affirmed his commitment to limited constitutional government. "Our government," he said, "has no special power except that granted it by the people. It is time to check and reverse the growth of government which shows signs of having grown beyond the consent of the governed." Further, "It is my intention to curb the size and influence of the federal establishment and to demand recognition of the distinction between the powers granted to the federal government and those reserved to the state or to the people. All of us need to be reminded that the federal government did not create the states; the states created the federal government."

In just a few short years, the people of America began to wake up and realize that they had to change their thinking. President Reagan helped to remind people that it was love of God, hard work, and a compassion toward our fellow citizens that made America great. Our country's military was strengthened during the 1980s as new threats to our nation began to develop. A stronger economy and a stronger military have helped the United States regain respect around the world. The communists in the former Soviet Union and Eastern Europe began to take steps toward a less repressive style of government and move away from their "Cold War" actions.

President Reagan's time in office was not without troubles, though. Early in his time in office, President Reagan was shot and almost killed. However, God preserved him and he recovered to full health. The economy was very bad for the first couple of years of his administration. Later in his administration, however, our financial system began to slowly improve, which continued into the 1990s. We tried to help the Middle Eastern nation of Lebanon overcome a deadly civil war by sending marines to that country, but many of them were killed and we were forced to leave the nation without accomplishing much good. We also supported those fighting against communists in Central America and in Afghanistan.

Our armed forces invaded the island of Grenada in 1983 to free it from an oppressive communist government and to protect American students who were attending medical school there.

In 1988, the American people elected George H. W. Bush, who had been President Reagan's Vice President, to be their nation's forty-first President. President Bush struggled during his four years in office trying to solve our nation's difficult economic and social problems, as well as some difficult foreign problems. As a matter of fact, President Bush had to send American soldiers to fight on two different occasions. We intervened in Panamanian affairs in 1989 and liberated that country from a military dictator.

Soon afterwards, President Bush had to send troops to the Middle East. In 1990 and 1991, a major military conflict arose in the country of Kuwait. This conflict is often called the Gulf War and was one of the shortest wars in American history. By God's grace, Americans and others helped the country of Kuwait to regain its freedom from the bloody occupation of the Iraqi army in 1991. Still, the Middle East continued to be a hot bed of violence and military conflict due to the fact that militant Islamist extremists were gaining power and influence over a growing number of countries in this region of the world. These leaders were committed to using any and all means, including terrorism, to spread their radical Islamic views to as many nations as possible.

In spite of many difficult problems, there were successes during President Bush's administration. Communism continued its decline in much of the world. The Soviet military was forced to leave Afghanistan in 1989. Then from 1989 to 1990, communist governments in Eastern Europe and Mongolia collapsed. This led to the reunification of Germany in 1990 and the dissolution of the Soviet Union into several countries in 1991. Third World communist movements also fell during this time, including Nicaragua, Ethiopia, and Afghanistan. In addition, the communist rebels of El Salvador had to give up the fight so they could participate in elections.

In 1992, William Jefferson Clinton was elected as the forty-second President of the United States. Many Americans voted for Mr. Clinton because they were dissatisfied with the sluggish American economy and wanted a change in leadership.

During President Clinton's first four years in office, he failed in his attempt to enlarge the size and scope of the Federal government in areas such as health care and education. By God's grace, very few of the unconstitutional programs put forward by Bill Clinton received the approval of the United States Congress. During these same years, Mr. Clinton was faced with several allegations of misconduct stemming from old business dealings, security problems in the White House, illegal campaign fund raising, as well as other issues.

President Clinton was also the first President in American history to publicly honor and support Americans who have chosen to live an ungodly homosexual lifestyle. He ordered our nation's military leaders to stop trying to exclude homosexuals from the military, and he hired several openly homosexual employees to work at the White House. The so-called "gay" and "lesbian" lifestyles were promoted by Mr. Clinton in spite of the fact that the Bible condemns such behavior as sinful and anti-family.

In 1996, in spite of the scandals and controversy, the American people decided to reelect Bill Clinton as President. Thanks to the efforts of many conservative leaders in Congress, the American economy and military was improved during the mid-

1990s. Most of these improvements were the result of Congress pressuring President Clinton to get rid of large and expensive government welfare programs and unconstitutional activities that had been in place for years. A stronger economy and better government policies made President Clinton popular enough to win a second term in office.

Later in Mr. Clinton's administration, he turned much of his attention to dealing with conflicts and wars in many parts of the world. In the 1990s, American soldiers were sent to Bosnia and Kosovo, in Eastern Europe, and Haiti—as well as to Africa and the Middle East. In a manner inconsistent with our nation's Constitution, President Clinton sent some of our soldiers to foreign lands under the control of leaders from the United Nations. Most of these so-called "peace keeping" missions were designed to keep small conflicts from developing into big wars.

The greatest threat to world peace in the late 1990s, however, came as a result of the failure of the U.S. government to protect American military secrets from falling into the hands of agents from Communist China. While President Clinton was still in office, Chinese agents were able to steal important military information that would enable them to launch long range nuclear missiles. Let us hope and pray that this security failure will not end up giving an evil Communist government in China the ability to fire nuclear bombs on American cities in the future.

President Clinton brought shame and disgrace upon the office of President during 1998, when he committed immoral sexual acts with a young woman who worked at the White House. To make matters worse, Mr. Clinton chose to lie directly to the American people and in a federal court regarding his adulterous affair, as he tried to hide his sin.

Mr. Clinton, however, decided not to resign in the days after he was caught lying under oath. As a result of this attempted cover-up, the House of Representatives voted on December 19, 1998, to impeach the President. The Senate of the United States, however, lacked the courage to confirm his removal. As a result, President Clinton was permitted to stay in office until his term was completed. This entire scandal and impeachment declaration has weakened the presidency and greatly tarnished the legacy of William J. Clinton.

In 2000, George W. Bush was elected as the forty-third President of the United States. The election between George W. Bush and Vice President Albert Gore was very close. It took a few weeks after the election was over before a large number of votes could be recounted and the winner officially announced.

Some readers of this book may be unaware of the fact that George W. Bush, the forty-third President of the United States, is actually the son of George H. W. Bush, who was the forty-first President. When George W. Bush was elected, he became the second person, as the son of a President, to have been elected President after his father held that office.

On September 11, 2001, President Bush and all loyal Americans were shocked and angered by an attack upon two major U.S. cities by radical Islamist terrorists. These attackers hijacked four American planes and managed to fly three of them into large buildings in New York City and Washington, D.C. Shortly after the attack, which was the worst single act of terrorism in U.S. history, President Bush declared war on any nation who supports or protects terrorist groups. American armed forces, along with those from other countries friendly to the United States, began to attack terrorist strongholds in Afghanistan in October 2001, overthrowing its pro-terrorist government.

President Bush warned the American people that the military effort against terrorist strongholds would be long, hard, and costly. Prior to the terrorist attack, President Bush had hoped to help the American economy to recover from a minor recession. In the months following the attack, however, it became more clear that the American economy would slip further into economic recession as the cost of fighting terrorism began to rise.

As the struggle against terrorism grew, President Bush asked Congress to approve the use of military force against Iraq in October of 2002. After months of failed negotiations through the United Nations, George W. Bush sent U.S. and British troops into Iraq to remove the Iraqi leader, Saddam Hussein, and to destroy any weapons or training camps that could be used by terrorist groups. This military action, called "Operation Iraqi Freedom" lasted from March 19 to May 1, 2003, although scattered resistance continued for an extended period of time.

The United States military forces succeeded in removing Saddam from power and freed the oppressed people of Iraq; however, U.S. forces now have the difficult task of rebuilding the nation and establishing a new stable government. President Bush and other government leaders acknowledge that it will take several years to transform Iraq into a peaceful nation capable of governing itself.

One positive result of the September eleventh attack, which killed over three thousand Americans, was that the people of the U.S. began to unite and support each other. The reality of terrorism simply underscores the truth of Scripture regarding the total depravity of man as well as man's need for salvation through the Prince of Peace.

Current problems and what can be done about them. As America begins the new millennium, we can see many problems. We have many problems in our cities and between the various races in America. Riots in Los Angeles and other cities in the 1990s are clear examples of these problems. Many people are concerned about the environment and the problems of pollution. One of the greatest current problems of our nation is how to deal with international terrorist groups. In addition, although keeping control of government spending has always been important, it has never been as much of a problem as it is today.

The federal government's main role under the United States Constitution is to protect the American people. The federal government was never supposed to be spending great sums of money to provide for the social needs of the American people. Nevertheless, since the 1930s, the role and power of the federal government in our society has been greatly expanded. This situation has become so bad since the 1950s that the government is now spending billions of dollars that it does not own, trying to meet the needs of various groups of people. Although Congress balanced the budget each year from 1998 to 2001, by the end of 2003 the American government still faced a seven trillion dollar debt! Such government overspending is fueled by socialistic tendencies, which are widespread among our elected representatives. This has made America less prosperous than it has previously been.

The federal government must get out of the business of social welfare before America is destroyed financially. The job of providing for the needs of the poor and needy should be done by churches and private charitable organizations like the Salvation Army. Christians must lead the American people by actions and statements to see their duty to serve the poor and the needy.

These problems, however, reflect an even deeper problem. A movement began to develop in our country that started to try to remove God from our society and destroy our nation's Christian heritage. Sadly, our country's Supreme Court ruled in 1962 that it was illegal for children to pray in the public schools. The Bible could no longer be taught in the public schools and the Ten Commandments could not be read in the classroom. In addition, in 1973, our Supreme Court ruled in the case known as *Roe vs. Wade* that it was no longer illegal for a mother to kill her unborn child. This ungodly ruling has encouraged the women of America to murder their own unborn babies in violation of God's Law that says "Thou shalt not kill."

When our courts and government leaders permitted God and the Bible to be removed from our society, they opened the way for many evil forces to gain power in our land. America in the twenty-first century is staggering under a heavy load of sin. Our land is losing its greatness because it is losing its moral goodness. Our nation's only hope is to turn away from lawlessness and immorality, and return to God and His Word. It is true that righteousness exalts a nation and that blessed is the nation whose God is the Lord.

What can you do now to help our country overcome these problems? To begin with, you can study God's Word, the Bible, so that you can learn about how you and our society should live. You can also study American history to learn about the principles of our country. As you have learned from this book, not everything that has happened in this country has been good, but there is much we could learn which should be applied to the United States today. The people who started the United States had definite ideas about running their government. They thought the people should make decisions about what kind of government they lived under. For over two hundred years, our government has operated according to the principles of these men. People in the United States have benefited from their kind of government. They have enjoyed a better life because every individual has had the opportunity to improve his way of life through education and hard work. Let all Americans, young and old, work and pray to the end that our nation may continue to be one nation, under God, with liberty and justice for all.

You should also pray for our President and others in authority over us that God would give them wisdom to lead our country out of the difficult military and economic problems that it is currently facing. In I Timothy 2:1-2, the Apostle Paul urged Timothy to pray "... [f]or kings, and all who are in authority in order that we may lead a quiet and peaceable life in all godliness and honesty."

Part of our prayers should also be for God to bring revival in this land and that leaders like George Whitefield and James McGready would rise up to be used by God to call many Americans to Himself. Finally, you can pray that God would raise up Christians like John Witherspoon, who would try to faithfully apply the Scripture to problems in our country.

As you grow up, you should try more and more faithfully to apply the Word of God to all of your life. Follow the Word of God when it states in I Corinthians 10:31: "Whether therefore, ye eat, or drink, or whatsoever ye do, do all to the glory of God." Only as more and more people faithfully serve God with their whole lives can America truly become great.

Summary. America was humbled by scandals and troubles during the 1970s. President Carter tried very hard to help America, but was unable to motivate the American people to change their ungodly and foolish thinking. President Ronald Reagan was used by God to wake up the people of America and to help begin the restoration of traditional moral and political values. America began to return to its former greatness during the 1980s. However, all of God's people must work hard in future years to promote additional reforms that are still desperately needed.

Our beloved country still has a long way to go in terms of needed reforms and changes. Unborn children still need to be protected from murderers. Our federal government still needs to learn how to spend less money so we can stop going into debt. Christian churches need to get busy and give poor people the spiritual and physical help they need in fulfillment of the Great Commission of our Lord Jesus Christ. Nevertheless, we must claim by faith that God is not finished using our nation. We must also act upon the words printed so clearly on our nation's Liberty Bell: "Proclaim liberty throughout all the land and unto all the inhabitants thereof" (Leviticus 25:10).

Comprehension Questions

1. What country was invaded by the Soviet Union in 1979?
2. In what Middle Eastern country were Americans held hostage by Muslim terrorists?
3. Did the image of the United States improve in the world during the 1970s?
4. Who was elected President of the United States in 1980?

5. What three things did President Ronald Reagan say that Americans needed to do if they wanted America to return to its greatness?
6. What Bible verse is printed on our nation's Liberty Bell?
7. Who was elected President of the United States in 2000?
8. On what date did the United States receive the worst terrorist attack in its history?

The Story of
NATIONS

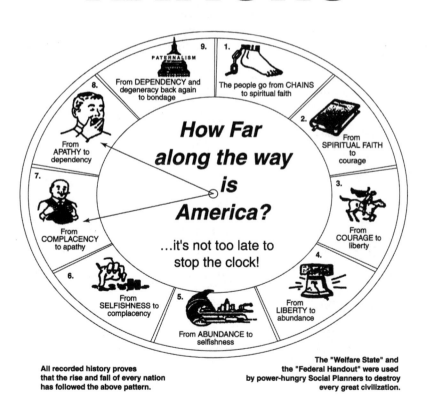

How Far *along the way is* America?

...it's not too late to stop the clock!

9. PATERNALISM
From DEPENDENCY and degeneracy back again to bondage

1. The people go from CHAINS to spiritual faith

2. From SPIRITUAL FAITH to courage

3. From COURAGE to liberty

4. From LIBERTY to abundance

5. From ABUNDANCE to selfishness

6. From SELFISHNESS to complacency

7. From COMPLACENCY to apathy

8. From APATHY to dependency

All recorded history proves that the rise and fall of every nation has followed the above pattern.

The "Welfare State" and the "Federal Handout" were used by power-hungry Social Planners to destroy every great civilization.

The History of Our Presidents

No.	Name	Born/Died	Years in Office	Home State
1	George Washington	1732-1799	1789-1797	VA
2	John Adams	1735-1826	1797-1801	MA
3	Thomas Jefferson	1743-1826	1801-1809	VA
4	James Madison	1751-1836	1809-1817	VA
5	James Monroe	1758-1831	1817-1825	VA
6	John Quincy Adams	1767-1848	1825-1829	MA
7	Andrew Jackson	1767-1845	1829-1837	TN
8	Martin Van Buren	1782-1862	1837-1841	NY
9	William Henry Harrison	1773-1841	1841	OH
10	John Tyler	1790-1862	1841-1845	VA
11	James K. Polk	1795-1849	1845-1849	TN
12	Zachary Taylor	1784-1850	1849-1850	LA
13	Millard Fillmore	1800-1874	1850-1853	NY
14	Franklin Pierce	1804-1869	1853-1857	NH
15	James Buchanan	1791-1868	1857-1861	PA
16	Abraham Lincoln	1809-1865	1861-1865	IL
17	Andrew Johnson	1808-1875	1865-1869	TN
18	Ulysses S. Grant	1822-1885	1869-1877	IL
19	Rutherford B. Hayes	1822-1893	1877-1881	OH
20	James A. Garfield	1831-1881	1881	OH
21	Chester A. Arthur	1830-1886	1881-1885	NY
22	Grover Cleveland	1837-1908	1885-1889	NY
23	Benjamin Harrison	1833-1901	1889-1893	IN
24	Grover Cleveland	1837-1908	1893-1897	NY
25	William McKinley	1843-1901	1897-1901	OH
26	Theodore Roosevelt	1858-1919	1901-1909	NY
27	William Howard Taft	1857-1930	1909-1913	OH
28	Woodrow Wilson	1856-1924	1913-1921	NJ
29	Warren G. Harding	1865-1923	1921-1923	OH
30	Calvin Coolidge	1872-1933	1923-1929	MA
31	Herbert Hoover	1874-1964	1929-1933	CA
32	Franklin D. Roosevelt	1882-1945	1933-1945	NY
33	Harry S. Truman	1884-1972	1945-1953	MO
34	Dwight D. Eisenhower	1890-1969	1953-1961	NY
35	John F. Kennedy	1917-1963	1961-1963	MA
36	Lyndon B. Johnson	1908-1973	1963-1969	TX
37	Richard M. Nixon	1913-1994	1969-1974	NY
38	Gerald R. Ford	1913-	1974-1977	MI
39	James E. Carter	1924-	1977-1981	GA
40	Ronald W. Reagan	1911-	1981-1989	CA
41	George H. W. Bush	1924-	1989-1993	TX
42	William J.Clinton	1946-	1993-2001	AR
43	George W. Bush	1946	2001-	TX

Important Facts on Our Fifty States and Territories

Name	Capital	Abbreviation	Date of Admission to Union	Number in Order of Admission
Alabama	Montgomery	AL	1819	22
Alaska	Juneau	AK	1959	49
Arizona	Phoenix	AZ	1912	48
Arkansas	Little Rock	AR	1836	25
California	Sacramento	CA	1850	31
Colorado	Denver	CO	1876	38
Connecticut	Hartford	CT	1788	5
Delaware	Dover	DE	1787	1
Florida	Tallahassee	FL	1845	27
Georgia	Atlanta	GA	1788	4
Hawaii	Honolulu	HI	1959	50
Idaho	Boise	ID	1890	43
Illinois	Springfield	IL	1818	21
Indiana	Indianapolis	IN	1816	19
Iowa	Des Moines	IA	1846	29
Kansas	Topeka	KS	1861	34
Kentucky	Frankfort	KY	1792	15
Louisiana	Baton Rouge	LA	1812	18
Maine	Augusta	ME	1820	23
Maryland	Annapolis	MD	1788	7
Massachusetts	Boston	MA	1788	6
Michigan	Lansing	MI	1837	26
Minnesota	St. Paul	MN	1858	32
Mississippi	Jackson	MS	1817	20
Missouri	Jefferson City	MO	1821	24
Montana	Helena	MT	1889	41
Nebraska	Lincoln	NE	1867	37
Nevada	Carson City	NV	1864	36
New Hampshire	Concord	NH	1788	9
New Jersey	Trenton	NJ	1787	3
New Mexico	Santa Fe	NM	1912	47
New York	Albany	NY	1788	11
North Carolina	Raleigh	NC	1789	12
North Dakota	Bismarck	ND	1889	39
Ohio	Columbus	OH	1803	17
Oklahoma	Oklahoma City	OK	1907	46

Name	Capital	Abbreviation	Date of Admission to Union	Number in Order of Admission
Oregon	Salem	OR	1859	33
Pennsylvania	Harrisburg	PA	1787	2
Rhode Island	Providence	RI	1790	13
South Carolina	Columbia	SC	1788	8
South Dakota	Pierre	SD	1889	40
Tennessee	Nashville	TN	1796	16
Texas	Austin	TX	1845	28
Utah	Salt Lake City	UT	1896	45
Vermont	Montpelier	VT	1791	14
Virginia	Richmond	VA	1788	10
Washington	Olympia	WA	1889	42
West Virginia	Charleston	WV	1863	35
Wisconsin	Madison	WI	1848	30
Wyoming	Cheyenne	WY	1890	44

Territories

Name	Capital	Abbreviation	Established or Acquired
American Samoa	Pago Pago	AS	1899
District of Columbia	Washington	DC	1791
Guam	Tamuning	GU	1898
Puerto Rico	San Juan	PR	1898
Virgin Islands	Christiansted	VI	1917